To Ta

Thank ... port.

It was Great meeting you.

Paying Attention to God

Beverly Freitag Weeks

Beverly Freitag Weeks

PUBLISH AMERICA

PublishAmerica
Baltimore

First printing

Softcover 978-1-4626-3164-3
PUBLISHED BY PUBLISHAMERICA, LLLP
www.publishamerica.com
Baltimore

Printed in the United States of America

Identity:

Some of the names have been changed to protect their identity and privacy.

THIS BOOK IS DEDICATED TO

Robert, my wonderful husband, my three awesome kids: Robert Ray, Roseanne Josephine, and John Joshua. Thank you for getting to know me and for accepting me. Without your love, support, and approval I couldn't have wrote this book.

Bio:

Beverly Freitag Weeks was born in Bellport, New York. She moved to Bonita Springs, Florida with her parents, sisters, and brothers when she was eleven years old. She lived in Bonita Springs for twenty five years. She met her husband when he was ten years old and she was eleven years old in Bonita Springs. After they grew up they got together and moved fifty miles away to Pine Island, Florida. They raised their kids on the island for six and a half years. Then they moved to Northern Florida. She is currently residing in Old Town (Dixie County) Florida with her husband Robert and their three kids Robert Ray, Roseanne Josephine, and John Joshua, and their eight dogs Rascal, Dixie, Rebel, Mullet, Buzz, Blu, Tela, and Molly, and her horse Spirit. Beverly's song that she wrote "Me and Momma Dreams" is published in "On The Road" song book. She loves cooking, baking, shooting pool and spending time with her husband and their three kids When she's not hanging out with her animals she loves to go fishing on her and Roberts boats. She also loves to lay out to keep her tan in their pool. She loves to read and write about real life. She has spent all her life learning how to live with and how to love her gifts from God.

Table of Contents

INTRODUCTION

My decision to write this book came on my daughter's 14th birthday, December 15, 2003. The day before I had finished one of my spiritual books and had started a funny book. I needed some laughs in my life. We had been living through a very hard financial year. We hadn't given up on our faith in God. But life was very hard. That morning as I sat at the kitchen table writing out my daughters birthday card. I wrote" Enjoy your special gifts and talents, use them wisely. They will amaze you everyday of your life." I sat and looked at those special words I had written. My daughter is so much like me with her gifts from God. She's still very young and has her own fine tuning to do in her life. She is very lucky to be growing up in our house. We've always been completely honest about these gifts. She's always been able to come to me and ask questions about our gifts. She's able to come home and tell me about the amazing things that have happened to her that day. I realized I needed to tell my story. I couldn't be afraid anymore.

I know there are millions of people out there just like me. I've read a lot of their books. I've seen them on TV. I've been researching this for two years so now it was time to do something with all my findings. I realized if I didn't open up my heart, mind and soul to the world. My sweet beautiful daughter might go through life thinking that she's different. I had lived that life. I wanted better for my daughter. We take after my mother but we didn't really talk about it openly. I just always knew when momma said something was gonna happen it always happened. Momma showed that to me even with Alzheimer's disease. She told me when my step dad was gonna die and he did. She stayed in the hospital with me that last night because she didn't want me to be alone when it happened and she wanted to be there with him.

So the constant demand and promise of silence about everything that happens in our house was broken on December 15, 2003. I broke the silence in my mind that morning but I didn't pick up the pen until 4:00 that afternoon.

My son and I went to the store to buy my daughter's birthday presents. Presents were all I was thinking about. Then my son Bobby Ray grabbed some real estate magazines. We had been looking for a house to buy. My husband Robbie was going to be getting money from his grandmother's estate soon. As I walked out the door I grabbed a real estate magazine too. I got home and all the houses were ten to fifty miles away from the beautiful island we called home that I didn't want to leave. But I started marking houses for hours. As I sat there I thought to myself if I move away I can write about my life and no one will know me. I can just lay low. I was still afraid to start writing this book.

Then my sister called me. She told me about her spiritual class that her and our other sister had been attending that was taught by a medium. The medium doesn't do readings during classes but was forced to do one by my beloved step-dad that had passed away two years ago. She told me about the message dad had for our other sister. To me this was also a sign for me from dad to pick up my pen and open my wonderful amazing life up to the world. So I got started writing that day and here almost six years later as I put my book onto my computer I am still afraid. Whenever I start second guessing myself I end up seeing so many signs and I have dreams to keep me writing this book.

I've been writing with my pen so afraid to get started on my computer and maybe finish the book. One night in my dreams my priest from my parish on that beautiful island we moved away from came to visit me. So hopefully I won't be afraid anymore. No more second guessing myself about this book. I have a great cheering section wanting me to finish this book. My husband Robert, my three kids Robert Ray, Roseanne Josephine, and John Joshua, my priest Father Ted, my deceased family members Daddy Ray, my brother Ray Ray, Step-Dad John and the most important one GOD. What more could I ask for. I have ESP, sixth sense, intuition, psychic, or whatever you want to call it. I didn't use to trust it all the time. I'd always second guess myself. I always thought I was very close to my family and friends, until my husband and kids came into my life. When my husband Robbie and our kids started talking and noticing my ESP I finally started believing in myself. I don't always like everyone I meet to know about my ESP.

I was thinking about all my family, friends and ex-husband that never really knew me. I've always been like this. I reckon I never let them all the way into my life. Maybe I let more of me out now that Robbie and the kids except this about me. I was always fearful that family and friends wouldn't like me or except me. Whatever the reason the only people that really know Beverly is Robbie, Bobby Ray, Roseanne, and John. I hope ya'll enjoy reading this book. I hope you see that I'm no different then you and your family. We all were born with these gifts from God. We just need to learn how to use them. I hope my stories about my life helps ya'll with your life. I hope this book helps ya'll learn to use and enjoy your gifts from God.

CHAPTER 1
THE BEGINNING OF A LONG JOURNEY

I've always known that I was different, so I spent all my life trying to fit in. I knew from a very young age that there was something about me that was strange. I just knew other kids didn't experience all these weird things. Some of it scared me. Some of it I just expected and accepted. I grew up in the sixties and seventies so none of this was talked about. I knew people would think I was crazy if I shared my life with them. So I always kept quiet about what I was going through. I shared some of the stuff with my sisters, but not everything. I couldn't share everything because I was trying to fit into this family. I had four sisters and two brothers. I come from a very Italian family. My mother is full blooded Italian. My father was full blooded German. So I am a half breed. When I was a child some of the grown ups that were Italians would say that I had the evil eye when I'd get angry.

When I was mad something about my facial expressions made them say that. To me as a child that meant I had evil in me. To me that explained all the strange things that happened in my life. I didn't understand back then that I had a gift from God. I started to understand it after a lot of research when I was forty years old. I started researching it trying to make sense of it and of my life. I now realize that this is a gift that's given to everyone to use when they're born. Most people don't use it because they don't understand it. I tried running away from my gift but it was such a big part of who I am that I finally quit running.

I've had a long journey to finding my gift. Now I love every part of it. I look forward to it. I look for the signs and dreams. I have fun with it. My first memory of life is laying in my bassinette in my parents bedroom. I don't know how old I was. My sisters brought their friends in to see their new baby sister. Everyone said how cute I was. Then they insulted me. They probably thought it was cute but I hated it. They called me Turk-a-Burk. I believe it was because I was plump like a turkey. That knick name stuck with me for many years. I was a plump child so it hurt every time they called me that.

My first memory of a out of body experience happened when I was about seven years old. My father had been sick with nose bleeds. They happened when he'd get really upset. With six kids close in age he had a lot of stress. So he was put into the hospital for a few days. Before he was put into the hospital I knew that he was going to be in the hospital. I don't know how I knew I just knew it. When he went into the hospital I thought I had caused it. Not from misbehaving but because I had the Italian evil eye. I thought I had put a curse on my own father. I was so upset. I wanted to go to the hospital to visit daddy with momma and the older kids. I was too young. One afternoon I was sitting there worried about what I had done to daddy. So I left my body sitting there at home and I went to the hospital. I didn't go inside because I was too young. I stood outside of his hospital room and looked through the window for a while. He looked ok, he was laughing about something that someone had said to him. So I went back to my body.

When daddy came home I didn't tell him about the out of body experience. I lied and told him that I had a dream that I went to visit him. I told him what the outside of the hospital that I had never been to looked like. I told him about his hospital room. He told me that my dream was really good cause that's what the hospital and the room looked like. He just laughed it off, he was just happy to be back home. I also thought that my visit had cured him. I figured that I had caused it with my evil eye, so then I thought I had cured it with my love and visit to the hospital. This was a lot for a seven year old to deal with. Most seven year olds biggest worry was what kind of snack was going to be in their lunchbox. This was just the beginning of a very confusing and scary childhood. No one to turn to. No one to talk to. No one who could help me. I was a very quiet, shy child. I was afraid to speak too much because of my secrets. I didn't want any to slip out. I had very bad speech problems.

Something else to be teased about, fat kid that couldn't talk. Then the show with my name in it became popular when I was a child. It was my favorite show. But then I was Beverly Hillbilly-fat kid-that couldn't talk. Everyone has baggage that they tote through their childhood and adulthood. I reckon I just had my fair share. Sometimes it just felt like it was too much. So here I was a seven year old convinced that I was evil because I saw things before they happened.

So I thought I caused them to happen. When in reality I had a gift from God. It sure didn't feel like a gift. I didn't have it fine tuned back then. I still have a lot of fine tuning to do with my gift. I'm learning more each day. Back to my childhood. I would have these strong feelings about different people. I wouldn't always see the exact things that were going to happen. I knew something was going to happen to certain people. I guess God knew I couldn't handle seeing too much at that young of a age. So when I had one of those feelings about a person, and if I just happened to be upset with the person. Then I thought I had put the evil eye on them. It wasn't the evil eye I learned later in life but it was a vision or premonition. Whatever you want to call it.

So when I was seven or eight years old I was upset with a close friends sister. I got that weird strange feeling about her. So I tried to make up with her, but kids being kids we talked about it but still couldn't agree on it. A few days later she died in a freak accident. I was devastated. I went home and went to bed and cried and prayed. I told God that I'd never get mad at another person as long as I lived. At seven years old this sounded easy. We all know its impossible. It did make me a much nicer child and adult. I always tried very hard to be more understanding of people that I didn't agree with. All that had happened was a vision. I knew something bad was going to happen to her. I didn't know exactly what it was going to be. She was the first person I knew that passed away. She was the first of many people that I'd have visions about.

I got with my second husband when I was thirty one years old. It didn't take him long to realize that I was different. He didn't understand it all in the beginning of our relationship. He always tried to make some kind of sense of all of it. He's not a traditional religious man. He doesn't go to church. He has his own beliefs. I was raised Catholic and we've raised our kids Catholic. My husband has helped me to become a calmer spiritual person. He has taught me to follow the signs God puts here for us. We're firm believers that what is meant to be will be. We're teaching our kids this too. When something unpleasant happens we tell them its just meant to be this way. Maybe someday you'll look back at this time in your life and understand this situation. The kids believe but sometimes they get aggravated about us saying that.

We believe there's no sense in getting all upset over things you can't change. The tears and yelling don't help anything. It just makes you feel worse. I come from a very high strung family. Always a lot of tears and yelling. My husband has taught me to live a calmer, healthier, more spiritual life. This feels like a brand new day to me. It is December 15,2001 my daughter Roseanne's 12th birthday and two months after my step dad John passed away from lung cancer. I feel happy these past few days. It doesn't mean I'm forgetting dad. He'll always have a place in my heart and mind. I've moved him from the sad place to the happy memory place. I've had a very hard two months since he passed away. I've gone through some hard grieving and a lot of guilt. I'm not completely over the sadness or guilt. But I'm ready to start my journey of healing. I'll never forget our four days and nights in the hospital together. I'm very thankful for that time we spent together in the hospital. A lot of it was hard on me. But it was worth it for all those laughs and smiles we shared. I always knew our bond was strong all those years. I just never realized how strong it was until the end.

I'm starting to feel proud of myself for the happiness I gave him in the hospital. Hopefully this will replace my guilt. I have learned a lot. If I'm ever in this kind of situation again. I will do some things different. I'll be better prepared for it. I won't be as scared. I'll be able to help the person even better. Thank you God for everything that I've gone through. I will survive. I will come out of this a better and stronger person. I started reading everything I could find on spiritual living, out of body experiences, and psychic ability. I just wanted to learn everything as I came out of my grieving for my dad. I felt like I was working towards something but I didn't know what it was until two years later when I started writing this book.

There seems to be a awakening in the world. People are welcoming the spirit world. Some say mediums are new. I remember as a child the big thing was people having séances to talk to people that had passed. Our society has always been curious of the dead. There will always be some non-believers. It is the job of the believers to educate the non-believers. Some people believe when you die that's it. They think once you're buried its over with. They don't believe that their soul lives on in the spirit world.

A lot of these non-believers don't become believers until they're faced with death. I've read a lot about near death experiences. These lucky people get to come back and tell their stories. Most everyone that has a near death experience comes back as a believer. Some of them even call out to God for help when they realize they can't take the pain or death alone. I watched my step dad call out for God's help just hours before he passed away. He knew he needed God and he became a believer. A lot of people become believers when someone close to them passes away. Most people can't handle a loved ones death without believing that they'll see their loved one in the spirit world/ the here after/ the other side/ HEAVEN.

Whatever you want to call it. Everyone has their own beliefs. I'm not here to tell you what's right or wrong. I don't have that answer. All I have is my own beliefs. It's what keeps me going in this crazy mixed up world. I don't try to change anyone elses beliefs. I just don't want anyone to tell me that I'm wrong. No one will know who's right or wrong until they pass away. I believe we'll all have a chance to chat about this in heaven. When I told people about this book, some of them told me that I shouldn't write this book. When I asked my husband and kids if I could write this book. They all said yes and have been very supportive of this project. They've reminded me of different things that have happened over the years that they wanted me to include in my book.

So this book isn't just mine, it's my families book too. If it wasn't for my husband and kids getting to know me so well. Paying close attention to all my day and night dreams, thoughts, warnings, and feelings. This book would have never happened. But more importantly I'd never have gotten to know myself. What my family saw in me was what I tried to hide from the world all my life. I hid it so well my sisters, brothers, parents, and friends never really got to know the real me. I was always afraid people would turn away from me if they got to know me. I was so scared of being labeled as a freak. I've had a few doubts while writing this book. I keep telling myself I have to keep writing so I can just be me. Reading psychic books and watching psychic's on TV has helped me to be true to myself and my gift. Watching Mediums on TV has been a huge help in not thinking that I'm crazy for talking to dead people. Mediums have helped me to feel normal.

I wonder how many people are really out there in the world like us that won't or can't embrace the real themselves. I've wrote very little the past four months. I told myself it was because I was stressed out living at my mom's house. I'd tell myself that I didn't have my mind in a peaceful spot so I couldn't write. The truth is I got scared of this book becoming a reality and letting my guard down. Nothing big has happened lately. Small stuff happens everyday of my life. I still have a lot of learning to do. I don't always act on the small stuff. Then when I'm proven right I get aggravated at myself for not speaking up. My life would be so much easier if I just follow my thoughts.

Some people call them your instincts. Whatever they're called we all have them. We all have the free choice to follow them. Anything that anyone does in life, you always know that there will be one of two outcomes. A good outcome or a bad outcome. So before you act you need to think about it. So many people second guess themselves. I think we all have the gift of insight.

Some of us might have more then just insight. Or we just use more. I use more. I'm not sure at this point in my life if I'd call myself psychic. I do know I have something very special inside me. I've spent so much of my life trying to get rid of it. I always just wanted to be like the rest of the people around me. I was so afraid of my gift. I give my husband Robbie and my kids Bobby Ray, Roseanne, and John all the credit for helping me to embrace my gift. If they weren't so excepting and understanding. I would have spent the rest of my life running away from myself.

This is who I am. This is who I chose to be on the other side. There's not many of us that use it on a daily basis. God gave it to us to make our lives easier to live. How we use it will determine how our lives will go. We cause our own bumps in the road of life. It's all a learning process. I'm not sure if anyone ever figures all of it out while they're living. I do know some people kinda float through life. I think these people have a lot of it figured out. Hopefully someday I'll be one of those people. Right now I'm like everyone else just trying to figure life out. My sister gave me a present years ago. It has brought me a lot of joy and happiness over the years. It's a small plastic see thru box with one hundred and thirty eight cards printed on both sides with beautiful Spiritual Quotes. I read them all the time.

They are quick quotes to give you a pick up or just to keep you close to God. When she bought me this present I'm sure she knew that I'd like it. I'm not sure if she realized that I would get this much use out of it for this many years. I love it and when I pass away it will get handed down to one of my kids. They all will enjoy it as much as I do. John reads them every time he's on my computer since I keep the box on my desk. All of my sisters are very special to me in so many ways. They are all my sisters and my best friends.

This sister has always been there for me no matter what, even if I was being dumb at the time. She'd have no problem telling me when I was being a jerk and give me a big hug while I was being a jerk. She'd always babysit my kids for me after my divorce and when I'd be in the hospital having a baby. She knew I was having such a hard time after the divorce with money. She would leave a care package for me and the kids. Food, diapers, snacks, and drinks for the kids. It was totally awesome to come home from working at the golf course and see a care package on the front steps. It made me feel so good to know someone cared and she took the time to show us how much she cared. My sister, her husband and kids welcomed my new boyfriend who later became my husband right into the family. He would come home from the store in the beginning and say I saw your sister and her kids and they all gave me a hug and kiss right in the middle of the store. I would laugh and say yeah that's how our family is. He finally got use to it.

Robbie and my brother-in-law ended up being good friends. They would go golfing together a lot before we moved to Pine Island. I was always really close to their kids since I would babysit them a lot when they were growing up. Since we all were so close my daughter was super close to my sisters youngest daughter. Whenever we go back home for vacation we always stay a few days with my sister and her husband. We feel so at home with them. Thank goodness our husbands just love each other. Family is so important. Everyone needs and deserves someone special like my sister and her husband in their lives. The love they've given me all these years makes me feel so special. What a great feeling.

My other sister is two years older then me but she always thought she was my second mother. She took very good care of me all through our childhoods.

She was the only one that knew what I was saying when I had my bad speech problems. So she always had to do my talking for me. I depended on her so much for so many years. We were closer then sisters we were more like twins. We looked a lot alike and a lot of people couldn't tell us apart. I finally got tired of saying I wasn't my sister and I started answering to her name. It was so hard on both of us when she got married. We both had a hard time not being together all the time. Then her husband did the unthinkable. He moved her away from Florida all the way to Texas. I was so angry. I was heartbroken. I had to face life alone for the first time in nineteen years. So when she moved back to town I was use to being on my own.

My sister wanted to start over where we had left off with her taking care of all my needs. So we had to learn how to be sisters since I had been on my own and had become a independent young lady. We had a few bumps in the road over the years. We have always loved each other and wanted each other to agree with our point of view. Out of all my sisters she always knew the most about me and my special gifts from God. I always could tell her everything. She always got so amazed by my stories about the strange things that happened in my life. Our lives were going in different directions when she came home but we both still loved life. We tried to stay close but our husbands were so different so it didn't work. We always talked about staying close like our mom and our favorite Aunt had stayed close all their lives. We learned it takes more then just sister love to stay close over the years. It takes work and commitment like any relationship. We always reconnect with each other after months or sometimes years of being apart.

My husband decided that we would be married on this sisters birthday. He would never commit to what the reason was for this choice. But I'm pretty sure it was because he knew that way he would never forget our anniversary since I am so close with my sister. I remember when I was about thirteen years old we were going roller skating with the teen club that we both belonged to. She told me that night she was high on life and it was contagious cause I got high on life that night too. We had such a great time just skating and hanging out with our friends. We didn't have to take anything to get high. She was with me when I gave birth to Roseanne and John. We keep in touch over the phone and with our minds.

My older sister is the coolest person I've ever known. She was always like a mom to me too. I reckon it was because I was the youngest that everyone mothered me a lot. She always took me with her when I was a kid. She's older then me so we always went to the coolest places. She let me move in with her when I was pregnant with my first child after my ex walked out on me. We had a great time living together. She taught me to cook stir fry so I was always able to get my kids to eat vegetables. She also was my babysitter for many years. It was so nice knowing my kids were safe at their aunts house. She taught me about plants and flowers. I love working in my garden thanks to my sister. No matter where I move to, be it fifty miles away or three hundred miles away. She will always come and visit me.

She makes sure she keeps me as part of the family. She never comes empty handed, there's always wonderful gifts. She has a way of making you feel like you're the most important person in the world. The only play I've been to was one she took me and our other sister to after a fancy dinner in a very expensive restaurant for our birthdays. Our birthdays are a month apart. I am going to take her to a play and dinner in New York City someday when I can afford it. Our kids grew up super close since we were so close. When I lived close she was the sister that would stop by all the time, it was so great. I miss that so much. We're a lot alike. I have her love for animals. I want to take care of every animal I meet. I am so lucky to have a sister like her in my life. She was by my side to see my first child Bobby Ray being born.

My other sister and I are the most alike and we didn't really spend that much time together when we were growing up with the age difference. We shared a room a few times and we always got along really well. I was tough like she was. I always thought she was so awesome. I wanted to be a cheerleader like she was but we moved so I didn't get to. She always took the time to teach me all her new cheers. She was a amazing poem writer. I wanted to write like she did but no matter how hard I tried I couldn't do it. We both found out that God and words were our life as adults. I started writing because she inspired me so much with all the things she wrote. She brought me back to God. I'll never be able to give her as good as gift as she has given me. My life has been so wonderful since I let God back into it.

She always lived far away from us but she always came for visits. She would always spoil me when she would come down. She'd take me places and buy me stuff. She would fix my hair and make up. We both loved to eat fast food and chocolate. The best compliment of my life came from her when she was reading some of my songs and told me I was a good song writer. Her approval means so much to me. I'm so happy that she shared God and writing with me.

My brother Ray Ray was her twin. He was killed by a hit and run driver in Texas one month after he turned twenty years old. I never got over his death. I am so much like my brother. I was a tomboy so I was like his little brother. He gave me his hand me down play clothes. He gave me his old cross when he got a new one. I wore that cross for many years with such pride. He was always showing me something with his chemistry set. I'll never forget the day he blew stuff up all over his bedroom. Mom had to paint his room, she couldn't get the walls cleaned. Ray and I laughed so hard that day. He always looked out for me when we were at the teen club dances. He would have been a great dad if he would have lived. He gave me so much love and attention all the time. He was a nice person and I try to be nice like he was. His smile would make you smile even if you didn't know why he was smiling. We're all better people for having our lives touched by Ray Ray.

My other brother was like my own child. I loved him with all my heart and soul. We were super close all of our lives. We had such a strong bond. He was my best friend. We played together and we learned together. When I got married I would have him come over all the time. We just had to be together. It was hard on both of us being apart. But I was always moving back home so we stayed close all those years. He was always such a giving person. He spoiled me and my kids with presents. It was hard on him when I moved away and we didn't see each other that much. Our lives went in different directions but when we would see each other it was like no time had gone by. We were just as close again. Then I moved far away and I have no idea why he got so mad at me but he did for about three years. So when we did see each other again it was just like no time had gone by. We talked and hugged like nothing had happened. We both know it happened. Time will tell if we get that bond back we thought nothing could ever mess up.

My momma is a very special woman. I always knew momma had ESP when I was a kid. That's what we called it back then in the 60's and 70's. Now you might say she is psychic, I'm not sure. I always knew I couldn't lie to her because she always knew the truth. Momma would always joke about the evil eye, ESP, and stuff like that. She would never talk about it seriously until I was a adult. Even then she didn't talk a lot about these things. You just knew if she said it then it would probably happen. When I was a young child my dad made us sell our piano. We were all very upset about selling it. Momma was mad about selling it. The man came to get the piano and I watched as they took it out of the house. I stood in the doorway once it was out. Momma went out on the front porch and was talking to the man. The man was giving momma a hard time. Boy momma got really mad at this man. He was standing on the front porch being mean to momma. I felt so bad for momma. He said something to her that made her real mad.

She said in Italian "Baf fa Nabla" as she clenched her left fist and slapped her right hand on her left muscle and threw her left arm in the air with her fist shaking so mad at this man. The man got so upset he fell off the steps backwards. I laughed so hard that my small five foot momma could stand up to this big man and not take any crap from him. I knew then that my mother was a force to be reckoned with. I also knew my mother was a very special and strong lady.

I was so proud of my mother since it was the sixties and men still thought they ruled the world. My mother and I were best friends. We had a blast when I was a child. We had an even bigger blast as adults. We just really like each other and have respect for each other. We did so much together boating, fishing, camping, cooking, baking, perming my hair what a mess, canning tomatos, shopping when she was taking me to the hospital cause I was in early labor. The mall was on the way and she needed to get my two sisters birthday presents. Of course she and I needed a hot fudge sundae after the shopping. We talked everyday on the phone or in person for so many years. She taught me how to be a wonderful wife and mother. I still call her a lot even though she has Alzheimers. We still get to hear each others voices. We still get to have a lot of laughs together. I hope it helps her, I know it helps me.

CHAPTER 2
CHILDHOOD

The first time I was begging them to make him stop. They told me to leave my body and come up there with them. They said they'd keep me safe. So I would leave my body on the bed crying. I'd float up into the picture with Jesus and Mary. We looked down at my body crying. I felt so sorry for my body down there. So Mary sent Jesus and me off to play in the garden. She said she'd watch my body. We ran around and played games with the other kids that were up there. There was always lots of kids running around. Jesus taught us to fly. When we wanted to fly we'd run real fast and we'd start going up into the sky. Once we were up we'd keep our legs moving like we were running to keep us flying. The faster we'd run the faster we'd fly.

The garden was a beautiful green grass sort of playground. There were beautiful flowers everywhere in the garden. It was so peaceful and safe there. Jesus as a adult was there too. He would sometimes sit on this big rock. The kids would go up to him and talk to him. He was so nice to all the kids. All the kids were so happy playing in their special garden. We all knew we were safe there with Jesus. We played on the playground and had fun.

Mary would call me back when daddy would get done tucking me in and leave my bedroom. She would tell me it was time to go back to my body. I didn't want to go back. I begged her to let me stay with her and Jesus. Mary told me I could slide back down into my body on their magic yellow slide. So I would get on the slide and slide back down into my body. I don't know how many times it happened. But I remember sliding back into my body a lot of nights. I would wake up in the morning and look up at my Jesus and Mary picture and look for my slide. When my dad quit tucking me in I'd still sometimes go up to my safe place with Mary and Jesus to go play with my friends. Even as a grown up I still go back there. I don't go as often now. I still have my Jesus and Mary picture hanging over my bed. It is Jesus as a child. Some people might say that the picture is of a beautiful garden with Jesus and Mary. It's not. It is kinda scary looking place on this picture. But it has brought me forty seven years of comfort.

I look at my picture every night before I go to sleep. My mother gave me the picture when I was twenty eight years old. Some people may say this was a dream that I had a lot of times. They may be right, I really don't know for sure. It felt and still feels very real to me. I never told anyone about this until I was an adult about forty years old. When I did talk about this I said it was a dream. Then I told my kids about it and said it was a dream. I never lie to my kids so I felt so bad. So I told my kids the truth about this, that I wasn't sure if it really happened or if it was a dream. I always wondered why did I remember it so well if it was just a dream. I also always wondered if it was just a dream, why did I keep having the same dream so many times over so many years. I always wondered if I'd ever meet any of those kids here on earth. Then it happened on July 28, 2003.

After my stepdad died in October 2001 I started reading everything I could get that had to do with dying, angels, near death experiences, out of body travel, and psychic ability. I had so many questions and I was ready for all the answers that I could find. I'd read usually two books a week. My husband commercial fished at night. So when I'd get the kids put to bed after we'd say our prayers every night. I'd stay awake and read for hours. I found this amazing book. I was amazed and in total awe of this woman that wrote this book. So then I got her other two books. All of her books were one better then the next. I wanted to share with everyone her name and the names of her books but I couldn't get in touch with her. I read what a woman had wrote to the author I cried my heart out. I could not believe what I had just read. So I read it again. She wrote that she went to this beautiful garden with Jesus and all the other little kids to play. This woman wrote about my garden. She was a child when she went there.

I curled up on my bed in a fetal position and I cried like a baby for this woman, for myself and for all the kids in our garden. Everything she wrote I had seen in my garden with Mary and Jesus. I was so shocked and amazed. When I read about my biggest secret of my life in this book. I said out loud to myself I always knew it was real. I finally realized for the first time in my life I was normal. I always felt so different from all the other kids and adults here on earth. Now I come to find out that I'm perfectly normal. I've just always stayed very connected to Jesus and God.

Thank you to this woman for having the courage to write about this to this author. Thank you to the author for realizing how wonderful a story this was to include it in her book. I read this in August 2003. A few weeks later I wrote the author a letter thanking her for her wonderful books and how much they had helped me. I never got the courage to mail that letter. Then in December 2003, I wrote the author another letter.

I thanked her again for her help for the past two years with her wonderful books. I never got the courage to mail that letter. So in December 2003, when I started this book I knew I had to have the courage like this woman had and include it in my book. Everyone that has ever been in that garden needs to know it wasn't just a dream. It was something so much more special and wonderful then just a dream. It was Jesus taking care of us in our time of need. Just like in the poem "Footprints". Jesus is always there to carry us when we need him. He will never leave you. People sometimes say that they found Jesus. He was never lost. He was always right there with you every step of your life from birth to death. God is always just a call away. All you have to say is God Please Help Me. He will be there.

I remember when I was seven or eight years old. I decided that I'd be a teacher. But I didn't want to teach regular classes. I remember sitting in my parents bathtub thinking that I wanted to help people with my stories. I thought to myself I need to do some living so I'd have stories to tell people to help them. I never became a teacher. I was inspired by my second grade teacher.

She was so nice and sweet to me. She was a great teacher. She is the reason that I've always wanted to be a writer. She gave me an A on my assignment "What did you do over summer vacation". I carried that paper around with me for weeks and showed every family member and every friend. I was so proud. It wasn't just the A, she also took the time to tell me what a good job I did on that paper. She was just such a amazing teacher. She was my teacher at Kreamer Street Elementary School in Bellport, New York. She never knew back then how much her caring and sweetness was helping me during the worse year of my life. I was in second grade. I was molested at home and raped at a neighbors house by a teenage boy. Thank God for teachers like my second grade teacher. Her caring saved me from going crazy during that horrible year.

Words cannot express how much she helped me or how important of a person she was in my life at that time. Her kindness to a shy little girl during one school year helped me live the rest of my life. When I got into my thirties a lot of friends and family members started coming to me with their problems. I was always considered the dumb kid of the family. No one would ever come to me for advice. I don't know how that changed. But it did and it was around the time when I came back to God. I'm sure that has got to have something to do with it. They'd come over or call me. It got to be where it was taking up so much of my time. I was working ten to twelve hours a day at the golf course. I worked as a equipment operator and a mower. All day at work every one always came to me with their problems. My husband and kids didn't like sharing me with the outside world when I'd get home. At first I didn't understand my family's side of it. Once I thought about it real hard I realized they weren't getting much of my time because of my job. Then when they had me I was on the phone helping people. I started cutting the phone calls and visits short. Then we moved fifty miles away from our home town. People quit dropping in since it was so far.

The phone calls slowed down a lot since it was a toll call to me now. But what I left in my home town I found in my new town. It started slow but before I knew it a lot of my new friends talked to me about their problems. I'd talk to them about my problems too. At the time I thought it was just our friendships. Now that I've moved away again I see it a little differently. I think my personality/psychic gift attracts people to me for advice. I have no problem helping people. I really enjoy it. I've tried to figure out how I can make it into my career. That way I'll still have time for my family. I've had several different ideas but I haven't followed through with any of them yet. Hopefully this book will be my first step in the right direction. I do miss all my wonderful friends I made on Pine Island. Those years will always be very special to me. I grew into my own woman on that island being away from all my sisters. My great friends on the island were like family to me.

I was about ten years old and I hung out with three boys who were my best friends. Two of the boys and I had been friends since we were born. One boy moved to the neighborhood when I was about seven or eight years old. One day we all decided to play with my Ouija Board.

I played with it all the time with my sisters. I believed in it completely. We took the board to one of the boys house and we set up outside. We asked it all kinds of silly kid questions. Then someone decided we should ask it how old our dad's would be when they died. So the two boys that I'd known since birth went first. They got answers that were a long time off. They were both happy. Then it was my turn with the new boy. We asked about my dad first but I wasn't ready for the answer. So in my brain I asked about the new boys dad. We got an old age that he would die. So finally I was ready. I just knew since everyone got these old ages that their dads would die that I'd get one too. So out loud I asked when the new boys dad would die. But in my brain I was asking when my dad would die. When I got the age of forty six years old. I got very upset. But the poor boy sitting across from me thought we were talking about his dad. He freaked out. He started screaming and crying. The other boys mom yelled out the window what was wrong, since we were always getting hurt. We went in and told her. She calmed the boy down and said that was enough of the Ouija board. Us four never played with the Ouija board again.

I was so upset on the inside. My dad was gonna die in seven years. I was never real close with my dad as a child. After that day I made it a point to get to know my dad. We became very close. I hoped the Ouija Board would be wrong. It wasn't. My dad passed away from lung cancer seven years later, at the young age of forty six years old. This was a lot to have on your mind for seven years of your childhood. I never asked the Ouija Board when anyone would die again. I didn't want to know. As I got older I realized that it was good that I found out when I did. It gave me a chance to like and love my dad. I had spent so many years hating him. So I had a chance to get to really know him. I got to enjoy all of his good qualities. He had a lot of good in him. I had always dwelled on the bad part of him. When my dad died I truly loved him and forgave him.

When I was eleven years old my parents decided to move to Florida. I had never even been out of New York. I was so upset. Then the dreams started at night before we moved to Florida. I had a dream about the road that we would live on. I had a dream that some of the kids in Florida had motors on their bikes. I also had a dream about the school I'd go to.

The school had the hallways outside and inside. This sounded crazy to a New York girl. There was big steel gates on the hallways that lead outside. After I had these dreams I told my sisters and friends in New York. Everyone just laughed at me. They said I was just scared about moving so I was dreaming crazy stuff about Florida. When I got to Florida I saw my dreams come true. It was a hour drive from the airport to our new home in Florida. When we turned down the road our new house was on I knew it cause it looked exactly like my dream. When I met the neighborhood kids I was amazed. They didn't ride bikes like we did in New York. They rode motor cycles, mini bikes, and dirt bikes. Those were the bikes with motors on them from my dream.

My first day of school was scary to start with since I had gone to school all my life with the same kids. That first day when I walked through those big steel gates I couldn't hardly believe it. Then as I walked down the halls and I turned down the next hall and I was outside but still in school. Those crazy outside halls in my dreams were real. They were in my new school in Florida. On my first day in Florida I was very unhappy. I wanted to be back in New York with all my family and friends. Dad and mom took us shopping since the truck with all our stuff wouldn't be there for a few more days. When we got home from shopping we got settled into our new home. Which I hated since it wasn't as nice or as big as our house in New York.

Once everyone was calmed down and everything was put away. Dad told mom he wanted to take her to the local tavern. The Dome. He wanted her to meet the town folk. Dad had come down a few days before us to get an apartment and a job. It was a small southern town. Not even a traffic light in the town. Just the blinking light close to the volunteer run fire house. Anyway mom was happy to go meet some people. Mom is very outgoing and loves people. She also hadn't gone anywhere all her life. Her life was her sister she had to leave in New York. She had never been away from all her family and friends so this was very hard for her too. But she always believed in Raymond's dreams. So they left and us kids hung out being miserable. When mom and dad got home mom was so excited. She had met a lot of really friendly people. She came home with fresh oranges and tangerines from a couple that dad introduced her to. She was so excited to tell me about this couple. She told me they had a son a year younger then me.

She told me the boy's name was Robbie just like my best friend I had left in New York. She told me about how this boy was being raised by his mother and a step father who also was his uncle. His real dad and step dad were brothers. She knew this would tug at my heart. She told me how Robbie and I would be the best of friends. But as she told me about this Florida Robbie, I didn't picture a friendship like I had with my New York Robbie. I stood there as a eleven year old girl falling in love with a boy I had never met. But I knew that my Florida Robbie would one day be the love of my life. My soul mate. Robbie and I became friendly but never the best friends my mom had hoped for. We always said hello and were polite to each other but that was it. We were both very shy. Never even a date through our teenage years or our twenties. Then one night it happened. I had been divorced for two years.

I walked into a local bar and there was Robbie. We both said Hi but this time he kissed me on the cheek and handed me a rose. He had just bought the rose for his mom but gave it to me. He asked me if he could buy me a drink and I said yes. We drank and danced the night away. After the bar closed we weren't ready to say good bye. So we bought a six pack of beer and we went for a walk on the beach. I had three kids from my previous marriage. They were Bobby Ray six years old, Roseanne two and a half, and John one and a half. We talked about the kids, he had met them a few times. He told me how he would raise them if we stayed together. We fell in love that night on that beach. We got married and he adopted my three kids and has raised them as if they were his own. The youngest one John even looks like Robbie. Robbie was thirty years old and I was thirty one years old when we got together. It took us twenty years to find our way back to each other. We've been together for nineteen years now. We both know this is forever. Robbie is my best friend and the love of my life. We are soul mates.

When I was fourteen years old and my sister was sixteen years old. Our big brother had moved to Texas to work for a while. He had been gone for about a year. He was planning on coming home for a surprise visit on Mothers Day. He had told our father and dad had only told me. My brother was buying a brand new custom pickup truck. This was a very big secret for a fourteen year old to keep. It was about a week before Mothers Day.

My sister told me of a dream she had that our brother died and it was on a Friday night and the moon was full. I told her it was just a dream don't worry about it. It was so hard not telling her this wonderful secret of dads. We should have told our parents about this dream. A few nights later we were on our way home from the Friday night dance. We had gotten a ride with a guy and a couple of our girlfriends. We were almost home and my sister saw the full moon and got hysterical crying. She whispered the dream to me again. I tried to calm her down. The guy stopped the car and we all talked about the dream and finally got my sister calmed down. The next day we found out our brother had died the night before. He was walking home and got ran over by a car. My sister and I talked about her dream after the horrible news about our brother. We both agreed that we should have told someone and for now on we'd tell if we ever had a friend and I have been best friends for almost forty years now and I let a job come between us. Never again. Jobs come and go best friends are forever if they are true best friends. Dreams and thoughts, pay attention to them. Share them and maybe help someone with them. I don't know if we can change anything or if things will still just go the same way. That will be one of those questions I will ask when I die and go to heaven.

Ray Ray died when I was fourteen years old. He was only twenty years old. I'm not sure how soon it was after he died. I think it was a few days later. Someone was visiting and sleeping in our bedroom. So my sister and I were sleeping in my brothers bedroom. I don't know what my parents were thinking by putting us in his room that soon after he passed away. I was laying in his bed and I was feeling strange being in his room. I wasn't asleep yet. My brother appeared in his room. He was standing there looking at my sister and I laying in his bed. I jumped out of bed and we hugged and kissed. He told me he was alright. He told me don't worry about him. He didn't look like a ghost. He didn't look dead. He just looked like I remembered him.

It was very confusing to me. He was the first person close to me to pass away. So in my young mind it wasn't a visit from the other side. I was convinced that he was alive and ok. When we got finished talking we said good bye and he didn't disappear like a ghost he walked out of his back door that led outside. When he died he had been living in Texas for a year. So I spent a lot of years believing he was alive and just wanted out of our family. That night felt so real to me. Years later when I came to terms that he had really passed away. It gave me so much comfort that he had come to say good-bye to me that night in his bedroom. When I was fifteen years old I felt like my life was over. My big brother had died the year before.

I just couldn't pull myself out of this horrible depression. Nothing in my life was going well. I had a lot of friends, I had four sisters, one brother, three brother in laws, my sister's boyfriend was also my best friend, a wonderful nephew, and two loving parents. I had boys that liked me. So what was my problem in life. Now that I look back I have no clue what my problem was. But at the time life was so hard.

My parents had been so torn apart when my brother was killed in the car accident. It was a hit and run so there never was closure on what happened. All we knew was he was ran over and killed. It was more then just depression over my brother.

I had such low self esteem. I was so lost. My parents were drinking more after losing my brother. So it was easy to make drinks for myself when no one was looking. The bar was well stocked from the funeral and it never got low after that. I would sit there drinking a screwdriver in the afternoon and mom thought I was drinking orange juice. She would say good for me I was getting my vitamin C. In the evening a rum and coke looked just like a coke to my parents. So I was a very self-medicated teenager. I was so unhappy with my life. I started thinking everyone would be better off if I wasn't around anymore. I thought I would be happy to just go ahead and go to heaven and be with my brother that had died. I thought about it for several weeks. I finally decided this was what I was gonna do and decided where and how to do it.

I was going to kill myself. I was going to commit suicide. They had just finished repairing the bridge down the street from my house. There was a lot of big pieces of concrete piled in the water. I figured if I pushed myself off the bridge backwards I'd hit my head on the concrete and smash my head. I thought if the impact didn't kill me it would surely knock me out and I could just drown to finish me off. I thought I had the perfect plan. No one knew what I was up to that day. I always went fishing by myself. As I said good bye to everyone they had no clue I was saying good bye forever so I thought. I got down to the bridge and it was perfect no one was around. I looked off the bridge at the concrete slabs one more time. I sat down and looked over my shoulder to make sure I was in the right place. I was so scared all of a sudden so I just kinda started rocking myself to get up the courage to do it to commit suicide. Then it happened. A car pulled up, It was ANGEL MICK. He was a guy I had a crush on for three years.

We always talked but that was it, we were friends. He just saved my life and he didn't even know. I knew from that moment on that I was supposed to live. I figure God sent Mick to save my life because he was the one person that I respected, admired, and liked so much. We talked for a while then he gave me a ride home and we hung out in my driveway talking. He came back over quite a lot for a few months and we hung out and talked a lot. He just stopped coming over. I was really upset and missed him a lot. Then I realized he had done what he was supposed to do and his work with me was over.

He saved my life that day and now I could handle my life and anything else life was gonna throw at me. I don't remember if I told him that he saved my life that day. If I didn't I'd like to tell him now. THANK YOU ANGEL MICK FOR SAVING MY LIFE THAT DAY ON MATHERSON BRIDGE. I am so glad he pulled up that day. I went on to live quite a full, happy, exciting, fun filled, awesome, wonderful life. Our lives crossed each others paths a few times since we lived in a small town. We brought our kids to the same daycare for a year. He was my sons little league baseball coach. I moved away from our small town. I'll never forget ANGEL MICK.

As a kid my favorite place to go was the dock at the river. My parents friend let us use her dock. We had our boat tied up at her dock. I'd go down to the dock everyday. It was only three houses away from our house. It was my job to make sure the boat was always bailed out. I'd go fishing from the dock. I had four crab traps tied to the dock to catch fresh blue crabs. I'd sit and watch the mullet jump. The manatee and its baby were so huge. I loved watching them play. The alligators always scared but amazed me. My friends and I had a fort one time not far from the dock. It was underground on the river. One day my dad and I were passing the fort in our boat and I showed him where the fort was. So he slowed down and all of a sudden we saw a alligator go into our fort. We both laughed and that was the end of that fort. The snook would plow up river. I'd fish for hours trying to gig a mullet or hook a snook. I fished there for about ten years. The only thing I'd catch on my line was blue crabs. I never caught a mullet or snook off that dock. I'd go sit on that dock when I was happy and enjoy the wildlife. I'd sit on that dock when I was sad and ask for Gods help. I was sitting on the dock one day when I was about fifteen years old.

As I cried I watched the blue crabs crawling on the rocks under the dock. I was crying because I missed my brother that had passed away. I saw a snook swim close to the dock. In the four years I had sat on the dock this was the first time a snook came that close to the dock. The snook stuck his head out of the water and laughed at me. I shook my head and looked away. I thought my eyes were playing tricks on me. I looked back down at the snook. It was still there laughing at me. I got very scared. Then I realized the only explanation for this snook laughing was it had to be a sign from God or my dead brother. I laughed with the snook. We sat there for about thirty minutes. Then the snook swam away. I never saw another snook that close to the dock again. After the snook left I was fine. No more tears that day. I realized that I'd be ok. I still missed my brother, but I knew God was taking care of him in heaven. As I sat there I knew if I told anyone this story they'd think I was crazy. I knew I experienced a very special event with God. For years after that when I was upset and sitting on that dock. I'd think about my laughing snook and I couldn't help but smile.

I never told anyone about that day until I was in my forties. I told my husband Robbie about my snook. We had a good laugh about it. By then he understood that I had a lot of strange things happen in my life. We both believed in signs from God. It helped me to deal with my sadness. I realized that life would go on. I knew I'd have to learn to live with my wonderful memories of my brother. God helps you all everyday. You just have to pay attention to the signs. Sometimes the signs are small, sometimes the signs are huge like my laughing snook.

When I was fifteen years old I was hanging out with my two best friends who were like sisters to me. We were at the local teen club dance. We left the dance and went to see a friend, he worked at the gas station. My one friend had broken up with her boyfriend the week before. She was sixteen years old. My other friend had just turned seventeen years old the day before. The ex-boyfriend pulled up with some friends and he started giving us a hard time. The guy that worked at the gas station and the ex-boyfriend got into a fight. Then the ex-boyfriend made some horrible threats and then he left. We were all shook up. We hung out at the gas station and we talked for a while. Then it was time for me to go home.

I told my best friends to be careful and I got a ride back to the dance from another friend that had pulled up. As my sister and I walked home from the dance I told her what had happened. My one best friend was also my brother in laws sister. We were family. When we got home I went to bed. I didn't tell my parents nothing about my crazy night. I was too upset to sleep. I just layed there thinking and I listened to the TV in the living room that my parents were watching. I knew I should tell my parents because there had been problems with the ex-boyfriend earlier that week and they had gotten a restraining order put on him. I also knew I'd get into big trouble if I told my parents that I had left the dance. What should I do? I didn't want my friends mad at me for telling. Well I layed there too long without telling. A special news report came on the TV. It said that there was a shooting in our small town. They gave the address and mom ran into my room and asked if that was where my friend lived. I said yes. It was midnight by now.

Mom called my brother in law and told him to come get daddy. He did and they went over there. A few minutes later my sister came and got mom. My sister and I sat in the living room waiting for them to come back. As I sat there I knew my best friend had died. I didn't say anything to my sister. I was scared and confused. Why was I sitting here thinking the worst. I should be praying for their safety. So I prayed but in my heart I knew it was too late for one of my bestfriends. Mom got home a couple of hours later. She told us that my bestfriend/brother in laws sister had died. She said my other best friend was on the way to the hospital. The ex-boyfriend had shot her and she had died. A child killed for no good reason.

Mom didn't give me much hope for my other best friend. Mom said she had talked to her in the ambulance while they were contacting her family. Mom had told her she'd be ok and was praying for this scared young girl. Mom was getting me ready for the worse in case my other best friend didn't make it. Another one of our friends was shot too. He was on his way to the hospital too. I told mom that I had left the teen club dance with my best friends earlier that night. I told everything that had happened. She was so angry with me but she knew I was in too much pain to be yelled at. I stayed up all night praying for my best friend and the boy that were fighting for their lives. They both survived their gun shot wounds.

He stayed in the hospital for two weeks. We've lost touch with him over the years. We see him once in a while. I'm sure the memories of that night will always be with him. The friend at the gas station grew up and became a police officer. I'm pretty sure that night had a lot to do with that career choice. I cried my heart out that night for my friends. It always bothered me how I knew that my friend was dead before anyone had told me. As I grew up and got to understand my gifts from God I've come to terms about how I knew that night before they told me.

The ex-boyfriend that had done the shootings got caught a week later. During that week I worried that he was going to come and shoot me. It was the longest week of my life. Thirty five years later he is still alive and well sitting on Florida's death row. My dear bestfriend/sister Jan only got to live to be sixteen years old. Her only mistake in her short life was breaking up with a crummy boyfriend. We were just starting our lives. Her's was cut way too short. She never got to fall in love and get married and have kids. She never got to find her soulmate and have true love. She never got to meet our four beautiful nieces. She never got to babysit those beautiful rowdy nieces. She never got to know that one niece that always reminded me of her. Her looks, her sweetness, her love for everyone and everything around her, and her passion for living life.

My other bestfriend/sister spent a month in the hospital. Then years of memories of that horrible night one day after she turned seventeen years old. She and I are still bestfriends to this day. We keep our bestfriend Jan in our hearts and memories. We still talk about her like it was just yesterday when we were all hanging out and cruising town in her car. From the store to the beach then back to the store then back to the beach all day long. We always wonder how she would have grown up if she would have had the chance. We'll always love and miss you.

REST IN PEACE JAN.

CHAPTER 3
FATHERS

Daddy Ray was told he had a daughter. He was happy but deep down he wanted a son. The good lord had blessed him with his fifth daughter. He had only one son. Ten years later he got his last child, his second son. It was the 60's and people treated girls and boys different. Not daddy. He taught all seven kids they could do anything. He wasn't the kind of dad that we were watching on TV in those days. He did the best job he knew how which wasn't always great. He sometimes drank a little too much. With seven kids maybe at times he needed those drinks to cope. He was a strong man in many ways. We sometimes saw his weakness peak out. Daddy taught us we could do anything and everything. He taught all of us to fish, play ball, mow the lawn, and work on his car. We helped him with anything he was doing. He spent time with us and taught us at the same time.

Momma stayed home and raised us kids. She put her dreams and ambitions on a back shelf. She raised kids for thirty eight years. Daddy sometimes worked two jobs. When he got home he always had a little energy left to play with us. He never was too tired to talk about our day. He would play baseball and hide and seek with us. He'd bring his golf clubs out and teach us to hit golf balls. When the balls ran out he would pick apples off the apple tree. We'd hit apples with momma yelling out the window she needed those apples for making pies and applesauce.

He'd take a few of us on his clam boat. We had to work then we could fish. The deal was you cleaned what you caught. We all learned to clean fish. He didn't have the time or energy to go to our ball games. When we got home he wanted to hear about the game play by play. One of the girls wanted a go go cage. He built the best go go cage and got her a pair of go go boots. Another girl wanted a hope chest. He got the biggest hope chest he could find. The twins wanted new bikes, they got matching bikes. The oldest girl wanted a stereo to play her albums on. She got a brand new stereo. I wanted a crab trap since the crabs kept falling off my fishing pole. He got me four crab traps from his buddy who's son I ended up married to twenty years later. Little brother wanted a BB gun, he got a new BB gun.

I needed to write about this part of Daddy Ray. This is the man I choose to remember. He had a lot of good in him. No matter what happened he did love and care very deeply about all of his children. He was a loving father. He loved being a dad. He also was the boogyman when he came and tucked me into bed. He left a lot of mental scars on his kids. Who knows who he would have been if that priest hadn't molested him seventy years ago. I was just seventeen years old and daddy Ray was sick. He went to the doctor for weeks that turned into months. He had pneumonia to start with but as the time went by he didn't get any better with the treatments he was receiving. It was September 1978 and daddy was only forty six years old.

He found out he had lung cancer. We were all very freaked out. They put him into the hospital very quickly to remove the lung that had the cancer. They opened him up and found that the cancer was already spreading to the other lung. They closed him up and told him they would do radiation and chemo and they gave him three months to live. Cancer was still pretty new back then and I had never known anyone that was told how long they might have to live. I prayed everyday. My mother and I did Novena's everyday. I just knew if we prayed and believed that he would be ok. Every time someone said something about how my daddy was dying, I'd get so angry and mad and I'd snap at them. I wanted everyone to believe and pray for him. I kept begging God to please let us keep him a little longer.

My daddy wasn't a great daddy or a perfect person for that matter. He had his baggage that he had to tote during his life. This doesn't really have a lot to do with this subject but maybe it will help one person out there. My daddy was molested by a priest when he was seven or eight years old, he was a alter boy. He wanted to be a priest himself until this happened. He quit going to church and being a alter boy. Daddy never molested any boys as far as we know. But he did molest me. He was molested seventy years ago. The scars still run deep in my memories of daddy. I openly hated daddy when I was very young. Everyone could tell and they all talked about it. I finally decided to try to like him. I found a very loving, caring, smart, funny, awesome daddy inside this jerk of a man. Boy was I surprised. So as the years went by and he quit molesting me Thank God. He and I developed such a close Father-Daughter connection.

So here I was watching my daddy dying a little more each day. I wasn't ready to lose him. I made sure I spent as much time with him as I could those last few months. It was now December 1978. I was hoping for a Christmas Miracle. Daddy was a jerk sometimes but I loved him with all my heart. I started dating a new boy about a month before daddy died. My boyfriend and I were at the drive-in one night shortly before daddy died. I had my first clear vision of my life that night. My boyfriend went to get us soda's and popcorn. For some reason I stayed in the truck.

I was looking at this bunch of trees near the screen. All of a sudden I went into my first vision. I saw my dads sister, his brother, and my two uncles and my sister. They all live up north in New York and we live in Florida. I saw them all coming down to Florida quickly and all of a sudden. I knew they were coming for daddy's funeral. I started crying so hard. I now knew my daddy was gonna die. I was scared and upset. My boyfriend got back to the truck and I was crying very badly. He asked me whats the matter? He must have thought I was crazy when I told him about the vision. It was the seventies, people didn't talk about things like this back then. He asked me if I wanted to go home right then and I said no, I didn't think it was gonna happen that night. I said we can go straight home after the movie. My vision came true about a week later.

My daddy kept getting worse. I overheard daddy ask momma to call the priest to give him his last rites. I cried. So when the priest got there mom, my brother, and I had to go outside. I'm not sure where mom and my brother went to. I stayed near the front door on the porch hoping and praying that the priest could heal daddy. I knew things were really bad because daddy didn't even go to church. He always sent us but he never went with us. When the priest came out of the house he was crying very hard. He hugged me and told me over and over how sorry he was. This was not what I had expected to happen. The priest and I cried our hearts out that day on the front porch. This was one of those tough old priests. Those last rites must have been some really tough ones for him to hear. Daddy had been getting treatments at the hospital then he'd come home for a few days. So the next day after his last rites he was feeling pretty good. I got my hopes back up again that maybe the priest had healed him. Dad sent my sister and I for some fried chicken.

Before I left I kissed him and hugged him like I always did when I got ready to go anywhere. He griped that my long hair fell in his face like he always did. Then we both laughed. I told him that I loved him. He told us to get going that he was hungry. I was on top of the world. I never asked if he did that to get us out of the house or if he was really hungry. On our way home with the chicken a ambulance came up behind us with lights and sirens going. We pulled off the road and we looked at each other and we both said its going to our house to get daddy. The tears started as soon as I saw it behind us. To this day thirty three years later I cry every time a ambulance comes up behind me when I'm driving. We followed it to our house. We got home and the ambulance was there and they were heading inside to get daddy. I got out of the car and started yelling and screaming for my little brother. He came running into my arms and we held each other and cried.

I was so scared that I didn't go up to daddy. I just wanted them to hurry up and make him feel better. Momma was yelling to me that it was gonna be ok. My sisters husband told her to stay with us kids that he'd go with momma and daddy. I knew in my heart that was gonna be the last time that I'd see my daddy. I didn't even go up to him and say good bye. I just watched them take him away. Mom and my brother in law stayed at the hospital for six hours. Dad told mom to go home and explain things to us kids. He told her he was ready to rest. That morning dad and mom had told my sister and uncle to fly down from New York on the next flight. So they were on their way down. Mom and my brother in law got home and I asked momma a bunch of questions.

Then I just felt the need to be alone so I went into the bathroom in mom's bedroom so no one would bother me. It was about thirty minutes after they got home. I heard the phone ring and I knew it was the hospital calling to tell us that dad had died. I heard everyone screaming and crying. I sat there and cried my eyes out then I went out to the living room and hugged and cried with my family. My sister and uncle arrived about thirty minutes later. My sister was heartbroken that she was too late to see daddy. She had tried so hard to get there before he had passed away. The rest of the relatives from my vision arrived the next day.

We had a funeral at the house and the priest came and spoke at the service. Dad was cremated so we had a service without his body. I never really felt like I had complete closure since I never saw him after he had passed. Maybe its better this way since my last memory of him is on the gurney going into the ambulance. And the happy memory of hugging and kissing him goodbye before we had left. I was so angry that my prayers weren't answered. I didn't understand what had gone wrong. I was very upset with God. It just wasn't fair. I knew my daddy wasn't the best person but I still needed and wanted him in my life. I took daddy dying very badly. I didn't go to church as often anymore. I even told the priest years later in confession that I was mad at God for taking my daddy.

As the years went by I tried to understand Gods reasoning for taking my daddy at such a young age. I wasn't mad anymore. I started praying more often again. My sister from out of state always talked to me about God. She never gave up on me. After years of talking on the phone and whenever she would come down for a visit. I finally told her that I was gonna start going to church again. I also got my kids enrolled in Sunday school. My sister saved me, my kids, and my husband. We put God back into our lives. God is in our life everyday all day long. I forgave God for taking my daddy. I forgave my daddy for being such a jerk that God had to take him so young. I put daddy where he belongs in my happy memories spot in my heart.

I grew up in a family that was always in a uproar. You never knew what was going to happen next. Any little thing might set my father off. I always hated the fighting and screaming. I always told myself when I grew up things would be different in my house. I was a shy and quiet little girl. When I played with my friends I was very out going and loud. I grew up and married a man just like my father. So I got a life just like my mothers life. I stayed in the marriage for ten years. I got divorced but the memories and nightmares lasted for years. I always said I wouldn't yell and fight with my husband. He was a abusive person and I became one too. I thought that was the only way to survive the marriage. Years later I learned to survive was to leave the abusive man and marriage. It took me having two kids and being pregnant with the third child to realize my kids were learning that life was always a uproar. I didn't want my kids to grow up like I did.

I left the marriage but that didn't calm my life down. My ex-husband still came over and turned our life upside down at all times of the day and night. The night before my oldest son Bobby Ray was to start kindergarten, my ex came over at 2:00 am to see him. He woke us up and told us he was going to war the next morning, so he was there telling us goodbye. He wasn't going into the war the next day. He wasn't even in the military. Then he left and wrecked his truck down the road so we had to drive him to his girlfriends house in the middle of the night. We got back and I had to get three kids put back to bed then get them all up early the next morning for my son's first day of school. He drove us crazy for two years. Then I fell in love with another man. My new boyfriend moved in with us and my ex husband still caused problems for a month. After a month he left us alone. I found the quiet, calm. wonderful life I had been looking for all my life. It was just as wonderful as I knew it could be.

It took me about five years to calm myself down. I should say it took my new husband about five years to calm me down. I was still a yeller. I would give the kids a smack on the butt if they did something wrong. My new husband Robbie finally taught me you don't have to yell or hit to get your point across. By yelling and hitting I had taught our kids to do the same thing. We're still trying to teach them not to yell and hit. They're getting a lot better but they still have a way to go. Hopefully they'll learn to calm down before they are adults. We don't want them to grow up and have crazy lives. We're trying to break the cycle. So when they have kids they won't yell and hit. We want our kids and grand kids to have calm lives. I'm not blaming my yelling and hitting on my parents. They raised us kids the best way they knew how. I'm sure with seven kids in the house it was hard for my parents.

Back in those days hitting kids was the way most people raised their kids. I had friends that got hit with belts, switches, or anything else their parents picked up when they were mad. We were really kinda lucky since we only got hit with their hands. Also our parents did more yelling then they did hitting. I'm not saying that I'm a perfect parent because I'm not. I'm still learning how to control my temper when my kids are driving me crazy. Kids do need to be taught right from wrong. There is a right and wrong way to teach them.

No one has a right to hit anyone in this world. Violence is not the answer. Many people say thats what is wrong with the younger generation. That they need a good whipping. I do not agree. My mother would make a wonderful homemade dinner every night. She would start preparing dinner everyday about 3:00pm. We ate dinner at 5:00pm every night. On Sundays we usually ate at 2:00pm. Everyone knew this in the family so no one should ever be late for dinner. With seven kids someone was late once in a while. That ruined dinner for everyone. My dad would yell at the late child. Then all through dinner everyone would be on edge, knowing he was in a bad mood. Then there was the split milk. Everyone tried so hard to be careful not to spill their milk. It seemed like it was only once in a while when it happened. It was probably about once or twice a week. When it happened everyone knew the drill and tried to get it cleaned up fast. It never mattered how fast we cleaned it up. The spiller still got yelled at. Then the rest of us were scared we would spill our milk. Of course some nights there would be two or three spilled milks.

During all this I thought to myself, when I grow up I won't yell at my kids when they spill a drink. Then you grow up and forget what it feels like to be a kid. I have three kids. We have had our share of spilt milk. I've done my fair share of yelling over spilt milk. One night as I was yelling and the milk spiller was crying. My oldest son Bobby Ray turned to me and said Rozie didn't spill it on purpose. Being a parent I said she should have been more careful. Bobby Ray is the comic of the family. So he says she was being as careful as she could be. What do you think she wanted to spill her milk in her plate and ruin her food. Do you think she wanted to get yelled at?

I looked at him mad at first, then as his words sunk into my brain. I realized I was acting just like my father. That was the last time I yelled about spilt milk. Rozie was eight years old at the time. That was thirteen years ago. My husband sometimes would still get a little upset over spilt drinks. But the kids and I would get it cleaned up as fast as we could. Being a parent isn't just about teaching our kids. It's also about paying attention to our kids and learning from them. We grow up and forget what its like to be a kid. I bet if every adult thought back to when they were a kid. They would remember thinking to themselves that when they grew up, they wouldn't make their kids feel bad like their parents made them feel bad.

Some where between childhood and adulthood we forget so many important things. I remember so many times that I didn't want to grow up. I always said I'd stay a kid at heart. In a lot of ways I have. Its so hard when you start raising your own kids. So much changes when you become a adult. I loved my job and career so much that sometimes my family came second. I thought that I had to be like this to keep this important job . So I could make sure I could support my kids in case anything happened with Robbie and I. I didn't realize that I was letting this happen. I always told myself that I was putting my family first. I would work all the overtime that was required of me. I thought my family could use the extra money. But what they really needed was me. My husband Robbie and our three kids never complained so I figured everything was perfect. But it was so far from perfect I had no clue. When I was home I was too tired to pay much attention to anyone. A few hugs and kisses and I thought that was enough for all of us. They wanted to talk to me and play with me.

They wanted to get to know their mother. I would go rollerblading with them and think I was spending a lot of time with them.

All they knew was that I was hot and tired. The kids would start a conversation with "mom are you hot and tired". If I said yes they would keep it short. When I said no we'd talk and play for hours. How I wish I would have or could have said no more often. I would come home and they would all be playing and be happy. A lot of times I'd come home and Robbie and the kids would be in the yard having a great time together. They never knew when I'd be coming home. I was so jealous. Then I'd end up getting mad over little things. I use to be jealous of the time my husband spent with our kids. I should have been happy that they all bonded so well. He had adopted my three kids and was a great daddy. I was so lucky to have him.

He commercial fished at night so he had them during the day and I had them at night. I was too tired at night to enjoy them the way I should have been. My career was my life. He knew the kids teachers. He knew the kids favorite cartoons. He'd even put our little girls hair up in cute hair styles for school. When I'd have a day off I'd have to ask Robbie what time was I supposed to pick the kids up from school. Robbie finally made me make a choice between my life and their life. I chose their life. I traded my career for my kids and my husband. It's a lot less money.

I now know my kids. We've had another chance to bond. I now have a wonderful relationship with all of my kids and I owe this to my husband Robbie for forcing me to trust in him and our love and faith to guide us through our life. The kids are now twenty, twenty one, and twenty five. I've been a huge part of their lives. I stayed home or worked part time from the time my youngest was in first grade until he was half way through eighth grade. I've known all of their teachers and I've even gone on quite a few field trips. I got to be a mother because my kids have a fantastic father. For five and a half years I had to go back to work full time. It was very hard to do after all these years but my husband got sick so it was my turn to step up to the plate like he did for me. We all did the best that we could do and we got the two youngest kids graduated from high school. I'll always be so happy that my husband let me enjoy our kids childhoods without being hot and tired.

I was just nineteen years old when I got my step-dad. It was hard for me at first. I only had my real dad for seventeen years. Step dad was always like a real dad to me. He wasn't a perfect person, but I don't know anyone that is perfect. Everyone makes mistakes in their lives. The good things he did in his life were so many more then the mistakes. He raised my little brother like he was his own child. He always told me family and a good job were the most important things in life. His family always came first in his life. He didn't talk a lot so when he did people stopped and listened. He was usually right when he did talk. Always right if you ask him. He loved my mom with all his heart. A holiday never passed without a present or flowers for mom and a holiday party for his family.

Even on his birthday he would have the party and him and mom would cook all the food. He always had his camera and video camera going during all the parties. He was a great grandpa. He was never too tired or sick to spend time with his grandkids. He loved the craziness of all his grandkids over at the same time. I kept moving back home so he built another bedroom onto the house. When I moved out the last time I didn't have a car. He let me use his van for eight months until I could afford to buy a car. He had a heart of gold. I could go on for hours with everything he did for me, my mom, my brother, my sisters, and his grandkids.

It came down to he did things for everyone. He never expected or asked for anything in return. All he ever wanted was to be a part of our big, crazy, loud, fun family. He always wanted every one to treat mom with love and respect. He believed that she deserved it. He bought big boats so there would be plenty of room for all the family to go out on the boats. No matter how good there was the bad thing he did to his granddaughter. So I had to choose to have a dad and mom or to be a judge and jury. I beat myself up for a lot of years if I chose right or wrong. I'll find out when I go to heaven to be judged. I decided that I was not God and it was not my job to judge. So I chose to keep my dad and mom. It caused a lot of tension over the years with the rest of the family.

My kids are grown now and they know everything that happened. They have thanked me for letting them keep their grandma and grandpa in their lives all those years. They were very close to their grandparents and they are happy that they had that special bond with them. So hopefully I chose right. I had to be who I am and that is a forgiving, loving, spiritual person. The last time I saw dad at his house was a strange visit. My kids and I went to dad and moms house for a visit. My husband told the kids and I to clean the yard and mow the lawn while we were there. He had been going down with our oldest son Bobby Ray and doing the yard work. We lived about fifty miles away. The rest of the family lived five to ten miles away. Dad was dying from lung cancer. He was our step father and the family had a problem with him. So when we got there we all went inside and said hi. Then I had the kids go outside to pick up the tree limbs that the storm a few days earlier had blown down. I was in the house talking to dad and mom. The kids started arguing about the yard work. I tried a couple of times to get them settled down and do the work.

Dad came outside and told them to stop doing the yard work. There was attitude in his voice of anger that I had never heard. He was not upset with the kids but I was upset with them. He wouldn't let them mow, he said he didn't care what the yard looked like. He always took such pride in his yard looking nice. He said "Let the next mother f----r worry about what this yard looks like. That day was the first time he spoke about dying. It scared me.

I felt so strange through the whole visit. As we said our good-byes and dad and mom stood on the front porch saying good bye like they always did. I was getting choked up. I got halfway down the driveway. I turned around and looked at dad one more time. It came to me that this would be the last time I'd see him on that porch. I started to cry. I got into the car and the kids all told me don't cry mommy. They said grandpa looks like he's getting better. They said look at him, his hair is growing back. I took one more look and sure enough I hadn't even noticed but his beautiful hair had grown back. But I still knew that was the last time I'd see him at home. It was the last time I saw my dad at home. I didn't tell the kids because they were so excited and happy about his hair growth. I just couldn't break their hearts right then.

I had always been truthful with them about their grandpa's illness. They knew for three years that grandpa was dying. They knew we didn't know when it was gonna happen. He was doing experimental drugs for three years hoping it would save his life. Also in case his kids or grandkids ever needed the cancer drugs to save their lives. Now that's love. We got the dreaded phone call on 10/5/2001 at 4:30am. When my husband answered the phone and said it's your sister. I said it can't be anything good. I thought dad had died. I was so happy to find out that he was just brought to the hospital. That meant I could see him one more time. She told me the ambulance had taken him to the hospital. I knew it was bad because dad had been fighting lung cancer for three years. They had told him three years earlier that there was no hope for recovery. He had been letting them experiment on him. He wasn't ready to die when they had offered him this chemo. He turned his three months to live into three years. He didn't sit there and wait to die. He got up everyday like he was going to work still.

He'd have his coffee and breakfast then he'd go outside and work on whatever project he had going at the time. He was a carpenter so he had a lot of wood projects going on. He made beautiful pipes and canes. When the chemo made him real sick he'd stay in bed late. I always knew when he did because momma would call me worried that he was in bed late. He said he wasn't going down without a fight. So I got directions from my sister how to get to the hospital. We decided that I'd go alone. My husband stayed home to get the kids off to school.

I left to go say good bye to my dad. As my sisters directions had me going back towards my house I pulled over and called her back on my cell phone. She told me I took a wrong turn. So she gave me more directions. I was coming from the opposite direction then what she came from when she went to the hospital. When I got to a dead end in some dark woods I called her back. She gave me more directions. I drove then I realized these were wrong so I called her back. I told her to ask dad how I can get there. I said dad can give me the directions better then you and he was in the back of an ambulance. We both laughed and dad told her how to get me to the hospital. She said she'd meet me out front of the hospital. We kept talking as I pulled into the parking lot. I asked her is that you the person I'm about to run over in the middle of the road. She said yes so I hung up. I stopped in front of her and she was still talking to me on the cell phone. I told her I already hung up and I'm gonna go park my car.

We walked into the emergency entrance to dads room. I was supposed to go over to mom and dads house on Sunday that had passed but I had the flu. I was so afraid to bring any germs into their house. So this was Friday and I was planning on going to mom and dads on Sunday that was coming up. When I walked in and saw dad hooked up to the machines and a oxygen mask on his face, I thought I need to say something funny. I told him "You couldn't wait until Sunday to see me you had to come to the hospital so I'd come see you". He laughed. I was really scared but I had to stay happy and confident for Dads sake. I knew he was a lot more afraid then I was right then.

My sister who turned out to be a angel from heaven that day and many days after that first hard day. We always teased her that she was momma's angel from heaven because mom always told this story to us when we were growing up. Mom was always psychic so maybe she knew my sister was gonna be her angel from heaven one day in the future. My sister was so strong and such a big help to dad, mom and to me. I wouldn't have been able to stay so strong all the days to come if it wasn't for her there by my side through all of it. So mom, my sister and I hung out in the emergency room with dad for about a hour. They asked dad if he wanted to be brought back by machines. He had to sign a paper saying he didn't want to be brought back.

When they got him a room we all went up to his room. We hung out and talked and laughed. We kept his spirits up. I had to leave for a couple of hours. I was filling in for the secretary at the fishhouse that day and had to go pay the fishermen. So I explained it all to dad and told him how sorry I was that I had to leave. They made us leave the room while they did some stuff to dad. While we were in the waiting room I told mom and my sister we need to call the family. They said its kinda early in the morning. So I started calling my brothers friends trying to find him. I left messages and about thirty minutes later my brother called back. He said he'd be up later would that be ok. I told him we really didn't know. I told mom and my sister to call dads sister when they got home and she would call his brothers. They had both been up all night and needed to go take a rest. So I left the hospital about 9:00am very upset that I had to leave.

I called mom's sister in New York and told her what was going on. My sister said she'd call our sister in Missouri. I got to work and worked as fast as I could. My husband Robbie told me I should spend the night at moms house so she wouldn't be alone. So I went home after work and packed some clothes in a over night bag. Then I went back to the hospital. I stopped in the hospital gift shop and got dad a stuffed lobster. He loves lobster. He had wanted Florida lobster a few months earlier so my husband Robbie and I bought him two Florida lobsters for his birthday.

We got him lobster, shrimp, and steak for his 60th birthday. He was so happy he loves steak and seafood. I was walking to the elevator and I saw dads brother. So we went up together. When I walked into dad's room I said real cheery "Dad look who I found downstairs". Dad was so happy to see him. Dad had worked for him for about twenty five years as a carpenter foreman. I was so happy that he had come to the hospital. Dad's sister and husband were there. I was so happy to see them. I've always liked her a lot. She told me a few days later that she didn't think that dad and her had been real close over the years. But you sure couldn't tell. Dad had always had good things to say about his sister and brothers. To hear them and watch them you would think they had always been super close. Dad was a very quiet, hard man to get through to. I got there at 2:00pm. I showed dad the lobster and told him I got it for him so he wouldn't have to be alone. I said when you get out of here I'll get you a real Florida lobster to eat.

I knew he wouldn't be getting out but I had to keep up the happy face for dads sake. He wasn't ready to give up. I wouldn't give up as long as he still had hope. We all talked and laughed. Dad liked his arms rubbed. So I started rubbing his arms on Friday afternoon. We started talking about a drink dad use to make. So I got my pen and paper out and had dad give me his recipe for this drink. Mom and my sister came back up to the hospital at 5:00pm after their naps. My brother and his girlfriend and kids came up about 7;00pm. Everyone took turns in the room with dad since it was real crowded with all of us in there. We took turns hanging out in the waiting room. My sister and I met the nicest woman in the waiting room. She was in her early 70's and was so full of life. Her husband was having heart problems a heart attack I think. She was there for hours alone. So all of our family had talked to her.

We were all afraid to leave since we didn't know what was going to happen to dad. My brother and girlfriend had to leave to get the kids home to bed. He told me to call him if dad got worse. Then the woman in the waiting room was told her husband was being moved to a different hospital. She was upset because it was about 10:30pm and she wasn't real sure how to get to the new hospital. So dads sister said one of us would take her. She said she wanted to drive her car if she could just follow someone there, so she could get back home from the hospital. So dads sister said my brother would and he said yes being as nice as he is.

So he went and told Dad bye and then left with the woman following him. My sister came into dad's room and said she was too tired to drive that she was gonna just sleep in the guest bed in dad's room. Remember my sister the angel from heaven. She said I could go spend the night with mom. Mom wasn't feeling too good so she didn't want to sleep at the hospital. Mom has a memory problem, she gets confused. We're all hoping its from the stress she's been under with dad's illness. A few years later we found out that mom has Alzheimers. I knew my sister was lying so I told her to come out into the hall. I said ok whats up. She started to lie again. I said no what's going on. She said you know he's dying and I don't want him to be alone. I had always loved and admired my sister. But at that moment I thought to myself this woman is so wonderful, special, giving, smart, sweet, caring, loving and truly a angel from heaven.

I said yeah you're right. I'll stay with dad you stay with mom. I'm not trying to take anything away from her but Dad and I were always super close. I had to be the one to stay with dad. She asked me if I was sure and I said yes. I was so scared but I had to do it. Mom came out and said what's going on. So we explained it to her. She said she should be the one to stay but she just couldn't do it. We told her she needed to go home and get some rest so she could be here for him the next day. So it was decided and I called my husband and told him. He said good he was glad that I was going to be with dad. So before you knew it everyone was gone. Dad and I were alone. I sat in the chair and rubbed his arm and we talked.

He asked how late did I usually stay up. I said I always stay up late. I told him if he got tired to tell me and I'd quit rubbing. He said he couldn't sleep. He hadn't slept since Wednesday night. I think he was afraid to go to sleep. So we stayed up until 1:00am. I told him I was gonna lay down to just wake me if he needed me. I still had the cough from my flu. He was coughing from his illness. We were a mess. So I went to sleep until 2:30am. Then I heard him coughing and I got up. I sat on my bed and rubbed his arm and we talked. He had to take his oxygen mask off to take sips of water. We had such a hard time with the straw. He decided the straw had to go. It wasn't much easier but we made it work, It was a slow process but he would finally get a drink. We stayed up until about 4:30am. He kept the lights on and the AC really cold. I froze all night with a jacket and blankets on. I just wanted him to be comfortable.

We got up at 6:00am. All through the night the nurses were in and out. They were GREAT. Saturday 10/6/2001 Dad's brother got there at 7:00am on Saturday morning. He and dad were so use to getting up early all those years to go to work. Thank goodness I'm a morning person too. I was so happy to see dad's brother. It had been a very long night. He asked me if I wanted some coffee, I said yes. He said how about something to eat I said no. He said how about a bagel. I said that sounds great. I hadn't eaten since lunch on Friday. I had just been drinking a lot of caffeine sodas to stay awake. After I ate I went to the rest room and got changed. Dad's sister got there about 8:30am. She said their other brother and wife would be here that afternoon. They live about five hours away. They kept bringing dad food. He tried to eat but he said it tasted bad.

Dad got tired of laying down so he wanted to sit up in the chair. We asked the nurses and they said yes he could. So he sat up in the chair for about two hours. He was able to keep the oxygen mask off for longer periods of time. Which was great but it was giving me false hope. Mom was planning on coming to the hospital first thing in the morning. My other sister was bringing mom up to the hospital. I was so happy that mom and that sister were going to get to spend some time together. I knew them and figured they'd stop for their breakfast. Dad had been asking for mom since 6:30am. So by 8:30am they still weren't there. So I called my sister and she said mom was taking a shower and then they'd be there. By 10:30am I was getting quite upset since dad had been asking for four hours. So there was no answer at mom's house. So I called my angel sister and she said they probably stopped to eat breakfast. They brought dads lunch and he wouldn't eat it.

His brother said he was going to the store and he left. He came back with a can of pork and beans and a can opener and a spoon. He opened it up for dad. Dad was so happy. He ate some of his beans. The nurse came in and he said dad needed some good southern food The nurse said ok she didn't care as long as he ate something. By the time mom got there around 12:00 dad was back in bed and tired out. I was so upset that she had missed out on those hours when he was feeling good. But years later I realized it was probably better that she did miss it since it gave me such false hope. My sister didn't want to see dad so she sat in the waiting room.

Some woman in the waiting room had seen me walk past several times barefooted. Yes barefooted in the hospital. I'm southern and I live in South Florida. What can I say thats me. So the woman was telling the people she was with how bad it was that I was barefooted. So my sister told me when I came by. I told the woman I was sorry that

I was offending her by being barefooted but I was southern and I hate shoes. I said I've been in this hospital for two days and I was gonna be comfortable. I told her she didn't need to be worrying or talking about me. Boy I was mad. She was mad too. She was acting like all that. I hate when people look down on me. She said a few smart mouth things and I just finally walked away. I felt really crummy now. I hate any upsets, arguing, or confrontations.

But when someone throws one my way I will stand up for myself and my family. I went and told dad what had just happened. He laughed and said don't put your shoes on. He loved to be barefooted too. Dad's other brother and wife got there about 1:30pm. He saw us rubbing dad and he joined right in. He went to the nurses station for some more cream. They said they didn't have any more cream. He wasn't leaving there until they got him more cream. He stood there with his empty bottle of cream waiting. So they finally found him some cream. He came back and he asked dad do you need your legs and feet rubbed too. Dad said sure. So he rubbed cream on dads legs and feet. I almost cried. That was the most amazing thing I'd ever seen in my life.

The love from brother to brother was just pouring out. I've always liked my step uncles before this. But now I have so much respect and love for them. The brotherly love between them and dad was the most beautiful thing in the world to witness. Dad was so happy. He loves his brothers and sister so much. It was so great to see how they rallied around dad in his time of need. His sister rubbed dad's arms for hours every time she was there, which was everyday for most of the day. Between her, mom, angel sister, and I one of us was always there with dad rubbing his arms and talking to him.

Saturday afternoon around 3:00pm I said I was going home to shower and see my kids. I hadn't seen my kids since Thursday night. I had to go home and explain to them about their grandpa. I missed my kids and husband a lot. On my way home I got a burger and fries and ate on the road again. I got home and talked to my husband. We decided the kids would go and see their grandpa on Sunday. The kids were mad they wanted to go back with me right then. They all made grandpa cards. John was the youngest and he had changed his name legally from Joshua to John like his grandpa six months earlier. John was ten years old. John gave me a stuffed animal to bring to grandpa. Then Roseanne gave me a stuffed animal for grandpa. The oldest boy Bobby Ray gave me a T-shirt with a rebel flag on it for grandpa. So I told the kids that they could give grandpa their presents tomorrow when they saw him but they wanted him to have them right then.

The kids were ten, eleven, and fourteen years old. So I packed a bag of clothes and took the presents. I kissed and hugged my kids a lot of times. I hated leaving them again but I had to be there for my dad. Then I was off to the hospital to spend the night with dad. I got back to the hospital at 7:30pm. When I got back to the hospital I had my cowboy boots on. I showed the woman who had a problem with my bare feet. I got to dads room and the doctor was in to see dad. Dad's sister and husband were there. His brother and wife from out of town were there. My brother was there. I was so happy to see my brother. The doctor told dad that he had pneumonia and he had a heart attack Thursday night. So dad wanted to change his code so they would bring him back. He said if it was the cancer killing him he'd go ahead and give up. But if it was a heart attack he still wanted to fight it.

The doctor was trying to talk him out of changing his code. The doctor knew it was the cancer and not the heart killing him but couldn't say that. It was a horrible scene to walk into. I wanted to turn around and run out the door. But I couldn't. Everyone was all trying to talk and make sense out of this horrible decision that had to be made. So I made my way through the crowd and took dads hand and said change his code now. So they said ok. The doctor went into the hall with some of the family. I stayed with dad. He explained it to me and I agreed. Even though I knew there probably wasn't much hope left. I knew he wasn't ready to give up. I would stand by his side and fight as long as he wanted to fight.

Then they called me out to the hallway. They asked me once again did I know that dad was dying. I said yes I know. I said he's not ready to die yet. I told them I can't dwell on him dying and keep a happy cheerful face for him. I told them he knows me too well. If I think about him dying he'll see it in my face. I told them all again he's not ready to die yet. So everyone finally agreed to his code. So they finally changed his code. He was happy. To me that's all that mattered at this point was his happiness. So after a little while everyone left except for my brother and I . We sat with dad and we talked about old times. Dad fell asleep for a few minutes and had a dream that he was cooking a steak. He was a great steak cooker. He looked over at my pillow and thought it was a ham. That kinda scared me but we made a joke about it.

My brother and I went downstairs to see if his girlfriend was done having her son's arm x-rayed. We met up with her and we went outside for a smoke. We talked and cried. The night before when we were outside talking and smoking he tried to be helpful and share some stories he had heard about when people died. He had scared me so badly. He said he didn't want me there when dad died. He said he had heard horrible stories from people about when someone dies. So he had shared these horrible stories with me which I didn't need to hear. I already knew the persons bodily functions let loose. But that didn't matter since dad had a bag for each bodily function. So there wouldn't be any mess. Then he told me how blood goes everywhere. NOT TRUE! But at the time I didn't know this. I tried to forget what he had told me. But it stayed in the back of my mind until the end. Nothing like that happened. He was trying to help but he just made me worry for nothing. I told him not to worry about me I'd be ok.

We went back up and he told Dad bye. It was about 9:30pm. Another night in the hospital. So after they left we hung out and talked and watched TV. I said I was going down for my last smoke for the night. As I was walking to the elevator I saw the woman who had a problem with my bare feet. I went up to her and told her I was very sorry for griping at her. I told her I was just really upset. I had been in the hospital for two days with my dad. I hadn't seen my kids in two days. I said my dad has a incurable disease called Scala Derma, he has lung cancer, pneumonia, and he had a heart attack and the doctors said that he is dying. I said I'm sure you're here because someone in your family is very sick too. I'm sure you're very upset too. I told her that

I'd pray for her and her family. She said thank you and that she was sorry too. I did pray for her but her dad died the next day.

I stopped and got me another caffeine soda to help me though the night. I got back into the room and got me some sleeping clothes and went and got changed for the night. I got back to the room and dad smiled like he did every time I walked into the room. I smiled back. This hospital room was filled with love. Dad had been coughing up a lot of blood and phlegm from the pneumonia. The nurses told me as long as he could cough it up that was good. They said if he couldn't get it all out I could help him by pulling it out for him with tissues and paper towels.

They showed me how to do it. They said when I could no longer do it they'd have to use the suction which was very painful. So of course I didn't want to cause my dad to go through anymore pain then he already had. So I would be up and down all night pulling blood and phlegm out of my dad. We'd have to take the oxygen mask off while we did it. Sometimes we'd have to put the mask back on for a few minutes then take it off quick and get some more phlegm out. It was so scary. I had never done anything like this before in my life. I didn't even like hospitals or anything that was gross or bloody. Anyway we went to bed at 12:30am on Saturday night. I layed there until 1:00am thinking I needed to talk to my husband. I needed to hear his voice. I was so scared. I needed his encouragement to help me make it through the night. At 1:00am my husband called me on my cell phone. I went out to the waiting room and talked to him. He said he just knew that I needed to talk to him. Robbie and I are just like that. We've used our brain waves like that a lot of times before.

He gave me the courage to face the rest of the night. I told him I was gonna come home the next day on Sunday and sleep for a few hours. I asked him if he would drive me back to the hospital Sunday evening and bring the kids up to see their grandpa like we had talked about earlier. He said yes he would. I just couldn't make the drive again. I told him I'd come home in the afternoon sometime. Then I went back to dads room. He asked who was on the phone. I told him it was Robbie. I asked if he needed a drink he said yes. So we gave him a drink and I went back to bed at 1:30am and slept until 3:30am when I heard his cup fall on the floor. I just rolled over. Then dad kicked my bed so I got up. He had tried getting a drink and spilled it on himself and the floor. So I dried him off and got him a drink.

Then I rubbed his arms and we talked. I pulled more blood and phlegm out. By 5:30am my hands were so swelled up from all the rubbing that I had done. I just kept rubbing. He told me to stop rubbing. He said put your hand on the bed and I did. He started rubbing my hand to get the swelling down. I let him rub each hand for a few minutes. Then I told him ok I'm fine let me rub your arms again. I told him not to worry about me that I was fine. He said he'd never stop worrying about me. He said it was really hard for him to switch roles with me.

He said he was supposed to take care of me not the other way around. We both laughed and we both knew it was my turn to take care of him. It was a emotional and physical strain and sometimes I wasn't sure how long I could keep going. Then I'd look at dad and see that he needed me there with him. He was so afraid but with me there he knew he could face anything as long as we faced it together. Some how I would keep going. We went to sleep about 6:00am. We slept or I should say I slept until 7:30am I don't know if dad ever slept. Sunday 10/7/2001 I woke up and I wanted coffee. But I drank my caffeine soda since it was right there in the room. Dad's sister got there about 8:30am. So I went and got changed then I got my coffee and a bagel. I came back up and ate and had my coffee in the room with dad. Dad's sister brought some liquid soap you rubbed on then you wiped off. So she and I gave dad a bath. We told him he'd have to get the nurses to do his private parts. He laughed and joked with us.

Angel sister called and said she was gonna bring mom to the hospital. I told her to rush mom along this morning. So they got there about 9:30am. So we all hung out in dad's room and in the waiting room. I told my sister what my plans were for that day about going home for a nap and to bring my kids back to see their grandpa. She said no I couldn't bring the kids. I told her yes I could I had already asked the nurses. She said that I was gonna scar my kids for life if

I brought them to the hospital. I explained to her that my kids have known for three years that grandpa was dying from cancer. I've made sure my kids understood that grandpa was living on borrowed time for three years. Grandpa dying was a part of their lives and childhood.

They had watched him getting sicker and thinner over the years. They love their grandpa with all their hearts. We had moved fifty miles away four years earlier. We still went to see mom and dad every two or three weeks. We always went over for mom and dads birthdays, mother and fathers day. They came to our house for X-mas dinners. Before we moved we saw them at least once a week. Usually two or three times a week. Mom and Dad came to our house for visits before we moved and after we moved. They came to every one of the kids church shows, school shows, and celebrations. Mom and Dad were Robbie and mine witnesses at our wedding. They were a huge part of our daily lives.

The kids would never forgive me if they didn't see their grandpa one more time. I had been worried all these days that he would die before I got the kids to the hospital to see him. Dad had already said he wanted to see the kids. Nobody was going to change my mind about this. Scare me yes, change my mind no. So now she planted the seed of doubt into my mind. Like I didn't have enough crap going on in my mind. So I told dad that I was going home for a nap and I'd be back with Robbie and the kids later that day, he said ok. I told him don't go anywhere before I get back. He knew and I knew what I meant. I was so scared that he'd die when I left that day. He promised he'd be there when I came back. That was the start to a very upsetting, messed up day.

I've looked back on it and wished that I could have kept it together better then I did. But you can't go back and change things. You just have to learn to live with your mistakes for the rest of your life. It's not easy but that's how life and people can mess with your head. It's not really the peoples fault or your own fault when things like this happens. This kind of grief, saddness, and stress is very hard on everyone that is involved. Its very hard for the sick person to be dealing with their illness and watching their family members falling apart all around them. I got home about 12:30pm. I talked to the kids and told them how much grandpa had loved the cards and presents. Robbie and I ate and talked.

Then I went to bed and slept for three hours. They got me up and we were all getting ready to go to the hospital. I got a phone call from my sister telling me not to come back to the hospital. She said that dad's brother in law was going to stay at the hospital that night with dad. I said no I'm staying at the hospital with dad. She said thats dad's family and they want him to stay. I said no I'm dad's daughter and I'm in charge of this. She said you're not in charge and don't bring your kids up here to the hospital. They don't think your kids should come. I told her too bad. I said Robbie and I are in charge of our kids and we're fixing to leave and go to the hospital with our kids so they can say good bye to their grandpa. I hung up on her. I was shaking and crying so badly I could barely talk to tell Robbie everything she had said. Robbie got me calmed back down. A few minutes later my other sister called me yelling at me. She said the same thing as my other sister had said. Then she asked me who put you in charge. I said I did and I hung up on her.

So then I was really upset. I'm the youngest of five daughters so they're all use to when they tell me to do something I always do it. Not this time. I can't remember if I called or if she called me but I talked to my Aunt. She is mom's sister who lives in New York. We are very close and she is always involved in our lives. She told me that I was doing the right thing and don't let your sisters upset you. She said if I could handle it I should be at the hospital since I wanted to be there. I told her thank you for always being there for me and helping me. So we hung up and I thought I could handle anything. I was wrong about being able to handle this kind of stress.

So then we left to go to the hospital. We got ten miles down the road and the cell phone rings. It's my sister again. So she's calmer but still trying to tell me not to come. I told her we were on our way there. She said she was still at the hospital, did I want her to wait there. I said no please go home. I told her she needed some rest. So she said ok she was gonna leave right then and take mom out to dinner then home.

Then she wanted to talk to Robbie and I said no, good bye and hung up on her again. Not a good idea. But she really didn't even want to talk to Robbie at this point. He was so mad that they were doing this to me. So the rest of the way to the hospital we laughed and joked with the kids. We wanted to keep everyone happy. We were all in a happy and upbeat mood when we got to the hospital.

We all knew this was probably going to be the last time we saw dad as a family. It was a very sad event for our family but we all knew this was something we needed to do as a family for dad. We turned down this long hallway and we saw my sister outside dad's room hysterical crying. Mom was hugging her. So of course we all think we're too late to see dad. Our happy faces turned to sad teary eyed faces. We were all heart broken. We all slowed down and looked at each other. It was the worst day and moment of my life. My poor babies faces. We were all hugging and kissing each other as we walked. All I could think was I didn't get the kids here fast enough. They were all thinking why didn't you bring us sooner. We got up to them and I said Dad died? They said no. I was so mad. I was so angry at all of them. I couldn't believe she did this to me and my family. What in the world was she thinking. She just made this harder for my kids. There was no need for this. She had seen us coming down the hall.

She should have went to the restroom or something. Anything but this crap. So she told me how sorry she was for yelling at me on the phone. I was so angry but I hugged her and mom. Then the kids hugged her and mom. Robbie hugged mom. So we went in to see dad. Then the nurse came in and asked us to step outside. So I told Robbie and he got aggravated cause he was talking to dad. So then we went back in. Then Rozie had to go to the rest room and I took her. So my sister came out in the hallway and started in on me again. I told her about her crying in the hallway was horrible for me and the kids. We went back in dads room.

John my youngest son was sitting next to me bugging me that he was ready to go. He was ten years old and very bored sitting in the hospital. I kept telling him daddy would take him home soon. I have no idea how long they stayed I started getting worried that I was scarring my kids for life by keeping them there too long. So I told Robbie that John was wanting to go. All the kids took turns holding his hand and saying good bye and that they loved him. They all wanted to hug and kiss him good bye like they always did. But they couldn't since he had so many tubes hooked up to him. So I walked out to the hallway with the kids. They were upset and I hugged and kissed all of them. Robbie was still in dad's room.

I made the worst mistake of my life when I walked back into the room and told Robbie again that the kids were ready to go. He was talking to dad. Robbie got up and I could tell he was upset. He walked out to the hallway and said that's the second time you've done that to me today. He said I was gonna leave in a minute. He said he wanted to finish talking to dad. So I said go back in there. He said no I'm done now. I begged him to please go back in there this might be the last time you see him. I said please don't make me have to live with this. This is so unfair. He wouldn't even go and say good bye to dad. At the time I didn't realize how hard this was for Robbie to be handling since dad and Robbie were very close. I tried so hard to do everything right for everyone involved but I ended up making a lot of mistakes and this was one of them. I was trying so hard to protect my kids that I hurt my husband. He said no he wasn't going back in and he hugged me and my family left no better then how we came into the hospital. I acted like a jerk to my husband and he acted like a jerk to me.

I know better then to tell him what to do like he's one of the kids. So now I get to keep this guilt the rest of my life. These are the things that happen when good hearted people try to plant seeds in your brain to help you. It doesn't always help you. You stop acting like yourself. You start acting crazy. I was heartbroken. I cried. I knew he hadn't finished talking to dad. When I walked back into the room dad said where's Robbie? I said he left and dad looked very sad. I was sad. Then my sister and mom left about fifteen minutes later. I was glad and mad. She couldn't have left sooner so we could have had a nice last visit with dad. Grief makes people do and say the craziest things. I went down for a smoke before they left and I cried like a baby. I walked past the chapel and told myself I would go in there later since I had missed church that morning.

I went back up and dad and I talked about EVERYTHING that had happened that day. He got me to laughing about all of it. He said he liked his brother in law but he was glad that I had come back. He calmed me back down. He said it was ok about Robbie. He said he would have liked to talk to Robbie longer. He was glad that Robbie had come up and brought the kids to see him. He said he wanted to make sure mom brought his heartburn pills the next day so I could give them to Robbie. He said he didn't need them anymore he had his morphine. We both laughed. He said he knew the kids were ready to go. He was really happy that he got to see the kids. He said it didn't hurt the kids seeing him in the hospital. He said it wasn't as good as seeing them at home. He said he wished he could have hugged and kissed them goodbye. He said him and I were a lot alike. He said we're not like those other people. He said Robbie was like us too. We just think different then most people. I told him I loved him and that I was getting hungry.

I told him I was going down to get some dinner. It was about 7:30pm. As I walked out of the room I thought I'll bring my food back up here so I can be in the room if dad needs me. So I stopped at the nurses station and asked them if it would be ok to eat my dinner in dads room. The nurses said it was fine with them but I had to ask dad. I knew he would be fine with it but I had to go ask him. I asked dad if he minded me eating in front of him. We both laughed. He said he didn't care. So I went downstairs to get my food.

On my way back up I decided to stop in the Chapel. I walked into the Chapel and signed in. I looked around and I didn't see any crosses or statues of Jesus, Mary, or Joseph. I got very upset. I'm Catholic so I expected to see some of these things. I thought to myself this isn't going to help me. I sat in a chair and looked at the wall that had doves on it. Then I bowed my head and shut my eyes and I started praying. I asked God for the strength to keep going. I prayed about what had happened with Robbie. I prayed for mom. I prayed that my sisters wouldn't torture me anymore. I prayed to be able to stay strong for dad. I told God I wasn't ready to give dad up yet, but if it was dad's time to go he could take him. I felt the Holy Spirit enter my body. My head lifted like in slow motion, like I wasn't the one moving it. When my head was up my eyes opened up. I knew I was filled with the Holy Spirit. I was so amazed. I could hardly believe what had just happened. I slowly got up and went to each book and bible and placed my hand on everyone of them. I knew I would be ok.

God had answered my prayers. I picked up my dinner and I kinda floated back upstairs. I asked dad if he needed anything when I got up to the room. I gave him a drink. Then I ate some of my food. Then I helped him when he started coughing up the phlegm. I pulled it out for him. It took me about two hours to eat my dinner because I kept stopping to help dad. It was ok though cause I was there to help dad. We talked and watched TV all night again. But it was ok cause I had gotten some good sleep at home. I kept fighting with myself about if he was gonna die or be ok. I wanted him to go back home again. We laughed and joked around a lot. We fought with that glass of water all night and that would make us laugh so hard.

10/8/2001 Monday, We got up early on Monday morning like we always did. I always thanked God in the mornings when I'd see that dad was still alive. Early is around five of six in the morning. I don't remember exactly. We were on spirit watch for a few hours. Dad said he wasn't ready to go yet. He said if I saw any spirits to tell him. He said if they were bad spirits he wanted me to scare them away. If they were good spirits to tell them he wasn't ready yet. He said that I would know they were bad spirits cause they would come in a group. He asked if I ever seen them in the movies. He said they always come in a group.

I told him yes I had seen them in the movies and I knew what he was talking about. Every flash of light or noise he wanted to know if that was the spirits. Dad wondered what it would be like after he died. He hoped he would be going to heaven. He said he didn't want to go to hell. He wondered how the world would change in the years to come. He said there was dinosaurs, there was the way the world is now. He wondered if the world would become a space age world. Dad and I had hope for him to get better until this morning. He was doing pretty good until about 8:00am. He took a turn for the worse. Dad and I both knew it didn't look good. That's when dad started talking about dying. I got very emotional and couldn't hold back the tears any longer. I turned my head to wipe my tears. I didn't want him to see me crying but when I turned back to look at him he was crying too. It was the first time in my life I saw my dad cry. He told me he didn't want me to be sad when he died.

I said I'm sorry but I will be very sad and I'll miss you a lot. We sat there and held hands and cried our hearts out for each other. I told him I would have to stay strong to help my husband Robbie raise our three kids. I was holding his hand and rubbing his arm with my other hand like I had been doing since Friday. He said he was afraid to die. He said he didn't know where he was going or what it would be like when he got there. I asked him once again did he want to see a priest or a preacher. He said no that he had me and I was his Angel and that I had all the religion in me that he needed. He was so scared to be alone after he died. I thought to myself God please help me to help Dad.

So it was like someone was feeding me the following words. These words just flowed out of me from heaven. I told him I'm holding your hand and when you die you will let go of my hand and you will go to heaven. I said my brother Ray Ray is up in heaven and he will take hold of your hand. Dad is my step-dad so he never met my brother who had died twenty six years earlier. I told dad Ray Ray is just like me. He will hold your hand and show you the ropes. I said he'll take you where you need to go and he will help you. Dad smiled and said ok and a look of peace came over him. He said he wasn't scared anymore. We both knew the end was coming. I was still very scared and upset. Dad's sister called me at about 9:00am.

I told her to come to the hospital right now. She understood and came. She stayed all day and evening. None of us knew how much longer we had with Dad. We all knew it was getting closer. The doctors and nurses told us there was nothing they could do for dad. So I was ready to take dad home. They said no he couldn't go home because he needed too much oxygen. They said he could only have that in a hospital. I was so confused by all of this and not knowing if anyone had spoken to his cancer doctors and what did they think. He had just had a blood transfusion on Wednesday. I wanted to know if all of this has anything to do with that. I kept asking all these questions but it just didn't seem like I was getting answers to any of my questions. I should have pushed more and harder. I hate when people make me become that aggressive person I keep down deep until I have to have her.

All I got from all my questions was a question from them. They asked if we wanted them to call Hope Hospice. We said yes. I thought ok this way his cancer doctors will tend him there until he passed away. I was so dumb and naive back then. Monday was a very long and confusing day. Dad wasn't talking that much. I was really worried after mine and dad's morning talk about him dying. I knew the end was coming and I was so scared. I was in and out of his room. Lots of smoking that day. My sister brought mom up about 10:00am that morning. I was out of the room for a few minutes and they called me into his room. He had taken the oxygen mask off and he wouldn't put it back on. He wanted to sit in the chair.

So we sat him up on the edge of the bed. The nurses, mom, and dad's sister were begging him to put his oxygen mask back on and he wouldn't. Mom said Bev do something. She told the nurses he'll listen to her. So I knelt down in front of dad and talked to him real calmly. I asked him if he wanted to sit in the chair, he said yes. I told him I'd get the nurse to help us put him in the chair. So the nurse came into the room. He yelled at her to get out. I told her I was so sorry. She was a real good sport about all of it. I got dad to put his oxygen mask back on. Then he asked me what was that on the floor. I looked where he pointed. I brushed my hand on it and said its nothing. He got upset and said it was trying to tell him something. So I got it back and held it and he said no maybe it wasn't talking. This was about 3:00pm.

He finally decided he'd lay back down. We got him settled. He didn't talk much after that. He just mostly layed there while we all took turns rubbing his arms. The lady from Hope Hospice got there about 4:30pm. She wanted to talk in the hallway. I said no this is dads life we're talking about so we will talk in his room. I wanted dad to hear what was going on. I didn't want to upset mom anymore then she was already. Mom was in the waiting room with dad's sister. So my brother, dad's brother in law, and I talked to the Hope Hospice woman. She said Dad couldn't hear us anyway. I looked over at Dad and saw that gleam in his eyes that I've seen so many times before. It was a look that we've given each other a million times before for a million different reasons. So I knew dad could hear us. I wanted him to know what was going on. So she layed it on the line for us. She said that they would take Dad the next day which was Tuesday.

She said they would disconnect his feeding tube on Wednesday. She said he'd probably die on Thursday or on Friday. My brother and I looked at each other with total horror on our faces. We both said no. She said the hospital couldn't do anything for him. She said he could lay in the hospital for a few days, weeks, or months before he died. My brother and I said so our choices are to starve our dad to death or let him lay in the hospital and suffer until he dies. We were so freaked out. I had expected a lot more then this from everyone. I had never in my life ever heard of anything like this. I kept looking at dad to see his reactions I knew he had heard the choices.

He didn't look like he liked them any better then we did. So I told them that dad had told me he didn't want to die slowly. So we decided to starve him to death. I was heartbroken. My brother and I hugged each other and cried. This was the hardest decision we ever had to make in our lives. The woman was really wonderful from Hope Hospice. She tried to make us feel better about our decision. But nobody could make us feel better. We now knew for sure that our dad would be dead in a few days. And we had handed down his death sentence. We went downstairs and we smoked and cried. We came back up and I called Robbie and I told him what was going on. I told him I'd come home after we got dad settled into Hope Hospice the next day. He tried to calm me down but I was a total wreck there was no calming me down. Then mom says that she is going to spend the night because she knows that dad is gonna die that night.

I didn't know if dad had told her anything. Or if she just had one of her strong feelings. But when mom says something like that you know its gonna happen. That's just the way momma is. So now I felt even worse cause I knew he was gonna die even sooner. My brother left then my sister left. Dad's sister and husband said they were going out to dinner and they would bring us back some dinner. So mom, me, and dad hung out. We rubbed his arms and talked. Dad quit talking sometime that evening. I'm not sure when he quit talking. After the Hope Hospice ordeal he had talked some. We pulled a lot of phlegm out. It was getting a lot harder to get it out. When they got back with our food mom and I went down stairs and ate. They stayed with dad. While we ate mom said again several times that dad was gonna die tonight so that's why she stayed because she didn't want me to go through it alone.

She said she needed to be there by his side when he passed away. After several times I got angry and begged her to quit saying it. I was so scared cause I knew if mom said it then it was going to happen. We went back up and I told them I was going to smoke. I asked dad's sister if she could wait until I came back up to leave. She said yes. On my way back up I stopped in the chapel again. I signed in. Then I sat down and I prayed. I felt the Holy Spirit come into my body. This time it wasn't as much as the day before. This confused me. It scared me. I was worried that I wouldn't be able to stay strong for dad that night.

I went back up and when dad's sister and husband got ready to leave I walked out into the hallway with them. Mom had been telling me over and over that she had to stay because she had a feeling that dad was gonna die that night. I kept telling her to quit saying it. I was getting so scared. So upset. So mad. I wasn't ready yet. But I knew her feelings are always right. So I knew this was it tonight. Dad's sister asked me was there anything she could do for me. I said yes PRAY for me. She said I'll do better then that I'll pray with you. So we hugged and she prayed. It was wonderful. So then they left. I went back into the room. Momma looked so sad sitting there holding dad's hand. I felt so bad for her. So we sat and talked for a while. The nurses came in and made sure we had enough blankets and pillows. The nurses were so great to me. So I sat in the chair and rubbed dad's arm.

Mom tried to sleep in the bed I had been sleeping in for a few days. We would doze off for a little while. Then dad would start coughing and we'd pull the phlegm and blood out. This went on all night like usual. I was so afraid that he'd die while I was pulling the phlegm out. It was so scary. It was about 3:30am. We were pulling the phlegm out. His oxygen mask was falling off. Nothing was working right. I tried four or five times to get the phlegm out this time. Momma was trying so hard to help me. I couldn't get it out this time. He was choking very badly. I had tissues, paper towels, phlegm and blood everywhere on the bed. I was freaking out. I finally gave up and hit the call button for the nurses. They came running in and put the suction machine on him to get the phlegm out.

He started tearing his tubes out. They yelled for me to grab his hands. I grabbed his two hands. Dad squeezed my hands so hard I thought he was gonna break them. Then he sat straight up and started screaming OH GOD, OH GOD, PLEASE HELP ME. I was crying so hard. I felt so bad that I had to put him through this pain. At the time I thought it happened because I didn't get enough of the Holy Spirit in me in the Chapel. But months later after a lot of guilt. I realized God didn't give me a lot of the Holy Spirit because it was time for dad to choose his destiny. When he yelled for Gods help, God came to him. Dad layed back down. He still held my hands but he was at peace. The nurses finished putting the tubes all back in. He was peaceful the rest of the night. He had chosen God. I told dad how sorry I was that I had failed him. The nurses had been telling me all along that he wouldn't die in front of me. They told me he was getting worse. I asked if they knew how much time he had left. They said they couldn't tell for sure but his vital signs were slowing down. The end was coming.

10/9/2001 Tuesday, The nurse told me again that he wouldn't die with me in the room. So when I got done talking to her we hugged and I cried. It was 6:00am we had made it through another night. I went out to the hallway and called dad's sister and husband and told them to come right now. I called my sister and left a message. I called my brother and he wanted to know if he could come later, I said no come right now. He said he was coming. I called angel sister and told her to come. These people didn't realize I wasn't just calling for them to come and say goodbye. I NEEDED THEM! Dad's sister and husband got there within thirty minutes.

No one else came. I called my brother back he said he wasn't coming. I was heartbroken that no one could come and help me and momma through this. I gave up on the phone calls. I finally said I'm going down to smoke. With the nurses talk eating at my brain. I told them to call me on my cell phone. I walked out the door and got in the hallway. I said to myself I didn't kiss dad good bye. I always kiss my dad good bye. I went back in and said I forgot to kiss dad good bye. I saw a twinkle in his eyes. I kissed him several times and I told him how much I loved him. I walked to the doorway and I stopped and looked back one more time.

It was the most beautiful picture I'd ever seen. Mom was sitting on one side of dad's bed holding his hand and rubbing his arm. Dad's sister was sitting on the other side of dad's bed holding his other hand and rubbing his other arm. Her husband was standing at the foot of the bed watching over all of them. Dad looked so happy, content, and peaceful. I turned and I walked out of the room knowing that was the last time that I'd see dad alive. I was so sad. They say as soon as I walked out the door he died. They let me get downstairs. They called me ten minutes later. He told me how dad had passed away as soon as I walked out the door. I said I'll be back up in a little while. I hung up the phone and cried and screamed and yelled. IT HURT SO BADLY! I called Robbie when I quit yelling.

He calmed me back down the best he could. I called my sister out of state. She always makes me feel better. She helped me so much. Then I went back up to dad's room. I sat in my chair and I started rubbing dad's arm. I couldn't stop. I called everyone and told them dad had died. My sister said she'd be right up to get mom. She got there 1 1/2 hours later. We sat with dad dead for 1 1/2 hours. It was very hard. I kept rubbing his arms. Mom has a memory problem. So she would ask about every fifteen minutes how come dad wasn't talking. Then we'd have to tell her again that dad had died. When it was finally time to go I didn't really want to leave him. When I looked at his dead body I could tell his spirit had gone to heaven so that did make me feel a lot better about leaving him. I hugged and kissed him and I cried. Mom said she wanted a few minutes alone with him. So I went out to the hall. She looked so sad and lonely sitting there holding his hand. I went back in after five minutes. She said she wasn't ready.

After twenty minutes I got her to finally say good bye. I felt so bad making her leave him. I knew how she felt because I didn't want to leave him either. As we were walking out I had such a empty feeling inside of me. I told everyone I loved them but please tell everyone that I didn't want no one to call me until tomorrow. They all understood. I was tired. I was drained. I was empty. I had nothing left to give. I just wanted to get home to Robbie and our kids.

Dad's sister and husband took me to the fishhouse to see Robbie. Then Robbie gave them some fish. Then they took me home. When we said good bye I knew I'd see them at the funeral. I also knew I wouldn't be seeing them anymore. I already missed them. They had helped me to stay strong all those days. I had stayed strong for Dad now I had to stay strong for my kids. I had to help my kids deal with losing their grandpa. They all knew it was coming but it didn't make it any easier when it happened. They were all heartbroken. As I copied this story onto my computer eight years later with my youngest son John sitting close by. John is now eighteen years old. I asked John if he was happy that we brought him to the hospital that day to say good-bye to his grandpa. He said yes he was glad that he got to go say good bye that day. I had asked Bobby Ray and Rozie the same question at different times.

They were both very happy that they had that chance to say good bye to grandpa in the hospital that day. They all agreed that they would have been mad if we hadn't brought them to the hospital. So Robbie and I were right about how we were raising our kids. We all miss dad a lot. We kept some of his ashes so dad lives with us now. He's moved with us a few times. Dad will always be a important part of our family. I felt so helpless that I couldn't save dad from death. I am very proud years later after a lot of thinking and a lot of studying on death. I feel like I helped him pass away as happy and calmly as possible. I just hope and pray when it's my time to pass away that I have a angel like me helping me to get ready to die like I helped dad get ready to die. He was truly at peace when he passed away. I believe dad went home to heaven

CHAPTER 4
MY KIDS

My kids knew that their grandpa was very sick and was going to die soon. After my dad died I came home and went to sleep for the rest of the day. I had been awake for so many hours in the hospital for those four days. I was exhausted. When I woke up I came out to the kitchen. I looked out the slider doors and saw my oldest son Bobby Ray working on his go-cart. I walked outside to tell him that his grandpa had passed away that morning. Before I could say anything Bobby Ray started talking. His grandpa had fixed his go-cart several times for him before he got too sick to work on it. Bobby Ray had been trying to get his clutch off for months. He had several grown men, some real mechanics try to get this clutch off over the past few months. No one could budge it.

Bobby Ray was so happy and excited. He told me he just got his clutch off. He couldn't wait to tell grandpa. I started crying and told him that grandpa had passed away that morning. He looked up at me with this big smile and said grandpa just helped me get this clutch off my go-cart. Then he stood up and hugged me and cried his heart out. Thank goodness for God, a young man's faith in God, and a grandpa's special goodbye to his fifteen year old grandson.

My dad told my oldest son Bobby Ray he could have his van before he died. We had it parked in the back yard. We had been fixing it up as we had the time and the money. One night I looked out the glass slider doors and told Bobby Ray that he had left a light on in the van. He looked out the doors and saw the light on in the van. He said he was sure he hadn't left a light on. We both walked out to the van and there was no light on. The moon wasn't up where it would be shining into the van. We got back to the house and we could see the light again. We tried turning lights on and off in the house to make the light go away in the van. We finally couldn't come up with a answer so we watched the van for a little while longer. Then we just shut the drapes. Another night Bobby Ray called me to the sliding doors. He said he saw someone in the van. I looked out the door and sure enough it looked like a man in the drivers seat. So we got the flashlights and our courage.

We went out to the van and no one was in the van. We finally decided it must be my dad that had passed away hanging out in the van. He loved that van. He had bought it brand new. He had it for over twenty years. We kept it for three years and we finally gave up on fixing it because there was so much wrong with it. Now years later I wish we would have kept working on it. I think these couple of events had us kinda spooked at the time.

I worked on a golf course mowing with a big mower. I'd mow the same grass with the same pattern everyday. This one morning it was about 10:00am. It wasn't hot because it was a very cloudy, breezy day. I wasn't tired because I had plenty of sleep that night and plenty of coffee that morning. Well I started feeling like I was gonna pass out. Whenever I'd get too hot or tired I'd stop and chill out. Well I kept mowing. I couldn't stop, I kept going and going. I felt really awful. Then all of a sudden I was watching myself mow. I thought I was having a stroke or heart attack. I thought I was dying. I was out of my body and floating above my mower. I was looking down at my body on the mower that was still mowing. Then I couldn't see my mower anymore.

I was floating in the air through all these beautiful white fluffy clouds. I thought I was floating up to heaven. Then I stopped and I was just floating in the sky so I looked down. I could see my three kids playing with a bunch of kids in a driveway. They were at a house that I had never seen before. So I thought I was dying and this was gonna be my kids new house. Then all of a sudden I was back on my mower and I saw one of my co-workers in front of me. I wanted him to talk to me and to bring me out of this. I stopped my mower but I couldn't talk. He moved out of my way but he didn't talk to me. I started mowing again. I was so afraid that I was dying. I went out of my body again. I saw my three kids all upset. All the kids with my kids were upset. Something was wrong. I mowed for about ten more minutes. I finally was able to stop the mower and come back to the present time. I grabbed my water jug and I started drinking water and pouring it all over myself. I was freaking out. Then my boss pulled up and said the secretary needed to talk to me. He told me to get into his cart. I said MY KIDS! He said no she just needs to talk to you. I knew it was my kids from the vision and from working there so long, they didn't pull you off the golf course like this unless it was bad news.

So I got into his cart and he took off driving really fast. I knew then it was my kids for sure or he wouldn't be driving so fast. I told him I feel like crap, and I almost passed out mowing. I was sweating really bad. He said its not even hot out today. So then I got scared that we'd wreck and I'd die. So I started yelling and cursing at him to slow down. I told him if we wrecked I was gonna get up and beat the crap out of him. Then I told him if we wrecked my kids wouldn't have a mother. When we got to the office I jumped out as he was still driving. The secretary told me my daughter who was three years old had gotten hurt.

So I went to the babysitters house to pick her up. The babysitter said she had gotten hurt at the babysitter's mother's house. Which I have never been to since it was in another town and I didn't know they were going there. She said the kids were playing on the driveway with her kids and her sisters kids. My daughter Rozie had fallen and cut her head. She said all the kids had all started yelling and screaming when Rozie got hurt. I took her to the hospital. I don't know which one of us felt worse me or Rozie. The doctor put a staple in the back of my little girls head. She got the staple in the head and I got the most massive headache of my life. I should have taken her home and cuddled and loved on my precious little girl. But I couldn't because I was required to go back to work.

I look back on this years later and I think what a fool I was back then. The worst they could have done was fire me. At the time I needed that job so badly and they knew it so I was like a puppet on a string. So I took Rozie back to the babysitters house and I went back to work. I drove past where I had mowed during all of this only three hours earlier. I had no memory of mowing parts of it. My mowing pattern was so far off from my normal pattern. After it was over and I had time to think about this amazing day. I realized how lucky I was to have this close connection with my kids even though I have to work for a living. I realized I needed to learn and embrace this gift. I still have a lot of work to do on myself. I'm still learning how to use it. I'll probably spend the rest of my life learning how to use and how to understand this precious gift from God. When my kids were little I'd have my back to them or they'd be in another room and I'd tell them to stop doing such or such.

They'd ask how did I know what they were doing. I'd say what all mom's say, I have eyes in the back of my head. I just always thought I had good mothers intuition. One night I was doing the dinner dishes and the kids came into the kitchen. The oldest boy Bobby Ray started moving my hair around with my daughter Roseanne and youngest son John watching very closely. I asked him what are you doing? They all answered together that they were looking for my eyes in the back of my head. So then I had to explain and try to convince them that I didn't have any eyes back there.

So then they all wanted to know how I always knew what they were doing. I said about a mothers intuition. They didn't believe me. They said that I had something more then just that. When they said that I thought back to when my oldest son Bobby Ray was three years old. I was pregnant with my daughter Roseanne. I was living with two other women. One woman had two daughters and the other one was my sister in law and she had three sons. It was a houseful with three mothers, six kids, and friends and family coming and going. There was never a dull moment in that house. We had a lot of fun as this mismatched family. I remembered the two women asking me how I always know when the kids were doing something wrong behind me or in another room. I had given them the mother intuition too. Or was it something more. Was it my gift from God? I didn't even know I had that part of it. Now I felt so bad that I said that to those two wonderful, loving mothers. These women cared so deeply for their kids. They were really good mothers. I hope and pray my stupid words about a mothers intuition didn't cause them any hurt feelings because they didn't have it. They were as good of mothers as I was, maybe they just didn't have their gifts from God working right. Maybe their gifts needed some fine tuning.

My son Bobby Ray was about ten years old. He went to spend the night at his best friends house. His friends mom is my best friend. She came over and picked him up to spend the night. She said she was going to drop the boys off at her house. Then she needed to go to the store. Her older son would be home to watch the boys. This was fine since the older son had watched the boys before with no problems.

We lived about a mile away from each other. It was about 9:00pm and the older son and his friend started picking on the younger boys. Bobby Ray got very scared of the teenage boys and he took off walking home in the dark. My son had never walked anywhere in the dark. He was crying and he was very afraid of the dark roads. He said he glanced down at the sidewalk and when he looked up there was a older man and his dog standing under the street light. The man started talking to Bobby Ray and told him he'd walk him home. Bobby Ray told the man the story of why he was walking home in the dark. He said the man was Italian or Mexican. He said he wasn't sure. He said it was dark and he never saw the man's face. He said the man had a hat on that he had only seen in very old movies. He was talking about a fedora. Anyway the man walked him to our house. The man stayed at the end of the driveway while my son came into the house. Then the man left.

My son Bobby Ray came into the house and told me and my sister his story. So of course I ran out of the house to thank the man for walking my little boy home. We lived on a dead end street. One way in one way out. I got out to the street and there was no one on our street. There wasn't enough time for a old man to walk down our street. But I ran down the street to see if he had gotten to the corner. There was no one around. He couldn't have gone through the backyard since it was all fenced orange groves. So all we could figure out was he must have been a ANGEL. I'm half Italian so I figured maybe it was my grandfather that had taken such good care of my son that night. Bobby Ray never saw the man and dog again. The sidewalk he met the man on was the same one Bobby Ray walked everyday to go to school. So he should have seen him again if he was a man. So we said our prayers that night and we thanked the ANGEL for taking such good care of Bobby Ray on his walk home.

My youngest son John started telling us he saw dead people when he was about eight years old. We were very concerned. He said it had been happening for a long time. So who knows what a long time is in a child's life. At first we thought a very active imagination. Then I thought to myself well he is my son. I've had so many amazing things happen in my life. So I told him that I believed him. Before he told me I always wondered why John wouldn't stay in a room alone.

When he told us about the dead people he said they only came when he was alone in a room. It explained why he was always so afraid at night, he always needed a night light. It was always a fight with his sister and brother that he shared a room with when they were young. He always hated sleeping in his bed. He would sleep on the floor of the bedroom and would some nights end up in the hallway where the light was on.

We're not sure when he started seeing these ghosts. But we do know they stopped coming when he was ten and a half years old. It was the same year his grandpa had died. I'm not sure if the two are connected. But I do know how much his grandpa loved him and how much he loved his grandpa. John said the dead people look different not from this world. They don't look scary. He said all the ghosts are always kids. John gets up and leaves the room when he sees them. When he comes back into the room they're gone. He said they always look like boys. I'll never know for sure if he saw ghosts during those years. But I do know the fear in his face and eyes was very real. I felt so helpless during those years. It's hard knowing your child really is seeing the boogeyman type of thing. I only hope my understanding, love, and stories about my life might have helped him through those tough years. We were all glad when they stopped. We were all very surprised when John started sleeping with all the lights and TV off at night. We were all so happy for him to know he had found peace in his night life.

My daughter was eight and a half years old in the third grade. She came home from school one day and told me this story and I thought how cool is this. This was the first time I saw that she had the gifts from God. Then a few weeks later I was at the school and the principal stopped me in the hallway. He told me the same story my daughter had told me and I got goosebumps. He was very flipped out and excited as he told me the story. I wasn't very surprised since this is my daughter we were talking about. He asked me if anything like this had happened before. I said no but I thought to myself I'm sure it will happen again. It was the beginning of amazing things for my daughter. She was like a kid with a new toy. She loved this gift and embraced it for many years. Roseanne and her gifts are the reason I started writing this book. Here's the story as it was told to me by Roseanne and her principal.

Roseanne was in the school library with her class. The principal walked into the library with a new girl to the school. The first person he came to was my daughter Roseanne. So he said Roseanne this is a new girl in your class. Roseanne said Hi Patti and the new girl said how do you know my name? The principal was shocked he hadn't introduced the girl to anyone yet. He said to Roseanne how did you know her name. Roseanne smiled and said I don't know and went off to find a book. The principal was still flipped out when he told me the story a few weeks later.

Roseanne later became a alter server at church. She always said her prayers. She was aware of God everyday not just on Sundays. She'd do the sign of the cross very often. She'd do it to thank God for different things. Her gifts blossomed as she grew up into a young lady. When we moved off our small island she said she'd never go to church anywhere else besides Our Lady of the Miraculous Medal Church. I thought she'll grow out of that and get over moving away. But she never did. She went to church a few times since we moved. But its nothing like the way it use to be. She use to go just about every Sunday. My husband and I made a agreement when the kids were very young. He made me promise I'd never force the kids to go to church. So whenever our kids were at church it was because they wanted to be there.

We told them if they decided to make their communions and confirmations they had to go to those Sunday school classes. So all three kids went through all their classes. We were very proud of them. So now the kids are 20,21, and 25 years old. The only one that goes to church with me now is our twenty year old son John. Our twenty five year old son BobbyRay says sometimes when they were kids that I'd guilt them into going to church. I didn't realize what I was doing at the time but I probably did do it since I'm a Italian Catholic mother. They may not go to church now but they all have God in their lives everyday. They still say their prayers. They all know that God is very important in their lives. When they don't do the right thing and something happens to them they believe thats Gods way of making them pay attention. I believe we did ok raising them to be good Christians. What more can you ask for when the day is done. Our kids are Happy, Healthy, God Loving People. Life is Good. Most of the time when one of my kids get hurt and I'm not with them I get a feeling that they're hurt or that something is wrong with them.

One evening my boyfriend Robbie and I dropped the kids off at my parents house. We were going to dinner at his mom's new boyfriends house. We got there and talked while he was finishing dinner. We sat down to eat dinner. In the middle of dinner I jumped up and said I need to call mom I forgot to leave her the phone number here. They all said sit down and enjoy your dinner the kids are fine with your parents. I should have just dialed the number but this was all new people I was around and didn't really want to start any crap. So I looked at the clock to see what time it was that I had jumped up out of my seat. So the rest of the evening all I could think of was getting back to mom's to my kids. Later when we went to pick the kids up from mom and dad's house. They told us how our youngest boy John who was three years old had gotten hit with a swing. They had taken him to the hospital since they had no way of getting in touch with us. John got a few stitches in his lip. I asked what time did this happen?

When they told me the time it was the same time that I had jumped up out of my seat and had wanted to call them.

Our thirteen year old son Bobby Ray had a ball game out of town. Our van was broke down so he got a ride with one of the players parents. I was sitting there in my pajamas writing. All of a sudden I knew my son had gotten hurt. So I got up and got dressed in case I had to help him into the house when he got home. When he got home I ran to the door and opened it for him. He had gotten hit with the baseball in the back. He was ok but he had a bruised back.

Bobby Ray was going to be in a play at school. He was so excited about it. That's all he talked about. He practiced so much for this show. A couple of days before the show he was at rehearsal in school. Bobby Ray and a girl classmate were goofing around during rehearsal like excited kids do sometimes. The teacher kicked both of them out of the show. He came home from school so upset. I told him I'd call the teacher but he said no he didn't want me to beg for him. We had all been planning on going to his show. The night of his show we were all disappointed about not going. Bobby Ray went to take his shower. When he came out of the bathroom he told me when he was looking in the mirror he could see the play in his mind. He said he could see a lot of things going wrong during the play. The next day at school he heard how a lot of things went wrong during the play.

His vision wasn't real clear but it had gotten the point across to him. It's not that he wanted the play to be a failure. But he didn't feel quite as bad after he saw that vision.

I stayed away from church for quite a few years. I still believed in God but I wasn't always practicing what I believed. I wasn't in touch with God except when I said my prayers at night. I'd go to mass occasionally. I was searching for myself. I went to a lot of different religion churches during that time. I was trying to decide what I should be and what religion to raise my children in. I had my first child baptized a Catholic. I still wasn't sure but I'd take my son to mass sometimes. Three and a half years later I had my daughter. Then fourteen months later I had my youngest son. I took the kids to mass once in a while. When my daughter started kindergarten I decided to enroll my kids into Sunday school at the Catholic church. This was after years of talking to my sister about God. She also has two kids about the same age as Bobby Ray and Roseanne so she had been telling me how much her kids enjoyed their church and classes. So she finally got me back to God now I needed to figure out the rest. The kids loved it and I loved it. We went to the church that I had grown up going to. It is a very big church and parish now. We fit right in and enjoyed going.

Then two years later my second husband wanted us to move fifty miles away to a beautiful island. Before we moved my husband brought home the island newspaper. I found the Catholic church in it and saw a picture of the new priest. I still hadn't agreed to move yet. When I looked at the picture of the priest, I knew he'd be a wonderful priest. I finally agreed to move to Pine Island. We found the most beautiful small church on this island. The parish members welcomed us with open arms. The priest is the most amazing, wonderful priest that I've ever met in my life. I've liked all the priests I've met over the years. This priest just had something extra special in him. I felt a great connection with him. My children liked him a lot too. It was such a joy to go to church. My two younger kids got baptized a few months after we moved to the island. They made their communions and confirmations in this small loving church. The two younger kids became alter servers. They were really good at it. They worked so well together. Everyone was always complimenting them. My older son would fill in as a usher whenever they needed him

He had wanted to be a alter server when he was young but I wouldn't allow it because of what had happened to my father. I will always regret that decision. I grew and learned and got more spiritual and was able to overcome so much to allow the younger ones to have that special time in their lives. Everyone always complimented me on how well behaved the kids were during mass. Of course it wasn't always easy keeping the kids quiet and behaved in church. My oldest son Bobby Ray liked to wear a suit and tie to church. People were amazed that a teenage boy would dress like that. He got a lot of compliments for dressing up for church. I am very happy and proud that my kids find time for God in their busy lives.

People always tell me what a good job I'm doing raising the kids. I enjoy the nice remarks. I know its not just me doing this. I have a wonderful, loving husband raising the kids too. My mother taught me so much while raising me. I take a lot of pride and pleasure in being a mom. Six years after we made this island our home, my husband decided he wanted to move back to our hometown. Roseanne and I were devastated. We didn't want to move. We loved our life on the island. We loved our church life. The boys were excited about the move. I kept putting the move off, hoping he'd change his mind. Robbie was on me everyday to pack more and to start telling the church and school that we were moving. Our parish had a new church built. The new church was as wonderful as the small church. The dedication of the new church was coming up. I was packing our lives up to move. Roseanne and John were chosen to be alter servers along with three other kids for the dedication. The morning of the dedication I told my husband that I'd tell the priest that this day would be the kids last day to serve. I was so sad that I couldn't change his mind. Our kids also were serving at the four thirty mass that day. The dedication was beautiful.

After mass there was a luncheon in the parish hall. We attended the luncheon. After lunch the boys went to the car. They didn't want to say any good byes. Roseanne and I went up to Father Ted and told him that we were moving. It was such a emotional thing for me to do. He said how he'd miss our family. He thanked Roseanne for being a alter server. I thanked him for welcoming us into the parish. He said how I made it easy to be welcomed. I could feel how sincere his words were. We told him we'd see him at mass in a couple of hours.

We went and said goodbye to the special parish members. Roseanne cried her eyes out. I kept it together barely. We went home for a couple of hours. We went to mass for the kids to serve their last time. I cried during the opening song. After mass I took a few pictures of the kids on the alter. Then a woman that we had known briefly took a picture of me and the kids in front of the alter. We went to say good bye to

Father Ted. As we waited our turn we said good bye to Deacon Fred who has been so much a big part of our lives in the parish. Our first neighbor on the island was also a parish member.

Our neighbors across the street Roy and Lily made our move to the island so much easier. They were wonderful to the kids and to us. Roy looked a lot like my dad and uncle. They didn't even get mad when Bobby Ray hit a golf ball through their screened in front porch. They always let Roseanne take walks with them around the neighborhood with her doll stroller. They never minded John and his friends loud playing and screaming. Lily told us to stop by the parish hall that they had leftover food for us from lunch. She really didn't know how badly we needed that food. Money had been really tight for a couple of months. They probably knew that I had gone to the church for help. What a hard thing to do. It's so hard to swallow your pride and ask for help.

It was our turn to say good bye to Father Ted. I got so upset saying good bye to Father Ted. He had been so much more then just the priest at church. As I told him how wonderful he was and how much we'd miss him. I broke down and started to cry. He told me what a good mother I was. He said there was something special about our family. He told me if I ever figured out what I was doing different raising my kids. That I should write a book to help others and make some money too. When he said these words I felt like he was looking into my soul. I was so shocked when he said this to me. When he said this to me I was in the middle of writing this book. I couldn't speak. I nodded my head with tears falling like rain. I said a last thank you and walked out of the church with my two kids. The kids were trying to calm me down. Then they asked me why didn't I tell Father Ted about the book I was writing. I said I'm not sure. He just shocked me when he mentioned about me writing a book.

Roseanne told me that's a sign from God that this book is a good idea. I knew she was right and John agreed. We went and got our food and cried and hugged our good friends and the kids Sunday school teachers. It was so hard saying good bye to these people that had become our extended family. We will always remember our six years at that great parish at Our Lady of Miraculous Medal Church. The people we met there will always be in our hearts and memories. The mass that last day was about being a prophet. I felt like it was for me. I had second guessed myself so many times while writing this book.

I learned at a young age to never talk religion. I was always told you don't talk religion or politics. Anytime I had broken that rule I had gotten into some heated debates about religion and God. So I felt like I was preaching about God in this book. After that beautiful mass about spreading the word of God. Then Father Ted saying I should write a book about raising my kids. I knew these were words from God. He was reassuring me that this book was the right thing for me to do at this time in my life. Hopefully I won't second guess this book again. I will let my words and the words of God flow onto these pages. I'm not trying to force anyone to turn to God. I'm just telling my story about how wonderful life can be when God is in your life everyday.

This will sound like a coincidence and it might be. That's what I thought at first too. I started to realize that I'd been wearing the same color as the priest at mass. It happened so many times that I got worried that he would notice too. So sometimes I'd go to my closet and pick something out. Then I'd lay it on my bed and get something different to wear. These times what I layed on my bed would be the color the priest would wear that day. I planned my outfit for the dedication for a few days. I went to my closet that morning and grabbed a different shirt. I got to church and sure enough my color matched the priest color. Coincidence or not. When I was a child growing up my mother would sit on our bed with us six kids at bedtime. We would all be holding our rosaries and we'd say our prayers together. It wasn't every night but it was a lot of nights. As we all got older it was left up to us to say our prayers at bedtime. I always remembered to say my prayers.

When I was about nine years old I added my own prayer to my regular prayers. I made up a prayer asking God to bless my mom and dad and then I would name each of my sisters and brothers. When we moved from New York to Florida. I added my aunts, uncles, and cousins. I didn't name each one but I'd think about each family as I said it. As I got older I added the names of husbands and girlfriends. Neither of my brothers have married. As sisters had babies I added nephews and nieces. As the divorces occurred and new husbands came into their lives I would add them. It took me years to take the ex-husbands out. Then the great nieces arrived.

It gave me a chance everyday to think about each person in my life that was important to me. When my children were old enough we'd sit on their beds several times a week and say our regular prayers together. Our dog Rascal even enjoys prayer time. He always comes in the bedroom with us when we say our prayers. Any other time he's right next to my husband. After a few years I told my kids about my special prayer I say. So they wanted to make up a special prayer too. They ask God to bless Mommy, Daddy, Bobby, Rozie, Johnny, Rascal, Dixie, Grandma, Grandpa, and everyone else they love. Whenever anyone they know is sick or just having a hard time they put that person into their prayer as long as needed.

I had a dream about my daughter on Monday night. In my dream there was something wrong with her but I couldn't find her. When her friends asked me where she was I started crying so hard. I kept looking for her to see if she was alive and ok. I couldn't find her so I was trying to keep the hope and faith that she was ok. When I first woke up I thought that I had dreamed that she had died. I was crying. Then before I got up out of bed I layed there and played my dream back through my mind. I realized that I hadn't seen her dead in my dream. So I knew she'd be ok. Now for the hard part. Should I tell her about the dream so she'll be extra careful for a few days. I was so upset. I told my husband about the dream. My dreams are sometimes just dreams, but sometimes they're visions of what's to come. I decided to not tell her. I was so stressed out during the next few days. During those days I prayed to God to please don't take my daughter away from me. I prayed to my dad, my step dad, and my brother who are all dead to take extra care of my daughter for the next few days.

A few days before the dream my husband Robbie had changed the kids curfew from 6:00 to 7:00pm. On Thursday night my daughter asked to go to her girlfriends house which was about five mobile homes down from ours. It was already 6:45pm. There was no school the next day. They were going to jump on the trampoline. So we said yes and my husband told her to be home at 8:15pm. That way she'd be home before it got dark at 8:30pm. When he said it I got a strong bad feeling. But I didn't say anything. At 8:00pm I sat on the love seat near the window so I could look out for Rozie coming home. I had such a really bad feeling. I tried watching TV but was so worried about her. At 8:15 she wasn't home and I knew my dream was coming true. I started praying. She came in about 8:35.

She was out of breath and I asked her what's wrong. She lied and said she had run home. She told us that she lost track of time. We believed her but thought there was more to the story. She left our room and I heard the front door open and then close. I watched her run to the fence and look down the road and then run back to the house. I thought and then said to Robbie some thing is going on. Before I could get up she bursts into our room crying so hard she could barely talk. She told us that she had been in a car wreck with two of her friends. The road they had wrecked on is one street over and the speed limit is only 15 miles per hour. The way she explained the wreck we thought it was a little fender bender with a mailbox and a tree. We were having a hard time trying to understand her. She had a scrape on her neck from the seat belt other then that she seemed fine. So we told her to go take a shower to help her calm down.

I went and called her friends parents. The friends sister said they were at the accident scene. I thought to myself Oh my God there's a accident scene. Then a car pulled up in the driveway. It was the friends dad. He said we needed to come to the accident scene. We went with him. I cried when I saw the van that my daughter had been in that had wrecked. The van was totaled out. I don't know how any of them survived the wreck. My daughter Rozie said before the wreck she got scared and said she was putting her seatbelt on and all the girls put their seatbelts on too. Rozie was in the front seat with her seat belt on and the airbag came out. This saved her from going through the windshield, which was smashed and pushed up close to the front seats.

When the accident started Rozie screamed "Oh my God". When the van quit moving, she climbed out of her window and fell on the ground into all the broken glass. She didn't know if she was dead or alive. She later told me that her step-grandpa was there with her. He was the only grandpa she ever knew. He had passed away three years earlier. We were living in his house at the time of the accident. She had scratches and bruises and a memory that will last a lifetime. She was grounded for a few weeks to make sure she remembered how wrong it was to ride with someone that wasn't old enough to be driving. I'm so happy I've made her wear her seatbelt all her life and she had the good sense to put it on. Thank goodness for that airbag. I'm so grateful to my step dad for being there with her when I couldn't be there. I'm very grateful and thankful to God for letting me keep my daughter.

I was getting ready to go to Easter Mass. My husband Robbie said we were going out on the boat when I got home. It was going to be us and our two kids, my mom, my brother, and his girlfriend. My son John didn't want to go to church with us. I was very sad but I didn't push the kids to go. While I was at church with my daughter Rozie and my mom, our youngest son John asked Robbie if he could stay at his friends house. They were going to ride his friends scooter instead of going on the boat. Robbie told him yes. John usually loves going to church and on the boat but riding this scooter was more fun. So we got to church early on Easter morning. Not early enough for us to all get a seat. We found a seat for my mother in the back row. Rozie and I stood behind her against the wall.

A man stood by me with his wife. A woman stood by Rozie with her husband. When mass started the priest told everyone to introduce yourselves to the people next to you. Well I've been going to the Catholic church for forty three years at that time and this was a first for me. Rozie and I went to church to thank God for letting her live through the accident a few days earlier. She hadn't gone to church since we moved her off the island. She loved that church and she loved Father Ted. It had been two months which was a very long time for her to not go to church. So the man next to me was named Ray. The woman next to Rozie was named Rosa. Rozie and I were between Ray and Rosa. Rozie and I both started laughing when Rosa told us her name.

We explained to her that I have a sister and brother that were twins and their names were Ray and Rosa. My brother had passed away twenty nine years earlier. I knew this was a welcome home message from my brother Ray. Rozie had swore she'd never go to church again if it wasn't on our island. So it was great when she finally went again and we were next to Ray and Rosa. What a beautiful welcome back to God. We got home from church and there was a note to meet Robbie and everyone at the boat. My son John walks in the door and tells me he was going to stay at his friends but he changed his mind. He wanted his friend to go on the boat with us. Which would have been fine except I had no way of checking with my husband. The friend was three years younger and we had only known him for two months. I wasn't really sure that I wanted the responsibility of watching a small child all day.

Our kids had grown up on the boat and swimming. So I said no which years later I look back and I should have brought the child it would have been the time of his life. So then John said he was going back to his friends house. I tried talking him into going on the boat. I didn't want to be out on the boat while he was riding the scooter. I didn't know what Robbie was thinking when he said yes. I had one of those bad feelings. Plus Rozie had just gotten into the car wreck three days earlier. I knew I was being a over protective mother. So then my son changes his mind again. He said he's going on the boat. I should have put my foot down right then but I didn't. He asked if he could walk his friend outside. I said yes. Then he walked back in and said he changed his mind again. He said he was staying at his friends. I argued and yelled at him. Which I don't do a lot of yelling at the kids unless they push me over the edge. But I was losing it completely. He finally left and we went to the boat.

As soon as my husband looked at me he knew I was upset. We had a few words to each other. I sat there during the boat ride praying to God to please keep my son safe. I was so scared. The feeling continued for a few hours. Robbie kept trying to cheer me up. I just couldn't shake this bad feeling no matter how hard I tried. Then all of a sudden I was fine. I didn't know why the bad feeling was gone. When I got home my son told me that him and his friend had gotten stopped by the police for riding the scooter on the road.

The police made them walk the scooter back to the friends house. The police stopped at our house to talk to us but we were on the boat. I felt so guilty for not being home to talk to the policeman. But I thanked that policeman in my brain over and over. He stopped my son from riding that scooter. I lost my bad feelings and got to enjoy a couple of hours on the boat. Who knows maybe the policeman changed what was going to happen. I'll never know what my bad feeling was. I'll never know what would have happened if anything that day. As far as I'm concerned that policeman happened to come by and he saved the day. Or God sent the policeman there that day to save the day. I believe prayers can change some outcomes.

My son Bobby Ray was eighteen years old when he told me he wished he had a normal family. He said that way he'd get away with more. I looked at him and he said he was just kidding. Of course I questioned him about it. He insisted he was kidding. I feel bad for him. It can't be easy having a mother like me. I think it partly had to do with what had happened earlier in the day. He told me he was throwing his futon away. Before he bought it I kept telling him not to buy it. I told him it wouldn't be good. Not because there's anything wrong with futons. I've known a lot of people that have them and they've lasted quite a while. I've even slept on my nieces futon and it was a great nights sleep. I had no good reason to give him for not buying it. So he bought it and sure enough it broke after just a couple months. I'm sure it had something to do with too many people on it at once. The kids wrestling on it. Anyway he brought me into his room and showed me where it was broken. He said I know you told me not to buy it and you were right. I hugged and kissed him. I asked him when will you ever start listening to me? He said probably never. I said when I tell you stuff it's not always momma just saying no. You know how I am I just know stuff. He said he knew that and he wished that he'd start listening to me more often.

My daughter Rozie was waiting for this football game all season. Her high school football team was playing the high school she would have gone to if we hadn't moved. So she was sure she'd get to see some of her old friends at the game. Well a couple of days before the big game I found out she had been riding to school with her girlfriends grandma. Not a real big deal except she had asked to ride with them a month earlier and we said no.

The grandma had just asked me a few weeks earlier and I said no. Not that I didn't trust her. We just wanted our daughter to meet some people on the bus since we had just moved again.

Also our way of thinking was less buses have accidents then cars. We had just moved back to the city and we were still trying to get use to all the traffic. So we would drop Rozie off at the bus stop in the morning thinking she was getting on the bus and then the grandma would pick her up and take her to school. If the grandma thought it was ok she should have been picking her up at our house. So anyway Rozie slipped up while chatting with me one night. So I got the truth out of her. I told her she had to tell her dad the next day. I never keep secrets from my husband. So she came home the next day and didn't tell her dad. I told her several more times to go talk to him. She didn't. So finally I called her into the room with us and we talked. By then he was mad that she didn't talk to him when she had first gotten home. So we usually decide on a punishment together. But this time he said no football game.

I was so upset because I knew how much this game meant to her. So then he got mad at me. So Rozie and I were both crying. We both went to our rooms and cried. As I layed there I thought how I hate eating dinner when I've been crying. I hate sitting there with my swollen eyes looking at my husband when we're mad at each other. Dinner got done cooking and the electric went off. It wasn't even raining out. We got to eat by candle light so no one could see my swollen cried out eyes. The electric stayed out all through dinner. It came back on about fifteen minutes after dinner was over just in time to run the dishwasher. The next day Rozie found out that the football game had gotten rained out. It hadn't rained in a couple of weeks. Just one of those strange rainy nights. So she didn't miss out on anything. But she hopefully learned a important lesson about not telling is just like lying. We also learned strange things happen all the time in our strange lives.

Our friends mom called him and said she was watching the news and that Robert Weeks had died in a car wreck. Robert Weeks is my husbands name. So our friend got really upset and called our other friend. He got really upset and had his wife call our house to talk to me. She called our house crying and Robert answered the phone. We all laughed about it.

About fifteen minutes later Robbie told me to call our son Robert (Bobby Ray) right now. I said "Oh God don't do this to me." Robbie said I'm not doing nothing call Bobby Ray now. I started crying. I couldn't get him on his phone. So I called his friends house and the kids answered and said they weren't back yet. So I asked if they could call Bobby Ray on his friends phone. Why I didn't just get the number, I just don't know. So I was crying and upset so the kid put the mother on the phone. I told her while crying that someone called and told us Robert Weeks was killed in a car wreck so I wanted to make sure Bobby Ray was ok. She said she'd call them and have Bobby Ray call home. So she gave the message perfect but the way I worded the message was messed up.

His friend got off the phone and said to Bobby Ray "Man I don't know how to tell ya this but your dad passed away." They both cried. So while they're parked on the side of the road crying. I have our daughter Rozie trying to call her police friend who was also friends with Bobby Ray. The policeman wasn't returning her call. So I was so afraid that he had heard that it was Bobby Ray and didn't want to call her until he knew everything. When I got off the phone I told Rozie and John to start praying that it wasn't Bobby Ray that had died. We all prayed very hard. Then the phone rang. It was Bobby Ray but I couldn't understand him. He was crying so hard. I kept saying is this you Bobby Ray. Finally he said yes it was him. I said oh Thank you God. I told him we were worried that it was you that got killed in the car wreck. As I talked he kept asking me "Where is Dad"? I said right here in his chair. I finally understood that he thought his dad was dead. So I said here talk to your daddy. So they talked and were both so happy that they were alive.

Rozie, John, and I hugged and kissed. We were so happy that Bobby Ray was safe and alive. You really know how much you love someone when you think they've passed away and they didn't. It's like you get another chance to love them. My husband and sons name is a very popular name in Florida. This had happened a few years earlier. It brought my husband and his brother closer. My husband Robbie is a third generation commercial fisherman.

My husbands cousin heard on the news that Robert Weeks had drowned while fishing. It sounded very possible at the time. So he called Robbie's brother and said he had heard that Robbie had died. So they all freaked out and finally tracked us down. We were at a motel for Bobby Ray's eighteenth birthday. They were all so happy that he was still alive. We turned on the TV and sure enough Robert Weeks had passed away fishing. Thank God it wasn't my Robert Weeks.

Our kids have grown up watching and learning about our gifts and their gifts from God. They believe in all of it but sometimes they forget to use it. They have lived all their lives with all of this around them on a daily basis. When they are focused they use their gifts. They have all prayed on me when I've been sick and have been able to heal me. I believe that is one of the most loving, special, and unselfish things you can do for someone. You just have to remember to not bring the pain into yourself. So many people make that mistake and say that they'd rather have the pain or illness then the person they are praying on have it. I've seen so many times where it goes into the person that's doing the praying. You just have to watch how you word your prayers. You want to help the person you're praying for but you don't want to make yourself sick. Everyone has different beliefs on this laying of hands healing. I believe anyone can do it with love and faith. It is

God doing the healing. He is just answering your prayers that you are praying for the sick person. I don't think I have any special powers. I just know that I have faith in a very special God that works miracles through us everyday.

CHAPTER 5
MOMS HOUSE

We were moving off our wonderful, beautiful island. I was so sad. We were getting ready to move back to our hometown. Our car wasn't running right. You could drive ten miles and then it would start to act like it was gonna stall out or it would just stall out. I had to drive the car since my husband Robbie was driving the moving truck. So Robbie went first with me following with his cousin following me. It was 6:00am. We drove the ten miles or so and the car started acting up. So I kept babying it to keep it running. My son Bobby Ray and our dog were with me. The dog started crying as soon as we left the house because he wanted to be in the truck with my husband. As soon as the car started messing up the dog quit crying. Bobby Ray and I started praying.

We were coming up to a tall bridge we had to get over with this car trying to stall out. When we went through the toll booth I ended up in front of my husband. As we started up the tall bridge the fastest I could get the car to go was twenty five miles a hour. The speed limit is fifty five miles per hour. We were so scared. Robbie and our daughter Rozie were behind us praying for us. Robbie's cousin and John were behind them praying for us. We got almost to the top and it sounded like it had stalled out. So I started pulling over to the emergency lane. Then all of a sudden it just took off and up and over the bridge we went. Down the bridge no problems. Thirty more miles to our hometown and no car problems. One month later the car is still running great. No new car parts, just a lot of praying. I still won't try to drive it over any more high bridges.

It was my birthday and my sister from another state called me to wish me a happy birthday. As we were talking I felt weird. I thought I was gonna pass out. I felt like something had come into me. I swayed forward like I was falling then I came back. I was upright and felt like something came right into me. I felt great after that. It was quite a awesome birthday talk. She is very spiritual so we were talking about God at the time these amazing things happened to me. She always helps me and empowers me with her spiritual talks. She has been my saving grace so many times in my life.

It's always been nice to have a sister that understands me completely. It has taken me years to open up myself completely to her. She might even read a few things in this book that she didn't know about me. My husband Robbie and our kids know me the best since I never had to hide anything from them. They always love me no matter how strange things have gotten over the years. My brother, my family, and I were living at mom's house taking care of her a few years after dad passed away. So my brother wanted to get mom's house put into his name. It was going to him in the will anyway so it didn't really matter to me anyway. So my brother and I were going to take our mom to the courthouse and get the house put into my brothers name. We have power of attorney over our mother. Mom agreed to putting the house in his name at first. Then she started yelling at us. She went back and forth like that for five hours. Finally we were walking down the driveway to get into the car to go to the courthouse.

All of a sudden it felt like someone or something grabbed me and stopped me from walking. I was so startled that I looked around to see what had just grabbed me. I didn't see anyone or anything. Then I told my brother no I'm not going. This may not sound like a big thing. But in my family it is, since I NEVER say no to a family member. He was shocked that I said no. I told him I had been having a bad feeling about this for two days. I try very hard to follow my feelings. They tried to talk me into going. I stood my ground and I didn't go. The power that grabbed me that day made me pay attention to my bad feelings.

My sister was having a party. She told me a few days ahead of time. The day of the party I decided that I wasn't going to the party. I was tired from working in mom's yard for a couple of days with Robbie and our kids. Also mom had been fighting with me and my brother for a couple of days. I was too tired and stressed out to go to the party. I was also very sad that I wasn't going. That night I tossed and turned all night. I kept waking up crying in my sleep. One of the times during the night I woke up and in my head someone was telling me it was gonna be ok. They told me my other sister was gonna pick me up the next morning and she was gonna take me out to breakfast. That night I had a dream that I was at a flea market. But it wasn't like any flea market that I'd been to before. This was in a wooden building up off the ground.

The next morning my sister called me and asked me out to breakfast. She came and picked me up and we had a wonderful breakfast. Then she took me to the next town to the flea market that was in my dream. We had a great time walking through the flea market. I told her that I knew she was coming. I asked her if she remembered when she had decided to ask me out. She didn't remember. She said maybe you put the thought into my head to take you out. Who knows how it all got started. I don't think I started it since I was hearing someone tell me about it. It was a great morning. My sister showed me so much love that day and it was just what I needed. Sister love is such a amazing pure love. It's the only love that is so close to a mother's love. Sister love is so caring and special. I'm so lucky to have four sisters that love me so much.

My family and I had been living with my mother and brother for six months. My brother's girlfriend moved in a few months later. She and I had put each other in our places the first time we met about eight months earlier. My brother and I were super close. It was more then just sister and brother, it was a super special unbelievable soul spirited bond. No one besides my brother and I ever really understood the bond we had. It amazed some people, it pissed a lot of people off. She was pissed off. I told her the first time I met her that I know a lot of stuff before it happens. She said she knew cause my brother had told her. I usually don't tell people this about me this quickly. I didn't even realize my brother knew this about me. So of course I knew what she was up to before I even met her. I usually don't let myself look into family's love lives unless trouble just jumps right out at me. Then I try to give advice. He didn't take my advice and I'm not sure but he probably told her about the advice I had given. So their relationship ended up destroying my brothers and mine.

What God made in thirty fours years was tore to pieces in about two years. They made it for a while then broke up. Who knows they might end up back together. They have a beautiful little girl together so they will always be connected. My brother and I were tore apart for four years. April 2009 I went down for my nieces wedding and I got to get my brother and my sister back into my life. My brother and sister both threw me away at the same time. I told my niece thank you for getting married and getting us put back together. So anyway back to 2004.

It was July of that year and I was really tired of not getting to move on with our lives. We had come to stay at mom's house to help my brother fix the place up. We were also waiting on my husbands inheritance so we could move about five hours away from our families. We wanted to move back to the country. City life just wasn't for us. We had done a lot of work at moms house. Then my brother pitched a fit and said he didn't want us to do anything else to the house. I wish he would have done that before we had worked our butts off for six months. We got mad at him since we still had a lot of work left to do. We had completely redone the back yard. He helped us one day for about a hour and this had been six months. He was supposed to get what he wanted to keep out of this big pile of junk in the back yard we had piled up. He never did it so we couldn't mow the back yard with all this junk in the middle of the yard.

So as the months went by the back yard became a jungle again. The grass was waist high. The weeds were taller then me. I'm 5'4, so anyway one night in the shower I started talking to my dads and my brother Ray Ray who are all in heaven. Yes strange but very effective. I promised my dad, step dad, and Ray Ray that I'd redo the back yard one more time if they'd let me move on with my life. I told them I would do it alone since my husband and kids had worked so hard fixing the yard up the first time. So I had to wait until my husband and kids were gone so I could sneak out there to do this work. I knew if they were home they'd help me. So I worked my butt off in that back yard all week. So about a week later I felt so sick all day. I took my temperature and I was normal. I told my husband that I was going to take a shower and hopefully I'd feel better.

I got into the shower and I started crying my eyes out. I felt so weak. I leaned up against the side of the shower. I prayed to God to make me feel better. I prayed to dad, step dad, and to my brother Ray Ray to please help me. I was so stressed out . I told God I know you don't give us more then we can handle. But you're really pushing me hard I just don't know how much more I can handle. I told God I needed a sign on what to do and how much longer we had to live at mom's house. I told God I don't want one of those small signs that I'm not sure if its really a sign or not. I need a big in my face sign.

Now years later I realize I really shouldn't order these signs from God. I should always just keep the faith that as long as I'm doing good then God will do good to me and everything will be just fine in its own time. God chooses what we go through we choose how we go through it. So I finally calmed myself down and finished my shower. I went to bed that night feeling a little better. I dreamed that we moved and loved the country town. A few nights later my husbands brother called and said we should be getting our money in about a week. My husbands brother and my step dad have the same name. So I figured it was a sign from my step dad.

Robbie mentioned that we were struggling to get money for school clothes for Roseanne and John. Robbie and I were fishing our butts off trying to make enough money for school clothes. A few minutes after Robbie got off the phone, his brother called us back. He told me he and his wife wanted to take the kids clothes shopping the next day. I was so happy. We had been really close with his brother when the kids were younger. For the past six years we had lived fifty miles away so we hadn't seen much of him and his wife. So the kids wanted me to go with them shopping. I felt like a terrible mother and I said no that they're doing this wonderful thing for us. It will give them all a chance to bond if I wasn't with them. The kids said yeah you're right momma. When I got alone I cried my eyes out that this was the first time I really couldn't afford to take my kids school clothes shopping.

It hurt so badly but at the same time I was so happy for his brother and wife to get a chance to do this awesome thing for us and to get to know our kids. Four years later as I copy this down for print here I am crying again.

Back to that day. Robbie had a fishing trip planned with his best friend and his son for the same day as the shopping trip. So I knew that I could get some work done in the yard. As I drove Robbie to his boat I told him about crying in the shower and about praying to God. He said you better finish that yard or we won't get our check next week. We both laughed. We didn't get the check for another four months. Before the kids left on their shopping trip my son John wanted to know what was I going to do while they were all gone. I told him I was gonna work in the back yard. He said you can't do that alone. I said yes I can. None of them knew that I had been sneaking back there working all week. He said don't work yourself too hard.

He asked what was I gonna wear on my feet. I said sneakers. He said no wear your rubber fishing boots. I told him I had thought about boots but thought they'd be too hot. He said wear the boots, so I wore the boots to keep John happy. All this love and concern came out of my thirteen year old son. It is wonderful being loved this much. I worked my butt off for two hours in the yard. I was moving stuff that was way too heavy for me to move. When it felt too heavy, I'd tell my dads and Ray Ray to come on and lift a little more. Then it would get lighter to move. I knew they were out in that yard helping me all those days of hard work. On this day it was one hundred degrees outside. I was sweating so bad my shirt was soaked through. I just kept on going so I could get it done so we could move on with our lives. Then my husband called for a ride. I got to the boat and it was pouring down rain. So I figured good I'll get a hour break to cool down. Six hours later it was still rainning. I had gotten most of the yard finished. I figured I'd be able to finish the rest the next day.

Thank goodness for the rain cause it stopped me from working too hard. As I did all this work in the yard my brother and his girlfriend layed in bed. Later that day the kids got home and they had such a good time with their Uncle and Aunt. When they started toting bags into the house I started tearing up but this time it was happy tears. I was gonna be happy if they got them one or two outfits each. They bought them everything. Six outfits each, shoes, socks, purse, earrings, two pairs of shoes for Rozie, dress shoes and sneakers, under garments, hair ties, backpacks, and then to top it all off school supplies. I was totally blown away by this much love and kindness.

I've never experienced anything like that before for my kids. We've gotten help during hard times before but never this much. I was so happy for the kids to receive that love and good time. They also took the kids out to lunch. The kids had a blast and got to know their uncle and aunt. I was happy for Robbie and I cause we had been so stressed out trying to make enough money for school shopping. I was happy for the kids uncle and aunt cause I knew it made them happy to be able to help us and to get to know the kids as teenagers. We all thanked them a million times. There just wasn't enough thank yous to express how much this meant to our whole family. A few hours later Rozie said mom I just don't understand it. I said what?

She said we haven't been real close to our uncle and aunt the past six years. Then they did this wonderful thing for us. Then there's family that we're super close to that didn't offer anything. Why is it like that? She really had me this time but I couldn't show it cause kids always think parents have all the answers, even a fourteen year old girl. So I told her it was because her uncle and aunt were wonderful loving people. It was just time for them to come back into our lives. I said what a wonderful, loving way to come back into our lives. The rest of the family is always there and we all help each other all the time in smaller ways. After I said it I thought I did have the answer. A few days later the uncle called up and said he couldn't buy our oldest son Bobby Ray school clothes since he was eighteen years old and out of school. So he and his wife had talked it over and wanted to give Bobby Ray a pickup truck. We were all so happy over their kindness towards our kids. Five years later we all have a wonderful relationship. We were just down there staying at their house a few weeks ago on vacation. You never know what act of kindness will change your life forever. We were able to move on with our life the next month.

It was August 10, 2004 a Tuesday evening. My husband Robbie had been watching a Tropical Storm on the weather channel for a day or two. We lived in Southwest Florida and hurricanes and tropical storms were part of our life every summer. We grew up with all our elders talking about Hurricane Donna and how bad she was and how we hadn't had a bad one since her so we were due to have one soon. So we're always paying attention to every storm. After dinner that night, Robbie asked me to call our friend. He said he wanted to dock our boat at his friends house. He wasn't sure if the storm would hit us but he knew he wasn't leaving his boat at the dock in the bay. I called our friend and he said sure we could park the boat there. He also said the storm wouldn't be here for another week.

The next day was Wednesday and it was a very hectic day. The morning started with coffee and the news that the Tropical Storm was heading toward us. We were living at my mother's house which is stressful to start with. I hadn't been getting along with my brother who was living there too in a few months. I dropped Robbie off at our boat at 10:00am. We were moving the boat further inland and hopefully it would stay safe.

While Robbie moved the boat I had to stop at the store to get John a new calculator. Then I had to go pick Robbie up at the new dock. Then we went home and I fixed us lunch. My husband watched the weather channel for the latest on the now Hurricane Charley. Robbie had told me correctly for twelve years where all the hurricanes and tropical storms would hit no matter what the weather channel had said. So when he told me on Wednesday afternoon to go buy water, lunch meat, bread, soda, and the fixins for a big noodle salad, I got really scared.

He said it was just in case. But I knew better. I knew right then that this was going to be a hurricane and that it was gonna come very close to us. The grocery store was already crazy at 2:00pm. I got back home and started laundry. I finally sat down and watched my soap opera The Guiding Light that I've been watching all of my life. After my one hour of peace for the day I got up and watered the dogs and played with them. Then I talked to each of my kids as they came home. I started dinner at 5:00pm. Robbie likes to eat dinner at 6:00pm. Our youngest son John helps me cook dinner quite often. I was ready to serve dinner and John asked me to make gravy to go on the cheesey mashed potatos. At first I didn't want to but I went ahead and made the gravy. The look on his face I knew I had to make the gravy without complaining. Of course it was homemade gravy. While I was cooking dinner I also fixed the window in my car that wouldn't go up.

I also folded and put away a load of laundry. Multitasking is my way of life and I really love every minute of it even on crazy days like this one. It was the best gravy that I've ever made. After dinner Roseanne heads to her room and I call her back like every night. I tell her she needs to stay in the living room so she can get the dishes done. So she sits and talks to us until her grandma starts to wash the dishes. So I tell Roseanne to get over there and dry the dishes. She had been at her friends house after school so she hadn't been much help around the house. Roseanne and Bobby Ray did tote the water jugs and all the groceries in the house for me. So after I put all the food away I asked Rozie to wash the dinner table. Instead of just washing the table she got on the floor and kissed the dog Rascal. He had dog food left on his mouth from dinner and it grossed her out. At that same moment I asked her to make Kool aid.

So when she started griping I thought it was at me but she says it was at the dog. So I got angry and we got into a argument about her not doing anything I had asked her to do that evening. I then went into the bedroom to watch a show on television with Robbie. I try to spend some time with him when I can. So ten minutes later during a commercial I went and checked my laundry. I came back then the next commercial I went to go make up with Roseanne. We made up and I noticed my son John wasn't in the house. I thought to myself I need to go check on him right now. I should have but I didn't go check on him. I usually follow my strong feelings but I didn't. He's thirteen years old and a normal teenage boy. He's always doing something.

I figured I'd finish the show with Robbie and then I'd go check on John. About ten minutes later we smelled something. Robbie said go see what that smell is. I knew it would be John.

I ran through the house looking for him then I went out the front door. No John. I ran back into the house and into the bedroom and into the bathroom yelling at Roseanne to move so I could open the back door into the shed. I opened the door and there was John. He looked pretty good. I thought to myself Thank God! I asked him what happened? He started explaining how he was going to weed eat the back yard. So he set the weed eater on the AC outside. He filled the gas tank up on the weed eater and over filled it. So gas had spilled into the AC. That's what we had smelled. So did his uncle my brother. When his uncle smelled the gas he opened his window and said John. That scared John and he jumped. When he jumped he cut his finger on the weed eater. So as he's telling me this story the poor kid is standing there bleeding and I hadn't even seen it yet. His uncle is walking around the back yard cursing.

I went to my room to get the bandages and medicine. I told Robbie what was going on. Then I went back to go doctor John up with so much guilt. Robbie came in and griped at John just a little bit. He told him I'm not mad at you but don't use tools without asking first. John was so upset and in so much pain. He wanted to know if dad and his uncle were mad at him. I said no don't worry about it. I told him you made a mistake. You were trying to do something good. I told him the story about when I was his age before weed eaters we had to use a sickle to cut weeds. I was trying to do something good too.

I wanted to surprise my dad too. When my dad got home from work laying block in the hot Florida sun on a nice hot summer day. He had to fix the plumbing. I cut a pipe when I was cutting the weeds down up against the house with the sickle. I got yelled at. I had cried and said I was so sorry to my dad. I swore that day I wouldn't yell at my kids every time they messed up. So even though I had a very hectic day all day long. I didn't yell at John when he messed up. But because it was such a hectic day I didn't slow down and go find John when I had that bad feeling about him. I should have taken the time to go find John as soon as I thought about him. I just wasn't paying close enough attention. I could have saved my son from messing up but the most important thing I could have saved him the pain of cutting his finger. I will slow down and pay more attention to my feelings and thoughts. Thank you God for it just being a cut finger. Yes I've learned my lesson. I will start taking my time and I'll start paying closer attention no matter whats going on around me.

Robbie said he wasn't sure how bad the hurricane would be but he thought we would get enough wind to lose our electric for a few days. I made extra ice for the coolers. On Thursday Robbie had me buy more lunch meat, canned foods, soda, and bread. My brothers girlfriend bought candles and batteries. We thought we were ready for the worst. Robbie watched the storm all night on the weather channel Wednesday night. He got a couple hours sleep. He was up most of Thursday night watching the weather channel. The weather reports were calling for the worst to hit about one hundred miles north of us.

Friday morning Robbie told me it doesn't matter what the TV is saying. He said we're going to get a lot of this hurricane. We were living in half mobile home and half house my step dad had built on. The wind from the hurricane would be coming toward the house half. Plus there was a lot of trees behind the house half that would slow down the wind. There was my husband Robbie, our oldest son Bobby Ray, our daughter Rozie, our youngest son John, my mother, my brother, his girlfriend, his dog, our dog, Johns dog, and me living in my mothers house. The eight of us were putting our lives in my husbands hands. He had always been right so I had faith in him when he said we were staying. I was scared but I had faith.

Robbie's cousin called from Pine Island a few hours before it hit. We were very surprised when he said he was staying. My sister called to tell us she loved us and we could go to her house. She was at our other sister's house. We said no we're staying. My sister from Missouri called to say she loved us and to give me a spiritual pep talk that I needed very badly. She told me that she'd be praying for us. She told me something I never knew. She said I could pray this storm away from us. I never knew you could pray about the weather. We talked about no matter how bad it got. She said just keep believing that we would be ok. No matter what, she said don't give the storm any power. My aunt who is mom's sister called from New York to say she loved us and to wish us luck. She was real worried about us like everyone else was.

When I was done with all the phone calls I went into the kids room to give them a pep talk. I told them all to start praying that the bad part of the storm would miss us. They were all really good at saying prayers for everything that needed a prayer. God is in our lives everyday not just on Sundays at church. Then I told them no matter how bad it gets just believe we will live. I told them if the roof blows off and you're being sucked out of the house keep praying and believing that you will live through it and you will survive. We were all scared but I wanted them to be ready for the worst. I knew if I told them that, they'd be ok if they kept praying. I figured at least if it got really bad and we got blown away from each other at least they'd have God there with them to comfort them.

Then Robbie yelled for me. He was at the other end of the house watching the storm on TV. He said call my cousin and tell him to leave the island right now. Robbie said tell him the hurricane is coming right toward him. I called and spoke to his girlfriend. I told her what Robbie had said. I told her a few times. We were hoping that they'd leave before the bridge got closed. A few days later we heard from his cousins mom that they left the island shortly before the hurricane hit. Back to the hurricane day. It was getting closer. We all went out on the front porch to make sure everything was in order outside before the storm hit. The firemen came past the house telling us to evacuate. It was such a strange feeling watching all our neighbors leaving. A shelter was out of the question with the three dogs.

Mom has Alzheimers so we didn't want to take her somewhere and get her all upset and confused. The number one reason for not leaving was my husband Robbie had always been right and he believed that we would be safe if we stayed. I kept praying and believing in my husband. We parked our car in the neighbors driveway. They had less trees in their yard. We told our son Bobby Ray to park his truck over there several times. My brother told him it would be fine in our driveway. He had his car in our driveway too. Our yard had a lot of trees so I don't know what they were thinking. It started to rain so we went inside. I knew they were both making a mistake by not moving the truck and the car.

The hurricane winds started. We lost electric and water immediately. We had our radio on. We sat in the living room. My brother, his girlfriend, and Bobby Ray went from the living room to my brothers bedroom. They went back and forth for a while. My husband sat on the couch very calm watching the hurricane through the living room window. Me, my mom, Rozie, John, and the dogs moved from chair to couch to other chairs. Robbie got up to look out the window better in case he had to move us to a different room. I finally sat on the floor on my knees praying in the living room. I could feel the floor moving up and down during the harder winds. I was so frightened. I told Robbie about the floor moving. The trees started falling in the yard. You could hear the hard wind coming before you saw it. I yelled out a few times when I saw trees falling.

I was on my knees praying my heart out. Rozie and I were the only two watching out the kitchen window when a huge tree started falling toward the window. Rozie opened her mouth to yell and nothing came out. I yelled so loud and prayed so much in those few seconds. It looked like it was going to come right into the side of the trailer. It fell along the side of the whole front of the trailer. It lightly brushed the front of the trailer. Some of the branches landed on the roof of the mobile home. Luckily none of the branches came through the roof. We all thanked God quickly for that close call. I don't know if my yelling and praying helped keep that tree out of the mobile home. But I believe it helped. Robbie told me not to yell again. After that scream, everyone came running from the bedroom.

Then my brother announces he's going to move his car. I tell my son he's not moving his truck so don't even ask. Robbie told my brother he didn't think that was a good idea. My brother put the rain coat on and said he only had one car. Robbie said yeah and you only have one life. My brother took the rain coat off and left the car where it was. The worst of the hurricane lasted about three hours. Toward the end of the hurricane my son John who was thirteen years old and I took his puppy into the shed to pee. He let her go and she ran out a opened door. The doors were all supposed to be closed. John went to go after her. I grabbed him and told him no. We argued for a minute then I told him the puppy probably went straight to the front door.

So we ran back into the house. The shed is attached to the house. I opened the front door and the puppy ran into the house. John and I were so happy. The storm was about over so we went ahead and ate some salad and sandwiches. We were finally calmed down. I then prayed for everyone in Florida to be safe from the hurricane. The hurricane hit thirty to sixty miles north of us. It hit hard on Pine Island which is where we had lived until seven months earlier. I prayed for all the people on Pine Island to be safe. My son's windshield in his truck got cracked from tree limbs falling on it. My brother's car got dented up from all the tree limbs falling on it. The yard was a complete mess. It took days of clean up. The first thing we had to do was get those big branches off the roof.

We didn't have electric and water for three days. The next morning I stood in line for coffee at the store for thirty minutes. I stood in line to use a pay phone for thirty minutes to call our family to tell them we survived the storm. All the stores close by ran out of ice and gas really fast. The lines for a burger in the next town over were crazy long. I stood in line for burgers for a hour and I was so happy for a hot meal when I got them. We got ice from my sister who lived in the next town over. She had made a lot of extra ice and they didn't lose power so she gave us the ice. It was so hot at night with no AC running. It really made you think about all the things you just take for granted. Living out of coolers for your food. No running water to wash and to flush the toilet. We had to get buckets of water out of the ditch to flush the toilet.

Mom's water comes from a pump and well. Our good friend invited us to dinner on the third night we were so happy to have a hot meal. We were all glad that dad's good house building withheld those hurricane winds. We were all very happy that Robbie was right once again. No matter what we went through during and after Hurricane Charley. We survived Hurricane Charley on August 13, 2004.

My daughter Roseanne and I were laying on my bed watching TV. Our family had been planning to move to Dixie County for a few months. We were waiting for my husbands grandma's estate to get settled. Roseanne turned to me and thanked me for taking her to open house at the high school. She thanked me for letting her go to this high school until we moved. She thanked God for a few things. Then she said "We're getting the money soon". She sounded so serious. I said how do you know? I said did someone tell you? She said no that she'd seen signs everywhere for the past week. She said she had been seeing a lot of things that had Dixie on it. So she knew we'd be moving to Dixie County soon. She said she had seen Dixie on the TV, in a magazine, and while riding down the street. So the next morning I told Robbie about it. Then Robbie, me, and our three kids, and our two dogs went out on our boat. When we got back from boating we were driving down the road. In front of our friends house was a plumbing van. On the side of the van in huge letters said DIXIE. In smaller letters it said something. We all saw that and started laughing. Roseanne said see I told ya'll I keep seeing Dixie signs.

Our life was very hectic living at mom's house. I was very upset that my younger brother and I weren't getting along. He wouldn't let me and Robbie fix anything else on mom's house. I was so stressed out. I felt like my real dad, step dad, and brother Ray Ray whom are all dead had pushed me to move to mom's house. Before the move I kept dreaming about them and they kept telling me to go home and help mom. I always tell Robbie about my dreams and he thought they wanted us to go help mom too. So seven and a half months later we were still living at mom's house. We had done a lot of work on the house and yard. Then my brother put a stop to the work. So during one of my stressed out crying moments I prayed and begged my dad's and my brother to help me figure out what to do next.

I wanted to leave mom's house. Not that I wanted to leave my mother. I just needed to move forward with my life. I yelled at my dead family for making me come home and not be able to finish what we came here to do. That night I went to bed very sad. I dreamed of my brother Ray Ray. I think about my big brother Ray Ray everyday. He's been dead for thirty four years. I don't dream about him very often. But when I do the dreams are so real. In my dream Ray Ray came back to Florida from Texas. He was living in Texas when he was killed. He was run over in a hit and run accident one month after his twenth birthday. In my dream he came home and said that he'd been alive all these years living in Texas. He stayed for a few months and helped get mom's house finished. Then he said he was going back to Texas to live his life. He said he'd be back for visits and all the family could go visit him in Texas. He told Robbie and I that we needed to get on with our lives. He said we should move out of mom's house and start living again. When I woke up that morning I was very confused. I was upset at first thinking maybe he never died. Then I reasoned with myself. I've always had a problem believing that Ray Ray was dead.

For years after his funeral I thought he was really alive living in Texas. I was in my thirties when I finally excepted his death. So when I dreamed that he was alive this time I was really upset. I told Robbie about my dream. We were still waiting on Robbie's money. So that morning we went to see the lawyer. The lawyer said it would be a few more months. This was Friday morning. On the way home Robbie said we've got to get a small loan to get moved and get back on our feet. Our credit was a little messed up since we had lost our truck ten months earlier.

I made a few calls for a loan. No luck on the loan. He said let's go to our favorite bar, maybe someone we know will come in. Before we left he called a buddy and the buddy said he'd go with Robbie on Monday to talk to the buddies dad for a loan. That wasn't a yes yet. So we went to the bar. We haven't been drinking much lately so this wasn't easy sitting in the bar waiting. A few hours passed and no one we could ask came in. Then we decided we were leaving after this beer and Pepsi and hope for the best on Monday. Then a guy we know walked in and he waved and said hi. A few minutes later Robbie went and sat with the guy. This guy is a really nice guy. We talk to him whenever we see him. He wasn't one of our best friends that we had grown up with.

I figured Robbie was just talking to him about life. Robbie needed someone to vent to. Then the guy got a telephone call and went outside. Robbie came back to our table he said that he had asked the guy for the loan. The guy said he would except he might have to send money up north to help care for his sick mom. The phone call was the call from his sister to tell him if he needed to send money. He came back in and asked Robbie if he wanted to go for a ride. The call was good news about his mom. She was doing better. He said since he got good news he was going to lend the money to us. He said he wanted to pass his good luck onto us. It all worked out just at the right time. So then we went to our friends house who was going to rent us two of his bedrooms in his house.

Our friend said it would be a few days since he had to give this other guy a chance first who wanted the room before we did. So we still didn't know if we were moving yet. On Sunday our friend came over and said we could move in. So we paid him and we moved in the next day on Monday. The move was bitter sweet. It was a new start for Robbie, myself, and our three kids. But it was so hard to leave my mother. I knew no one would take care of my mother as good as I did. Momma was heartbroken watching us pack up to leave. She asked us to stay several times. She told us we didn't have to go. She knew she wouldn't be taken care of as good by anyone but me. It was even hard to leave my brother even though we had been fighting so badly. It was the end to a Season. There's a Time and Season for everyone and everything.

I was so sad and happy at the same time. So we finally got all moved into our new house. We were only planning on staying for a few months then we were Dixie County bound. On Monday night we called on a few sleeper sofas. We were planning on spending fifty to one hundred dollars on a sofa. Some were sold, some weren't home. Robbie said that means there's one cheaper at a store. I said let's go to the used sofas store. So we went the next day. Robbie stopped at this other store first but they were closed. We got to the sofa store and found a nice sleeper sofa for $14.99 we bought it. Everything was falling into place. So we were doing what Ray Ray told us to do. We were starting to live again. Thank You Ray Ray for coming to me in that dream and helping us to feel like we did all we could do for mom.

We were free to go and start living our lives again. Ray Ray freed me without the guilt I would have had if I would have left on my own. We begged momma to move with us to Dixie County. She said she already knew how good Robbie and I would take care of her. She said it was the rest of the families turn to step up. She said she wanted to see what the rest of them were made of. She felt the need to give them all a chance to take care of her. Like I said earlier in this book Momma is psychic. So I don't know if she thought they needed to do this for their own personal growth or what. I was very sad to leave my mother. Four years after I left they put her in a nursing home. They all did their best with our mother. Everyone's best is different.

CHAPTER 6
THOUGHTS, VISIONS, FEELINGS, AND DREAMS

I worked with a woman for a while. We became friends and we did a lot of talking. We'd tell each other stories about our lives. We really connected. Sometimes she'd tell me a story and then tell me why she did something. I'd listen then I'd tell her bull crap you did that because such and such. She'd look at me completely shocked. She would never tell me if I was right but the look on her face told me that I was right that I was reading her right. But you always question yourself when you don't know for sure.

I worked with a woman and a teenage girl. We all became very close friends. A lot of times before they said something I knew what they were fixing to say. I'm not sure if this was from us being such good friends or was there more to it. I'd sometimes get angry with this one boss I had for stuff he'd say. Sometimes I'd get mad at him for things I thought he was thinking and he didn't say. Did I just know him that well or did I hear his thoughts?

I use to be really bad about finishing peoples sentences for them. I always thought I knew what they were going to say. I finally decided that I could tell a lot more about myself if I let them finish what they were gonna say and I could see if it was what I was thinking. Its not always important to prove to other people that I'm right. But when you're younger it felt kinda good to show people that I wasn't that dumb little kid that they all thought I was. Once I grew into myself and had been loved by my husband Robbie for a few years I realized as long as I knew that my gifts from God were working that was good enough for me.

Sometimes I feel like I'm so in tune with people. I sometimes wonder if the thoughts in my head are mine or their thoughts. I know its possible since I've read about other people like this. Some people have to have physical contact with a person to get their thoughts.

Some people can just pass by someone and hear their thoughts. I don't know how you would ever know for sure if they are your thoughts or the persons that you are close to. It seems like when there is no eye contact there are no thoughts jumping into my head. Sometimes its a wonderful gift from God. I'll get a thought and talk to the person about it.

They always act like they really needed to talk about that subject. It doesn't happen all the time. I'd probably go crazy if it did. I almost didn't put this part of me in the book. I was trying to go to sleep one night and this part came into my head. So I decided to put it in the book. I was worried about what people would think about me again. I've only told one of my sisters about this and it was just last month. Well it was last month when I wrote that part but now its been about five years ago. I reckon it was my first step to opening up about thoughts jumping. So many thoughts have jumped in the past five years.

People will sit there and tell me something and I know its bull cause I hear the real story in my head not in my ears. It's been quite interesting raising teenagers with this gift. I can ask them for the truth until I'm blue in the face and they keep giving me this bull story. I'm sitting there knowing its bull but don't always know how to get the truth out of them. My youngest son John is the easiest one to get the truth out of when I tell him that I know that what he's saying isn't whats really going on. My two older kids will stick to their stories a lot longer but will finally tell me the truth after I drive them nuts telling them that I know the truth. Some things I still question myself on which is normal I reckon since I don't know for sure unless someone tells me and validates my thoughts or their thoughts that have jumped into my head.

Its kinda funny sometimes some of the crap people will try to tell you to cover the real story. Its very hard sometimes to not say you're full of crap. But I usually don't say much anymore. But sometimes I just can't hold it in. There have been many of the kids friends that try to tell me a bull story and I'll tell them the real story. Needless to say it embarrasses the kids when I do this. Rozie says that I'm being mean when I do it, so I try to not do it too often. I worked with this one guy for about two years one time. He was a really nice guy but I could see right through him and hear his thoughts too much. So I always second guessed everything I thought that I heard. Sometimes I'd think there is no way he could be thinking this, he's always talking about going to church. None of it was really bad it was just stuff that people like to keep to themselves. Towards the end he and I fought all the time. He would make me so mad and I'd make him so mad. Then sometimes he'd be so sweet to me. He had a wonderful side to him.

Finally I said to myself this is bull and I started back reading my spiritual books to try to get myself back in the right frame of mind. This guy was driving me crazy. So I finally got my head back where I needed it to be. When I'd see him I'd be so sweet. I was trying very hard to keep his thoughts from jumping into my head. When they would jump I'd stay nice and calm no matter how crummy the thoughts were about me or anyone else. So this one day he walked in and I knew he was fixing to try to upset me. Then he said Beverly I'm gonna get you really upset. I said no you're not but give it your best shot. So he did and I told him no I'm not upset. A few weeks later a few of us were all talking and for some reason he just started saying all these truths about himself that most people never share with anyone. I couldn't believe it and I told him so. I told him I always knew he was like that and I couldn't believe he was telling us all of this. So then he started saying what, what, I'm like what. I told him thanks for telling me cause now I know I'm ok. Now I know what I was thinking was right.

I was starting to feel so guilty that I was thinking anything bad about this man. None of it was anything really bad and no I'm not going to give any examples. So I finally told him just read my book. When he reads this book and realizes nothing got pass me all those years. I didn't have to walk around bragging about how I go to church every Sunday. Which is a great thing but you need to take God out of that church with you. So many people walk out of the door of the church and they leave God at the church door. They don't think about him again until next Sunday when they walk back through those doors and pick God up again. So many people don't go to church at all but they still live with God. They connect with God everywhere they go. God is not just inside of a church building. Its great to pray in church with your family and community. But you can connect with God anywhere. God is out on that boat, in that tree stand in the woods, on that golf course, in your yard, in your house, at that ball game, at the car races, you can't go anywhere and not be with God. God Is everywhere.

He had his fishing license numbers clipped onto his net. The marine patrol said the numbers were supposed to be sewn on. So the marine patrol took all of his net. He came home and told me the story. Then he told me how we had to cut our deep net in half. So it was about midnight and we went out to the front yard and started getting our deep net ready to be cut in half the next day. So as we were getting it ready I told Robbie about my vision earlier that evening about him cutting his net in half. He told me for now on please tell me when these visions happen. He said maybe we could have avoided losing our net. We got the net back a few months later when that fishing season was over that we used that net for.

On the way home from church on Saturday night our youngest son John asked if dad was going fishing that night? I said yes I think he is. John said "I have a bad feeling about him going fishing tonight." I said well you better tell daddy. He said no cause what if it doesn't mean nothing and he misses a night of fishing. I said you'll feel worse if he goes and something bad happens. When we got home the kids went out to play. I told Robbie about John's bad feeling. When John came in Robbie questioned him about his bad feeling. He explained to John for now on tell him about any feelings he gets. Robbie didn't go fishing that night. As he was getting ready the next night he asked all of us if anyone had any bad feelings. We all said no. He went down to the boat. He went to go to the restroom but someone was in it. No one was ever in that restroom. As he walked across the parking lot he saw the marine patrol so he didn't go fishing. He came home and said Johns bad feeling was a day early we all laughed. We always watch out for all the signs. They're everywhere if you can open yourself up to them and pay attention. I've gone against the signs to end up finding disaster in the direction I had chosen.

When I follow the signs its always smooth sailing. Now its kinda like a game looking for the signs. My son Bobby Ray was fourteen years old. He went to spend the night at a new friends house. I knew the boys grandmother and where they lived. I forgot to get the phone number. Early the next morning I went up to the corner like every morning to get my newspaper. I pulled up and saw the accident scene. There was a car wrecked. It didn't look very bad. But all of a sudden I felt death. I knew that there was a dead teenage boy. I got so scared and upset. So I finally got out of my car. I talked to some people that said that their grandson was in the car. Then I left as I drove I cried hysterically. I was worried that my son was in the car but I couldn't walk up to the car. I got home and told my husband, he tried to calm me down. He told me to go pick our son up. But I was too upset to drive past the accident again. So I waited. Our son came home three hours later. I was so happy that he was ok. But I cried my heart out for my friend and her teenage son that had died in that horrible accident.

When my step-dad passed away I expected him to come say good-bye to me in my dreams. My real dad didn't come to say good-bye. But I figured my real dad knew the trouble I had dealing with my brothers death after his visit. So I figured my real dad didn't want to confuse me. My real dad died when I was seventeen years old. It was so soon after losing my brother. Years later my real dad would come to see me in my dreams. As the days passed and my step-dad didn't come I got upset that maybe he'd be like my real dad and not come. Finally about a week after he died he showed up in my dreams. In my dream all my family and I were in a hospital different then the one he had died in. We were all in this waiting room. One by one everyone went in to say good-bye to dad. I kept waiting for my turn. I was the last one to go in. As I walked through that white door into this brightly lit hallway. I didn't know what to expect.

I looked down the hallway to my right. Dad called my name and I turned to the left. There he was sitting up on a hospital bed in the hallway. I walked down to him. He looked great. No oxygen mask. He told me he was dead but he was ok. He just wanted to come and tell me thank you for those days and nights we spent in the hospital before he died. He told me I helped him so much. He told me how much he loved me.

We hugged and kissed and I told him I loved him and I missed him. Then I went back through the door to the waiting room. We had said goodbye to dad and we were all happy. The family and I left in good spirits. We all had closure. That was dads way of telling us he was ok and that he wasn't afraid anymore. Everything was fine now. He was at peace and that gave us peace. I'm rewriting this seven years after it all happened and it feels like it happened yesterday. It didn't feel like a dream. I needed dad to come and say good-bye to me so he did. He did it in a dream as to not scare me. Some call it a dream I call it a visit. When I woke up I was so happy that dad had come to visit me.

Bobby Ray had broken up with his girlfriend a few weeks earlier. I had never met the girl. After they were broken up for almost two weeks. I was taking a shower one night. I started thinking about this girlfriend I didn't even know. I thought to myself why am I thinking about her. That night he came home from work and told me that they had gotten back together. I told him well that explains why I was thinking about her during my peaceful shower. We all laughed.

Robbie and I were sitting talking. All of a sudden I said do you want a leftover sloppy joe and potato salad. He said yeah I was just thinking that's what I wanted. He explained that he didn't think of it a few seconds ago. It was just in his brain and I said it. He looked so surprised. I thought to myself its not like you haven't lived with me all these years. I reckon it will keep surprising him.

My daughter Roseanne, my son John, and our dogs and I were going to the grocery store to pickup a few things. Mom asked me to get some ice cream. She wanted chocolate and vanilla swirl. I asked if she wanted chocolate syrup. She said no. I wanted the syrup. As we drove I thought to myself Roseanne wants cookies and cream. I thought that would solve my syrup problem. But I had already promised mom the swirl. We got to the ice cream section and I started laughing. I told Roseanne you got your wish there is no swirl ice cream. I guess we'll have to get your cookies and cream and I'll get my syrup. She laughed and asked how did you know I was wishing for cookies and cream on the way here.

I just smiled at her and we hugged and she said how she loved it that we were like this. Our kids went to a weekend Hope Hospice camp after their grandpa had passed away. I left in plenty of time to pick them up on time. I was almost there and people in the car next to me pointed to my tire. There was a gas station right there so I pulled in. I had a real nice truck with all newer tires. I pulled up to the air and it was out of order. So I called my husband and his cousin came with his air pump. We pumped the tire up and a big bubble came up on the side of the tire. So he told me to drive slow and he'd follow me and we'd change it when we got home. I got there to pick the kids up last. They had gotten to say good-bye to everyone. The counselors gave us a bunch of leftover snacks and drinks. When Roseanne got into the truck she said during the bus ride she had prayed real hard that I'd be last to pick them up. She wanted to spend as much time with all of her new friends as she could. She said she didn't mean for me to get a flat tire. We all laughed and teased her for making the tire go flat.

I dropped my daughter Roseanne and her girlfriends off at their eighth grade graduation prom. Roseanne said mom please come late so I can have time to say good bye to everyone. I told her I'd try but you know how your dad is. So when it got close to time to go pick them up my husband told me. I tried to give her a few more minutes by taking my time getting ready to leave. Then I got into my car that we had recently bought. I started the car and turned on the head lights. I didn't have any dash lights. So I played with the buttons for a few minutes. Then I finally went into the house and asked my husband. He came out and messed with the buttons. Finally we got the dash lights on. When I got to the school they were some of the last kids to be picked up. Roseanne told me thank you for being late but you didn't have to be that late. I explained to her what had happened and we all laughed. We didn't explain it to her new girlfriend. It was too soon.

I was laying down listening to the TV and my husband and brother talking. All of a sudden I saw my son standing in his brothers bedroom talking to a little boy about six years old. Then I saw my son John and the little boy walk out of the bedroom. John told me with his mind for me to come into the bedroom.

I went into the bedroom and John and the little boy were just standing there. I started talking to the boy with my mind. I was asking him who was he? He looked like he was fixing to answer me and then the vision was over. My whole body jerked and I sat up. I was still in the living room. My husband looked at me like I was crazy. A vision or a very short dream?

I drove past a new shell shop in my hometown that I had just moved back to. I had one of my feelings about it but I didn't understand it. That afternoon I was taking a shower and thought about a shell shop in another town that was my customer. When I got out of the shower I got a letter from the shell shop from out of town with a order. I spoke to the woman the next day and she told me how she also owns the shell shop in my hometown.

After I got the kids off to school I went into the bathroom to get dressed. My nose hurt all of a sudden so I blew it. It bled for no reason out of one side. I thought to myself that was strange. Later that day my daughter Rozie came home from school and told us she had pierced her nose on the school bus that morning because someone had bet her five dollars that she wouldn't do it. It was the same side of the nose that had hurt me and bled that morning about the same time of the morning.

Our two teenage kids wanted to go to the movies on Friday night. They started talking about it on Monday. I told them yes that they could go. On Thursday my husband and I drove past the movie theater and I got one of my strange feelings. All of a sudden I didn't want them to go to the movie the next day but I had no good reason to say no. The next day Robbie and I were driving home and he was complaining about the traffic. I said I'll have to drive in it in a few hours to take the kids to the movies. Then it hit me that could be my excuse for them to not go to the movie that night. So Robbie and I agreed the traffic was too bad for the movie. The kids were disappointed but they understood because the bus ride drove through all that bad traffic. The next morning I awoke to the news on TV. It was saying that a thirteen year old boy was stabbed at the movie theater. It was the same one that my kids were wanting to go to the night before. The boy that was stabbed was also a boy that they knew from school. I was on my way to work and I was praying really hard for Robbie to have a healing.

I prayed to God, Jesus, Holy Spirit, all of our deceased family members. I had tears in my eyes, I was so upset, so alone, so afraid for Robbie. My cell phone rang when I was done praying. It said RES, I answered and no one was there. I wondered who it was for a minute. Then I realized it was a response to my prayer. It was a message from God, Jesus, Holy Spirit, Heaven and our family. They were telling me everything will be ok.

I was packing my car to go to the corner of the road to sell smoked mullet dip. I had most of my stuff packed in the car. I thought about my plastic bags and thought to myself I really don't need my bags for just the dip. I reasoned with myself that they were in good sturdy containers. As I got ready to leave I had this over whelming sense that I needed these plastic bags. So I usually follow these strong feelings so I went to the room and got my bags feeling kinda silly. As I pulled up to the corner there were two boys on their bikes in my parking spot. So I stopped and watched them waiting for them to move. They both looked really upset. I saw that they both had grocery bags hanging from their handle bars. They were both trying to hold onto big sports drink bottles. I asked them if they needed some bags. They were so happy as they both said yes. So I doubled bagged two bags and helped the one boy that had the two sports drink bottles in his arms put them into the bags.

He asked if the other boy could have a bag too. I said sure and got two more bags and helped the other boy. Both boys thanked me. I told them I know how hard it is to carry groceries on a bike, that I've done it before too. I told them how every time my son Bobby Ray would go get a gallon of milk for me. That he would always drop the milk and I'd end up with a half of gallon of milk dripping everywhere. I was laughing and smiling as I told my story. Both boys started laughing and said that their milk had dropped and how it just exploded when it dropped. I looked over at the milk bag and sure enough it was dripping.

So I'm sure their upset faces when I first pulled up was due to worrying what their parents would say about the dripping milk. I was glad my story about my son cheered them up. Hopefully their parents were understanding about the dropped milk. I told them how the first time Bobby Ray dropped the milk my husband and I were kinda hard on him.

After that we pretty much expected it. So it just became a family joke. At this time Bobby Ray was eighteen years old and drove a pickup truck to get the milk. I told them you'd think the milk is safe now. Nope. Now it rolls off the seat of the truck onto the floor. I still get beat up milk. The boys laughed and then thanked me several more times and then they were on their way down the dirt road to hopefully understanding parents. After they left I thought how lucky I am that my eighteen year old son Bobby Ray is still sweet and caring enough to take the time to go get my milk for me.

I layed down in bed to go to sleep. Instead I went into a vision. No big deal I have a lot of visions. I knew I was in a vision. I saw water splashing in my face. I was trying to figure out what the vision meant as it was happening. Before I could figure out what it meant my son walked into my room and asked to use my phone. I came out of the vision and said yes to him. Then I wondered if he had anything to do with my vision. After he left the room I tried to go back into the vision but I couldn't get back into it. The next day I was on the boat with my husband fishing. We were throwing our cast nets for mullet. I caught two sand brim and I shook them out of my net onto the deck of the boat. Then I bent over to pick them up to put them into the fish box. There was some water on the deck and both sand brim were flopping their tails in the water. I reached down to pick up the fish one in each hand. The water started splashing in my face. No problem with the first fish. The second fish kept flopping and splashing water in my face. I remembered my vision the night before and as I did I grabbed the fish and cut both of my fingers really bad on its sharp gills. Besides hurting really bad my fingers started to bleed really bad. I've got to figure out my visions better. It will save me a lot of pain. My visions don't always give me enough details to know exactly what is going to happen. I'm not sure if these visions are so I can change bad things from happening. I've gotta pay better attention.

I was on my way to work. There was a car accident in Cross City where the speed limit is thirty five miles per hour. I had to stop near the accident until I could get into the other lane to drive past the accident. There was a car in front of me then the accident. As I sat there I felt death. I knew someone had just died. I felt so sad.

I was glad that I was running a little late that day and had gotten here after the accident. As I drove past they were still working the accident and I thought to myself that there's no reason to think that someone had died but I just knew. I thought about the accident all day at work. When one of the police woman came in shopping I talked to her about the accident without coming right out and asking if the person had died in the small car. She didn't come right out and tell me but I knew. Two days later the newspaper came out and on the front page was the accident. The woman that was driving the car didn't stop when the truck stopped in front of her to turn. She ran into the back of the truck. Her name was just like my name. I got so upset. This was too strange even for me. How weird is that. It gets even stranger. A week later I'm driving right in the same spot of the accident and a truck stops in front of me to turn. I scream Oh my God and I start to slow down. My son John was in the truck with me. He said mom don't be so crazy. We weren't even close to that truck. It scared me so badly. I thought about how easy it was to get into a wreck. I thought about the poor woman who had died a week earlier with my name in the same spot and the same thing had happened. Was it a warning or a coincidence.

Robbie got major back surgery done on January 31, 2008. The hospital is fifty miles away so we decided it would be easier if I just stayed at the hospital with Robbie instead of trying to drive back and forth for five days. The kids were old enough to stay by themselves or so we thought. Bobby Ray was almost twenty two years old. Roseanne was eighteen years old. John was one month from being seventeen years old. So we talked to them everyday several times a day. The operation was done on a Thursday. The kids all came up the next night which was Friday night. We begged them to not go out while we were gone. I didn't wanna be worrying about them while I was helping Robbie.

Rozie said she was going out after she brought her brothers home that night. She said she'd stay home the rest of the time when she got off of work. I told the boys to just hang out around the house after work and school. How hard could that be. So they all promised to be good. They told me don't worry about us. So Saturday afternoon the calls started the boys wanted to go here and there. We said no please just stay home.

In the middle of the night Robbie and I were both awoken at the same moment. We talked for a few minutes about how strange it was the way we were woken up like something had caused us to wake up. So we got up it was about 2:00am. We started walking the halls. I started praying for the safety for our kids. I was so worried about the kids at that moment. We stayed up the rest of the night we couldn't fall back to sleep. The next morning our son John called and said please don't be too hard on Bobby Ray. I knew it was bad news. Sure enough he wrecked his truck the night before coming home from a party. He totaled his truck out. He doesn't know how he got out of the truck. I asked him what time did this happen? He said about 2:00am. He had gone out Saturday night even though I had begged him a hundred times to please stay home with his brother while we were gone.

He had dropped John off at a friends house and was supposed to pick John back up. Thank goodness he didn't pick John back up before the wreck. The truck was in such bad shape I just don't know how he survived it with the few bumps and bruises that he received. He said his grandpa was there with him. He doesn't know how he got out of the truck. Maybe grandpa pulled him out. Grandpa was deceased but he still takes such good care of his grandkids during wrecks. All I can figure out is when he wrecked he must have yelled for us and we heard him even though we were sleeping fifty miles away. As soon as I woke up I had started praying to God to keep our kids safe. Prayers work very quickly. God took care of our son that night. Thank you God for keeping Bobby Ray alive that night. Thank you dad/grandpa for being there with your grandson.

I thought about how a friend of ours didn't have our new phone number. We hadn't talked to him in about five months. A few days later he showed up in our driveway which he had never been to before. We had moved three hundred miles away from our home town. We live six miles from town out in the woods. He asked the mail lady where did we live.

I thought about my husbands cousin that we hadn't seen in a few years. A few hours later my husband called from his cousins house. He had run into him and was gonna stay a few nights with him while he was fishing in our home town. There is really no way for me to tell if my thoughts and feelings about people are right.

The only way is when people slip up and reveal there inner most thoughts and feelings to me. Which usually doesn't happen until I've been around the person for quite a while. Sometimes its months but sometimes its years. In the years cases I always second guess myself and my ability to read people. Very seldom am I wrong about people. I usually read a person within the first few minutes of meeting them. I always know if I'm gonna like them or not. I usually don't change my mind about liking someone. Sometimes I'll just learn how to deal with the person to make my life easier. It doesn't mean I like them. It just means I know this person is gonna be in my life for a while and I figure out the best way to deal with them. I give everyone a fair chance to prove me wrong.

It's not my fault some people are just rotten and treat people like crap. I never like seeing anyone being treated badly even if they're a jerk themselves. Some people are jerks because they're trying to hide their true selves from the world. Everyone you meet has a lot of baggage. Life throws a lot of stuff at everyone and you gotta figure out how to deal with it and keep a happy out look on life. Some people love me, some people hate me. I use to get so upset over the ones that hated me. Now I think the ones that hate me know that I can see them for who and what they are. When they finally settle down and try to get to know me they usually end up at least liking me because I'm really a nice person. My biggest problem is that I don't lie and I speak my mind way too much.

My mom always said if you didn't tell that was just like lying. She hated for any of us kids to lie to her. Now years later I understand why she didn't want us to lie besides all mothers don't want their kids to lie. But mainly because she was psychic and knew when we were lying. As a child I was very quiet. I played softball on a girls team when I was twelve years old. I still didn't speak well. The pitchers name was very hard for me to say.

It was a very easy name, but not for me. . So being on a team you would have to shout out your team mates names to throw the ball to you. As I walked to every practice and game I would say her name over and over and over again. I could never get it right when I would yell it out on that ball field.

I liked her a lot but I prayed to God to please put me on a different team next year then what he put her on. I still say a lot of words wrong. My husband tries to help me when I say words wrong. Robbie is a big help to me. As I got older I decided to start talking with a lot of help from my mom. She was very outgoing like I am now. She begged me to talk when I started working for her and my dad in their sub and pizza shop when I was fourteen years old. She would get so mad at me when I wouldn't talk to her customers. So it just finally got easier to keep the peace with mom I started to talk to everyone. I worked for them until I was seventeen years old. By then she had me talking pretty good.

Now I never shut up. The people that know me now have a hard time believing that I was ever quiet. I was also quiet for all those years because I knew I was very different. If only my mother would have talked to me about the spiritual things as a child, maybe I would have understood myself better. As I got older she opened up more to me about all that and how important prayers were. Before that it was just go to church on Sundays and pay attention. Well they didn't teach everything I needed to know in church or Sunday school. Some of it is just by living and experiencing it you learn about it.

Momma had heart surgery in 1988. When she got out of the hospital she told us this beautiful story. Some believed, some didn't believe. I always believed. She said she had died during surgery and that she went to heaven. When she got there she saw her next door neighbor friend that had recently died. Mom was confused why this woman met her in heaven and not any of the many family members that were deceased. The neighbor lady said to mom you can't stay in heaven. You have to go back to your body and take care of your husband. Mom told her my husband is fine he doesn't need me. The lady said your husband is going to need you soon.

Mom said she was very upset because she wanted to stay in heaven. She said it was so peaceful and beautiful in heaven. She didn't understand what her friend was talking about but she finally said ok that she'd go back and she said good bye to her friend. So mom went back to her body. When mom told this story we all laughed because Dad was in perfect health.

About three years later Dad got very sick. Mom took care of him for ten years until he passed away. Mom always remembered her visit to heaven and finally was able to understand it when Dad got sick. Dad was so happy that she was there taking care of him for those ten years of his illness.

I call this part of my life spacing out. I'm not sure what it is or what causes it to happen. It use to happen quite often. It was kinda a joke when my husband Robbie first noticed it. He would talk to me while I was sitting there with my eyes open and I wouldn't answer him. I wouldn't hear him. He would talk louder to get my attention. Then I'd jump and he'd ask me where were you and I'd tell him whatever I was thinking about. No big deal right. As the years went by he started to pay more attention to me when I'd space out. He says I look like I'm gone when I space out. When I come back I feel like I've been gone. I don't hear or see anything that's gone on around me while I'm spaced out. No one has ever noticed it all my life except for Robbie.

Now I understand so much of my life. People and teachers use to get so mad at me for not paying attention. I was spacing out back then too. I remember as a kid in school looking out the window. It would feel like I'd leave my body in class and I'd go where ever my mind took me. At the time I just thought it was daydreaming. Now I think it was more like a out of body experience. I remember trying to stop it by talking more to my classmates so I'd stay in the moment. That back fired on me cause then the teacher would put me alone, against the blackboard for talking too much. She thought I'd pay more attention. But I'd just space out more. Robbie and I were watching TV. I spaced out. I came back when I heard the toilet flush and he walked back into the living room. He saw that I was startled so he knew I had been spaced out. He walked in front of me while I was watching TV and I never saw him. Day dreams or out of body experiences.

Some days I'm in a bad mood for whatever the reason is. I end up spreading my grouchy mood onto other poor innocent people that happen to get in my path that day. Other days I'm in a great mood. I embrace my gifts like a mother embraces her baby. I'll wake up and thank God for another day. Some people say January 1st gives you a chance to start a new year off fresh. You get that chance every morning when you wake up.

You have the power to have a good day or a bad day. You can spread your happy smile to everyone you come into contact with that day. You have the power to make other people smile or cry each day. Some say they have no power over their moods. No control over their life. Each person comes into this world alone and goes out alone. Everything they do in between is totally in their control. No one can keep you from smiling and laughing. The next time you smile or laugh look around at the people near you. Someone will be smiling or laughing with you or even at you.

But what does it matter as long as you've made someone happy that day. It might be the only smile they receive that day. It might be the only smile that they smile that day. Some people are very alone in this crowded busy world. Young and old people. If you make one person happy each day then you've done something good with your gift from God. One day I watched as a bad mood spread onto a innocent child. A woman wanted to return a childs outfit she didn't have a receipt. Our policy says you need a receipt. My manager was a unhappy woman and gave her a lot of needless crap because she didn't have a receipt. The woman was in a happy, good mood when this started. She had spoken to me first and I couldn't help her. The woman got done with the return and her child said something. She snapped and was so nasty to that poor innocent child. All because my manager had been so nasty to her.

Please be careful where you put your bad moods. Spread your good moods all over the place. Try to keep your bad moods to yourself for everyone's sake. I was shopping just the other day and a mother and child were in line. The cashier who also is the manager was having a hard time with the transaction. The manager knew what she was doing but there was a problem. The customer starts telling the manager how to do her job. All cash register computers are different. The woman kept telling the manager to just push the button. The manager was being so nice and the woman got mad. Then her child said something and got yelled at for no good reason.

My daughter Rozie and I are very close even during her teenage years. My sisters teenage daughter had been living with her father for the past few years. My sister had been living alone. My sister and her daughter were going through the normal teenage struggles. They hadn't been talking much lately. Roseanne saw her cousin at a school football game.

When Roseanne came home we sat and talked about the game and everyone she had seen. She told me about seeing her cousin. So then we got to talking about her cousin and mother. We talked about how we wished they could have a relationship like ours. We wished they'd start talking a lot and spending time together We also wished that my niece would move back in with her mother. We thought it would be good for both of them. As I told my daughter good night I told her to pray for them. When I went to bed I prayed for them. We talked about them a few more times that week. One week later my sister and niece talked on the phone. Then they spent the day together. My niece told her mom she wanted to move back in with her. I saw my sister the day after she was with her daughter. She was so happy and excited. I didn't tell her about my daughter and my prayers. I wanted her to make her decision on her own. I told her I thought it was great that her daughter wanted to come back home. That evening I was telling my daughter about it. My youngest son John was sitting there too. My daughter was so happy that our prayers were answered so quickly. My son smiled at us and said ya'll are so weird. It still surprises him that prayers work so well. I don't know why since his whole life has been involved with prayers and God.

My son went to spend the night at his cousins house. I was worried about the boys going bike riding. His cousin had more freedom then we had given John. John was use to living on small Pine Island and now we lived in the city. I wanted John to have fun but this bike riding issue weighed heavy on my mind and heart. I kept telling myself that I was worrying too much about them bike riding. My son left during the day so I was sure that they'd have two days of bike riding around town. The second day I saw the cousins grandpa. He told me the boys were out bike riding. When the grandpa left I went back to my smoked mullet. I sat down on the back of the car and I prayed and prayed for my son's safety. I was so upset. I kept praying all day on and off. At 5:00pm I told my husband I was going to my sisters house if it was ok with him. As I drove down the road I prayed again for my son's safety. When I got home a hour later my son was home safe. He had wrecked on the bike and had quite a bit of road rash. But he was safe. I thanked God for answering my prayers.

Some would say that my prayers weren't answered since he got hurt. I figure if I hadn't been praying that he could have gotten hurt a lot worse. So to me God did answer my prayers.

I had a dream about one of my childhood friends. I was still good friends with her brother. That morning I asked her brother about her and he said she had just gotten to their mom's house the day before for a visit. On Tuesday night I dreamed about work and all the people I worked with. On Wednesday night I dreamed about work and all the people I worked with. On Thursday I got to work and asked my boss what was going on. I didn't tell him that I'd been dreaming about work and all the people I worked with. He just wouldn't have understood. He said everyone had been talking about me while I was gone. He said that it wasn't good stuff.

I dreamed that I was at the fishhouse with my husband Robbie. We were at the boat ramp. Which this was a normal thing for us to be doing in real life. The fishhouse looked a little bit different in my dream. Then I saw my first dad Raymond. He said he was going fishing with one of our fisherman friends. I said I'd wait for him at the fishhouse. The only problem with this was in real life we didn't fish at that fishhouse anymore. I don't know why we were standing at the boat ramp. Raymond told me to go home. He said my work here was done. He said it was time to go home and help my mom. I said no I wanted to spend time with him. My dad and the fisherman ran down a long dock like in a big tunnel.

I ran to the dock. My dad Raymond yelled back to me one more time and said go home Beverly. My dad Raymond had died already in 1978. Before they came out with a red soda, I had a dream about it. At the time I drank the regular soda just about everyday. In my dream I was at a party. All of the food was bright colors. My regular soda was red. It tasted great. When the red soda came out I was so freaked out I wouldn't even try it. This was one of my dreams that I had written down. So there it was written down on paper before it came out. My kids finally talked me into tasting it after it had been out for a few months. It tasted great just like in my dream. I had a dream about writing with a female. I know her good in my dream. She has blond hair. I had no idea who she was when I woke up. Five months later my sister came down for a visit I was so shocked to see that she had blond hair.

All of us girls in the family have dark hair. She is also a writer. We started writing together. I had a dream about a lady from church. I wasn't close friends with her and I couldn't figure out why she'd be in my dreams. A few days later a close friend from church just came up to me and started telling me that this lady was having so many problems in her life. I hadn't even asked questions about her or said anything about my dream. I had a dream Robbie and I were at a wedding at the fishhouse. In the dream the manager was my full time boss. The next year in real life Robbie and I went to a wedding at the fishhouse. I was also working there full time. The manager was my boss. I had a dream about the family being at our house for a cook out. There was a little boy about two years old. Rozie fed him a big plate of food in his crib. He looked just like my step brothers son when he was younger. A few days later I was reading the newspaper from back home. I read that my step brothers ex wife had died. She was the mother of the child in the crib in my dream. I dreamed that I took off running and started to fly. I jumped on the trampoline a few times. Then I flew up higher into the sky. I fly by kicking my legs like I'm running. This has been a recurring dream all my life. This is the first time the trampoline was in my dream. I always had this dream when I'd dream of heaven or was I really in heaven. I'll never know until I really go to heaven. I believe it was more than just a dream.

I was starting to second guess myself as a mother. Was I trying to be too good of a mother. In the process was I smothering my children with my time with them. By doing this was I stunting their growth as individuals. I was so confused. When Robbie and I decided that I would be a stay at home mother and work part time when needed mother. I had decided I would spend as much time with the kids as I could. They were seven, eight, and eleven years old at this time. That was about seven years ago. I had enjoyed the past seven years and hoped the kids had. Now I was looking at all the mothers around me wondering if I had messed up. After a couple of weeks of stressing out over this the dream came one night. In the dream we were going to watch a baseball game. People I knew were playing. A lot of my friends from my childhood were there to watch. Just as my husband, our kids and I were walking to our seats. Our son John came up to me and asked me if I could help him and his friend.

In the dream I told him I didn't want to miss the game and the fun of talking to my old friends. He said it will just take a minute. So I went with him just to where we couldn't see the game. They had what looked like a big go cart. They were working on it. If we got it fixed they explained to me that you could drive it on the road or fly it in the air. I started working on it with John and his friend. I looked up once and said I'm missing the game. John said but aren't you having fun with me. I said yes so we kept working. The game got over and everyone came up to us and asked if we had fixed it. We said no. They said you wasted your time and missed the game. We said we didn't waste our time cause we were having fun and enjoying being together. The game didn't matter. When I woke up from my dream I knew that dream was from God. He was letting me know that as long as I was having fun and enjoying being with my kids then thats what I should be doing.

I was so happy. I thanked God for the dream. I now know the way I mother my kids is right for me. It may not be right for someone else. Everyone has to choose their own way to be in this world. It's called free will. We all have it. Every human being is in charge of their life, body, mind and soul. What you choose to do with it is up to you.

What you choose will affect people around you. But you still have to choose what is right for you. People will continue to tell me to take more time for myself. Now I won't second guess myself. I will just reply "I will have plenty of time for myself once the kids are raised". I'll probably have too much time. It's now about six years later and I miss all that craziness when the kids were little. The kids were eighteen, nineteen, and twenty three and the oldest moved out for six months. I was getting use to Bobby Ray being moved out then he moved to Ohio to work for a few months. Hopefully he comes back to Florida soon. The past four years I had to go back to work because Robbie got sick. I've had to work some nights and I've missed some kids events. It's been the hardest four years of my life. But just like when we chose for me to stay home with the kids. We've chosen to give Robbie some time off work while he recovers from his illness and back surgery. I miss the kids and Robbie so much. I'm so glad that I took those years off from work to be with our family.

I could have lived in the brand new big house and worked while raising them. We went and looked at the house to have it built on property my parents were gonna give us. We chose to live in a rented apartment and have me home most of the time for the family. I don't think I would have this special bond that I have with my kids if I would have worked all those years. I don't mean to offend anyone that chooses or has to work while raising kids. I had to work when they were very young and I missed a lot that I could never get back. It usually takes both parents working to be able to pay the bills. A lot of woman don't get a choice they just have to do the best they can while being a working mom. I cherish all those special memories I have from spending so much time with my kids.

I always wanted to have another baby but I had my tubes tied after John. I've prayed so many prayers to God. I reckon God thinks I don't need another child. I lost my first child in a miscarriage during my third month. Then I wasn't able to get pregnant again for almost five years. I didn't think that I was ever going to be able to be a mother. So when it finally happened I was so happy. Being a wife and mother has been the happiest years of my life. Now my life is changing since the kids are raised.

During my youngest sons last year of high school I had a very hard time. I was so sad that it was almost over. Once it was over it felt like a big load was lifted. I enjoyed all of it but now I'm enjoying my next phase of my life. Its like a new adventure. My husband always says I don't like change but we've been through so many changes during our life together. I face them a little scared but with open arms.

I sometimes wonder why do I have these dreams and visions if I can't change what is going to happen. I understand the things I have control to change. I just don't understand these things that I have no control over. For almost three days I felt like blood was dripping down my left leg. I kept looking at my leg but there wasn't anything there. I knew that I'd be getting hurt and that I would bleed. I knew this was a sign. So I was trying to be extra careful. On the third day it happened. I was working in my moms flower bed. I was trimming plants back. I kept being careful of my leg. I kept checking for blood on the leg that felt like blood was dripping down.

Then it happened. I stabbed myself in the left arm with the clippers. I pulled the clippers out of my arm and the blood started pouring out. I put my right had over the wound quickly to try to stop the blood. I ran into the house and got a bunch of paper towels to stop the bleeding. I walked back outside still holding the towels on my arm. Then I remembered the leg. I looked down and sure enough where I had felt the blood dripping for three days. There was blood dripping down my leg in the exact spot I had felt it for days. It was blood from my bleeding arm. I wiped the blood off my leg and the feeling of dripping blood went away finally after three days. This vision/feeling has taught me a important lesson. The whole time I felt the dripping blood on my leg I was convinced that I would cut my leg. I now know I have to really pay attention to the signs and to the signs that I don't get.

We found the property and mobile home we wanted to buy. We went and looked at it that evening. My husband said we needed to put a offer in the next day before someone else did. I called the next day and set up a appointment with the realtor for two days later to see the inside of the house. The family was so excited. The night before we were going to see it I was soaking in the tub.

I was thinking about the house and I thought in my head we're never going to live there. So to make myself feel better I thought maybe we're buying it and selling it to our son. This place was too good to pass up. The next morning I called the realtor. She said someone had put in a offer the same day I had called her. The house wasn't meant to be ours and I felt that while I was soaking in the tub that night.

I was at a outdoor concert one day. A lot of different bands had played all day. I enjoyed all the singers. I was drawn to the stage during one of the bands performing. I was drawn to one of the members of the band. I watched him play and I saw him as a star but not a superstar. I really don't know how to explain it. I was quite confused about it. Then I heard how he had played with some big name singers. So to me he was already a star. This vision made no sense to me until a few days later. He got into traffic accident and died. I cried for this star that I didn't even know. My step dad John would come to me in my dreams.

He let me know he was dead and only back for a short time. He went grocery shopping this one time cause my brother wasn't doing the grocery shopping as good as he should have. We were at mom's house in my dream. Dad had stocked the house up with food again. He told me he understood the problem I was having. He didn't give me a solution or did he. There was a big spider hanging down over my head as I was soaking in a tub. The tub swayed back and forth under the spider under the grape light in the living room. It was near the TV. I got out of the tub. I told my brother about the spider. My sister and Rozie scared the spider away. Dad said he knew I didn't want to fight with my brother about the grocery shopping. He knew thats why I quit doing the shopping. He said he wasn't mad at me. Dad talked to us with his brain no words were spoken.

Mom was so happy to have dad around even if it was for a short time. When I woke up I wrote the dream down on a piece of paper for my book. Then I set it aside. I started writing other stuff on a different paper. I wasn't sure if I was gonna use it for my book or not. I got up to let the dog outside across the house. After I sat back down the paper about my dream about Dad slid across my folder about twelve inches. No breeze to blow it. I picked it up and tried to figure out what I should write on it.

So I wrote about it sliding then turned it over and put it back in its spot. Then I sat here and read my old dream papers. The last dream written was about dads last visit to me. I realized he wanted this dream in my book and in my dream log. So I just wrote all this down. Thats why he slid the paper. I think he was trying to tell me to start writing my dreams down again. He wants me to keep better track of my dreams. They can help me in the future. A few weeks later I found out what dad was trying to tell me with the bath tub. The hot water in mom's bath tub wasn't working. The other part of my dream that night was about a friend that had lost his leg due to complications during a operation in real life. In my dream he was walking fine. I don't know if this friend is alive or dead. I haven't seen him in about seven years. In my dream Robbie brought my friend over to see me in the grocery store. My friend had a box of medicine in his hand. He showed me the 1-800# and said call that and everything will be ok.

I hugged him and thanked him. After I wrote this dream down I went to my medicine cabinet and got the medicine and found the 1-800#. I wonder if it means anything. Maybe there's a message. Should I change the numbers into letters from the telephone. Or am I just going completely crazy. I later found out it wasn't that phone number that I needed to call. I needed to call a 1-800# to a woman to save my truck. The medicine is made by the same name as the woman. I didn't understand the connection until it was too late. The truck got repossessed. But I did learn a important lesson about paying more attention to my dreams.

When I awoke from the dream about my dad going grocery shopping. I knew he was trying to tell me mom needed groceries. I called her up and sure enough she said she had given my brother money yesterday to get groceries and he hadn't come back yet. But to be fair to my brother, my mom does have a memory problem at this time. So I told her about my dream about my dad. She was so happy to know dad was still looking out for her. She said dad knew who to go to in a dream to get his message across. I asked her if she had enough food for the day. She said yes, I told her I'd call her tomorrow and if my brother hadn't come back I'd come over and take her grocery shopping.

I lived fifty miles from my mom. Then I asked her if she had anything to drink. I asked her if she had any bottled water left. She said no that she had been melting ice cubes in a glass and drinking the water as the ice cubes melted. She said she didn't want to boil them in a pot. She asked me if I knew how long it took to melt a ice cube. I said no, how long. She said quite a while. We both laughed. I told her to look in what use to be the pantry when dad was alive. I had saw bottled water when I was there a few days earlier. She looked and found plenty of water. She was so happy. She now had water and could make ice tea. We laughed and joked about how wonderful dad is even though he's not in this world any longer. He's still taking care of things. He knew momma needed help and he came to me in my dreams and had me help her. He'll always be with us. That is a very comforting thought to know we have a angel in heaven helping us through this life. I was working on a golf course on beautiful Pine Island, Florida. I became good friends with a older man that worked there part time.

He hadn't been feeling too good for a couple of weeks. Everyday he worked I griped at him that he needed to go to the doctor. I asked him if he had told the boss or his wife how bad he was feeling. He said no. He was so worried about getting the rest of his house painted. He didn't have time to slow down right then. I finally couldn't take it anymore so I told him that I was gonna tell the boss and his wife if he didn't get to the doctor. He promised he'd go to the doctors the next day. As he drove me home that day I got such a strange feeling. I felt like this was going to be the last time he would drive me home. I just figured that I'd get my van fixed and not need a ride. I didn't want to get out of the truck that day. I kept saying good bye. I finally let the feeling pass. He had the next day off and I was hoping he was spending it at the doctor.

The day after when he wasn't to work on time I knew something was wrong. The other guys joked around saying the only way he'd be late was if he had died. When they said it I knew it was true. I told my boss to call his house. I knew the guys were just joking like usual but I could feel that something was bad wrong with him. I was so upset as I went out to the golf course to work. My boss came out a few minutes later with the bad news. My dear friend had passed away the night he had dropped me off after work. I was so sad. I cried my heart out for my dear friend. Then I wondered if I could have saved him if I would have told the boss and his wife how sick he had been feeling. I had such guilt. But he was the macho old school type of man.

A real manly man. He would have been so angry if this woman from work had interfered in his private life. I will always question my judgement on this man and what I should have done. If there's ever a next time I would rather have him mad at me then not have him around to be mad at me. I always think about him when I play golf at that golf course. After he passed I became good friends with another co worker. I was good friends with all the guys I worked with but some of them and I just bonded more or just worked together more. I'm not sure which it was. This co worker wasn't feeling well either. So after our friend died he told me how bad he had been feeling. He said he was gonna go to the doctor. So needless to say I was always bugging him to get it taken care of. He didn't have a wife or any family close by for me to tell. So we stayed good friends until we both quit the golf course.

We lived on a small island so we did run into each other once in a while. I heard he was mowing at the cemetery. I didn't see him for a few weeks and I knew something was very wrong. I saw one of our other golf course buddies and he said our friend had died. I was heartbroken. I cried my heart out for my friend. I just couldn't understand why God had taken these two awesome men. They both still had so much love and sweetness to give and to share. I was very confused and upset about losing two good friends. I wish I could say that was the end of losing my golf course friends but it wasn't the end. This one co worker was my sons age and was a friend of my sons. He was being home-schooled by his mother. He was fifteen or sixteen, I can't remember. We got along great from the first day. We had a blast and we did a lot of laughing and a lot of riding. I always let him drive since he had so much fun when he drove. When he'd drive too crazy I'd tell him that I was gonna drive if he didn't slow down. So then he'd weave through the trees. Then we'd really laugh so hard. We'd talk about my kids, his parents, his dreams of the future.

He'd talk about his mom a lot. He was so happy that he was home-schooling and he was seeing a lot more of his mom. He just thought the world of his mom. When I'd listen to him talk about his mom I'd think to myself that I hope and pray my son talks that good and that much about me to people. He had so much love and respect for her. He talked a lot about his dad too but I think I remembered so much more about his mom since I am a mom. They did such a good job raising him. He had so much good in him and he was so full of life and energy. He was one of the sweetest, well mannered, caring kids that I'd ever met. After he quit the golf course I'd always see him around the island. I'd always give him rides and I'd always lecture him on doing something great with his life. He had greatness in him just waiting to pour out. So the years went by and I'd always give him pep talks when I'd see him.

One night I pulled into the gas station and up to the pump. My two sons were with me. There was my golf course friend who also was my sons friend. He said Hi and I turned and looked at him and said hi. It was always good to see him. He had one of those special smiles that always made you smile.

When I looked at him there was a bright white light glowing all around him. I thought to myself thats strange but beautiful. Then I thought it must be from the gas station bright lights shining at night. I thought about those bright lights surrounding him a few times the next few days. Four days after we saw him he passed away. I was devastated. He was so young only nineteen years old. He had so much good to offer this world. I was so busy that night at the gas station. I didn't take the time with him that I usually did. I didn't even give him a lecture that night. This last night was just hi, how's it going, what are ya up to, see ya. I reckon that was all the good bye our friendship needed.

I probably couldn't have changed how any of it would have turned out. But you never know when its gonna be the last time you talk to anyone. You never know if what you say to someone will change anything that person does. You should always take that extra minute to say what you want to say to someone. You might not have the next time you see them to tell them something. No matter how little or how big a thing it is. You should always try to make a difference in every ones life. I will always remember that beautiful smile of his and all the laughter we shared. I miss seeing him around our island. Rest in peace my dear friend.

CHAPTER 7
HEALINGS AND MIRACLE CURES

My oldest son Bobby Ray was about fourteen years old. He came down with the flu. He had a cough, runny nose, sore throat, and a fever. So the first day like any good mother I gave him flu medicine and medicine for the fever. The next day he was worse. I didn't have any flu symptoms. On the second day he was laying on the couch just so miserable. I sat down next to him. I touched his forehead to check to see if his fever had come down after he had taken his medicine. It was still very hot. I kissed his forehead and touched his face and I started praying. I begged God to take this flu out of my son. I told God I'd rather be sick then to see my child this sick. I hugged and kissed my son and told him how I'd trade places with him if I could. The next day my son got up completely healed. There was no flu symptoms left. It was like he hadn't even been sick in bed for two days. I woke up just as sick as he had been. It took me over a week to get better.

At the time we joked around about how mom took the flu out of Bobby Ray and put it into herself. As time went on and I did a lot of reading about this sort of thing. I realized that's exactly what I had done. So I read a lot more about laying of hands for healing. I learned how to do it without putting the pain or illness into your own body. I still sometime mess up and end up with it in my body. When this happens I'm still not really sure what I do wrong. So I only do this for my kids and husband. I do the laying of hands healing on my kids for headaches, stomach aches, colds, and flu's. I got a lot better at it as the years went by. It turned out that we were able to raise our kids through ten years of their childhoods without ever having to go to the doctor. I'd take them for all their childhood shots. They had their chicken pox before we started this praying.

I believe in doctors when you need them. We just didn't need one for ten years. I never even thought to try to heal myself. About three years after my son's healing, I did heal myself. I was up all night sick. I was sick all morning. Then I called my mom and I decided to go see her. She wanted to take me out to lunch. As I started my drive I was so sick to my stomach.

I wondered to myself if I could make the hour drive without having to stop. Then I thought to myself I heal my kids all the time. So I rubbed my stomach and prayed for a few minutes. I was healed. I felt great. I couldn't believe that I hadn't tried to heal myself before this. My mom and I went out to a wonderful lunch. I told my kids about my healing that night. They thought it was great. Then they asked me why I heal them all the time and I don't heal their dad. I told them that I've tried to heal Robbie a lot of times. I told them I think it works on them because they believe. I told them I don't think dad believes that I can heal him. So I told my husband about this conversation with the kids. I told him I'd try to heal him again if he could believe. He told me to try it. I prayed and rubbed his back. He didn't have a healing. His back felt a little better. But I think that was from the rubbing. The healing comes from God, I am just God's helper.

Hopefully someday he'll totally believe in me and I'll be able to heal his back. It's not that I have any special powers. I have the power of prayer and faith. Anyone and everyone can have it if they want it. I believe God does all the healing. I believe we are able to help people heal with our prayers. I believe some people need their medicine. They believe the medicine will cure them and it does. I've had pains that I wasn't able to cure with my prayers. I don't really understand why it doesn't always work. I do keep the faith that it will heal. I keep praying and believing that God will cure me when the time is right for me to be cured.

My son John had been a alter server at the Catholic Church for two years. On this one afternoon we were getting ready for church. He was going to be a alter server that day. He was crying that he had a very bad headache. I was in a hurry so I told him to take some medicine. He said no he didn't want any medicine. My kids hated taking medicine. They had to be very sick before they would take medicine. John asked Roseanne if she'd serve for him that day. She said no because she had served for him the week before. So while I got ready he layed on the couch with a wet wash cloth on his forehead. On the way to church he complained about his headache. As we were walking across the parking lot I finally had a few minutes to think. I asked John if I could try praying his headache away. He said yes please. So as we walked I put my hand on his forehead and I prayed until we got in the church.

He went to serve and I hoped and prayed that his headache would go away. He looked good during church. He did all his serving perfect. After church I asked him about his headache. He said it went away after I prayed with him walking through the parking lot of the church. I should have taken the time to pray for him as soon as he told me about his headache. But I was in a hurry to get ready for church. I still sometimes forget to just slow down and ask for God's help. God is always there ready to help. You just have to slow down and ask God to help you. Everyone has this gift. It's God's gift of prayer that we all have. I was so proud of my kids for wanting to be alter servers. They loved being servers for Father Ted. He is such a wonderful Priest. I hope my kids find another priest in their lifetimes that is as awesome as Father Ted.

All priests have been getting a very bad rap for the bad priests. Which I do understand since my father had a problem with a priest in the 1940's. I don't know exactly what happened to him but I do know it messed him up very badly. Then it messed my life up very, very, very badly. It messed me up so badly that I wouldn't allow my oldest son Bobby Ray to be a alter server. By the time the younger kids started asking to be servers I was dealing with my fathers bad memories much better. He passed away from lung cancer when I was seventeen years old. So something that happened in the 1940's was still causing problems to kids that never knew the people in the year 2000. People don't realize what they do can still be effecting peoples lives sixty years later. So watch how you live your life. Make sure your grandkids and great grandkids have happy stories to tell about you.

My daughter Roseanne was laying in bed close to tears when I walked into her bedroom. I asked her what was wrong. She said she had a bad stomach ache, cramps, and her back hurt real bad. I told her to take some medicine. She said no. I told her I'd bring her the medicine. She said no. My kids will only take medicine if we force them to take it. So I sat down next to her. I asked her if she wanted me to try praying and rubbing the pain away. She said yes. I rubbed her stomach area lightly with my hand and prayed for her pain to go away. After a few minutes I told her to lay on her side. Then I rubbed her back lightly and prayed. Then she layed back on her back. I asked her how she felt and she said her cramps were still hurting.

So I rubbed her lower stomach and prayed. When I finished I asked her how she felt. She sat up hugged and kissed me and thanked me. She said she felt so much better. She got up out of bed and was fine. I'm sure some people would say it was just a stomach ache and it just went away. My daughter and I know how bad it was. We believe God healed her. I did the loving touch and praying so I helped her to heal. It's not that I'm so special. I ask for God's help and healing. I take the time to help someone else without getting anything in return. I do the praying. The person knows I care and love them by the prayers and my loving touch.

It was almost a year after dad died. To be exact it was ten months after dad had passed away. I got a phone call at work from my sister that they had taken mom to the hospital and it didn't look good. I knew mom had been feeling sick the past few days. But I thought it was more like a stomach virus. Mom had been in perfect health except for the Alzheimer's disease she had for the past four years. My sister said it might be cancer, that they were still running tests. She made it sound like mom could die any minute. My husband was sitting there seeing me starting to fall apart. I hung up the phone and in between sobs retold the story. He told me to calm down, that my sisters always over react to everything. He said mom will probably out live all of us. But he said that I needed to get off work right then and go to the hospital to see for myself.

So I took off to the same hospital my father had died in ten months earlier. I had the room and floor number in my hand as I walked through those same halls I had spent so many hours in when dad was there. I stopped in the same bathroom that I had changed my clothes in and had cried a million tears in just ten months earlier. I stopped this time in the bathroom to try to pull myself together before I walk past dads room where he died to go see mom. Mom was just three doors down from where dad had passed away. Thank God mom had Alzheimer's, she had no idea that this was the same place. I walked into her room with my happy, cheerful face and attitude that I put on just for these occasions. The actress in me comes out in full bloom when I need it. This actress mode my mother had taught me ever since I could remember. I think I was two or three years old when I started realizing how my mother could change her attitude in a moments notice.

My mother the unpaid actress. So I sat and talked for a few hours. She looked so bad, but everyone looks bad laying in a hospital bed. I was so scared. I didn't want to leave in case she died. My oldest sister said she was going to stay overnight with mom like I had with dad. It was finally time for me to leave. My sister asked me for my jacket I was wearing. If it was any jacket but this one it would have been fine. But this one was the one I wore for four days in this hospital three doors down. I didn't want to give it up but I did, I thought maybe it would keep her warm and give her the strength she would need to spend the night in the hospital. So I left feeling very scared and depressed. I called a few hours later to see if they knew anything. They didn't know anything new yet. I called the next morning and they were still doing tests.

So my sister said don't come to the hospital cause mom will be getting out today. So I kept calling every few hours for a couple of days and I was always told about the same thing. They kept saying she'd be getting out soon so don't bother coming to the hospital. She finally got out three days later. My sisters information was all I had since I hadn't talked to a doctor. So I was told she was dying of liver cancer. She had about twenty spots on her liver. They said she probably had breast cancer too. She had a big lump on her breast. So I called her when she got home. I told her that I would come see her right then. She said no please don't come until I feel better. She said

I don't want you to waste a visit. She said wait until we can go out to lunch. So not wanting to upset her I let these phone calls go like this for about a week. I lived fifty miles away. So one day after our call I got off the phone crying my eyes out that my mom didn't want to see me. My husband told me give it a couple more days or just get in the truck and go see her right now. So I decided to give it a few more days. So I decided to call the hospital and try to speak to the doctor. Of course I couldn't talk to her doctor. So I spoke to a male nurse. He explained several times how he couldn't give me any information.

I broke down crying and explained that I was told my mother was dying of cancer. I told him how I just lost my dad ten months earlier three doors from her hospital room to cancer. He told me again he was so sorry he couldn't tell me anything.

Who knows maybe he remembered seeing me in the hospital for four days and nights with my dad. He said what I can tell you is that she probably won't be dying anytime soon. I said so she's not dying of cancer and he repeated what he had said and said thats all I can tell you. I finally understood he was telling me without telling me because he could tell in my voice that I was falling completely apart. I got off the phone feeling much better. So I called my aunt in New York and told her the good news.

So that night I went to bed with mom on my brain. I prayed to God and to my real dad, my brother in heaven, and my step dad to tell me what to do. My step dad came to me in a dream. He told me he was dead but he was fine. He said he was worried about mom. He told me I needed to help her. I needed to go see her. So I promised him that I would go see her soon. The next morning I called and she told me the same thing don't come yet. So I called mom's family doctor of about twenty years. I knew the doctor, nurses and receptionists very well, since I took mom to a lot of her doctor visits. I had also gone to this doctor when I was younger. So I explained to the receptionist what my sisters had told me about mom dying and about the cancer. I was crying in between the words I spoke. She said she hadn't heard about any of this but if I held on she'd ask the doctor. Just then the doctor walked out of a room and she told him that it was me on the phone.

She told him what I was calling about. He laughed and said mom would probably out live all of us including him. He then looked at her chart and said there wasn't any cancer. The spots on her liver weren't cancer. I thanked them several times.

I called my aunt who is mom's only sister who lives in New York and we're in Florida. I gave her the good news and she was so happy. But we both had that question why were we told this horrible news? I called my brother and told him the good news. He had the same question why were we told this? I finally called my sisters and asked why did you tell us this? Their answer was this is what the doctor had said to them. The news seemed to change some to the doctor said the liver spots could turn into cancer in the future. I was so confused. So that night I went to bed and after I said my prayers I just started talking to mom like I was standing in her bedroom. I'm not real sure what happened next.

Some would say I fell asleep and had this wonderful dream about being in my mothers bedroom talking to her while she layed in her bed looking like she could die any minute. But some would say what I say, these are the believers. They'd say that I had a OUT OF BODY EXPERIENCE. I traveled fifty miles to be with my mother that night. I told her how much I loved her and still needed her. I told her how much my three kids loved her and needed their grandmother. I gave her tough love like she had taught me to use when needed. I told her if she didn't get up and start living again that she would die soon in that bed. We cried and laughed together in her bedroom. We hugged and kissed. She promised me that she would get up the next day. So I left and went back to my body.

I woke up the next morning not sure if it was a dream or a true out of body experience. Then the phone rang. I answered it and it was mom. She said she was up and out of bed. She then thanked me for coming to see her that night. She told me what a wonderful daughter I was and how much she loved me. Then on the phone she repeated some of the things I had told her the night before. She thanked me so many times for saving her. I realized this was one of the most special things to happen in my life. I was so happy. After we hung up I thought the only problem with this was I experienced it with my mother who has Alzheimer's disease. I was a little disappointed but I decided right then it didn't matter. I would tell my husband, kids, sisters, and brother. Whoever believed me great. The others oh well it didn't matter. I know it happened. All that mattered to me was I saved my mothers life. She told me to wait a couple of days until she got her appetite back. So a few days later we went out for a wonderful lunch.

I still didn't know for sure if she was still dying on the inside. She looked great on the outside. My two sisters were still telling me to get myself ready for moms death. So they set up more tests. I said I'd take her for the tests. I wanted to know the test results from the doctors not from how my sisters understood the doctors. I was gonna get first hand information for now on. I took mom for the test on her breast. It was a fatty cyst. No cancer. We were both so happy. We went out to lunch to celebrate. I took her back to the hospital for another series of tests. Everything came back perfect. Mom had a clean bill of health. Nothing was wrong with her.

She was in perfect health besides the Alzheimer's disease. Which is a very horrible disease but cancer is a lot worst. So what caused the illness, lost of weight, the throwing up, no appetite, laying in bed for weeks, the four day hospital stay. All I could ever come up with was depression. She was depressed from my step dad John dying ten months earlier. He was her whole world. They had twenty wonderful years together. They were always on the go and living until his illness took their lives away. My sister from Missouri had been down for a visit a month before mom's illness. When my sister left and went back to Missouri mom got real depressed and had gone to bed. So depression can do some crazy things to you and to the people around you. My sister that lived out of state in Missouri was still convinced that mom was dying soon.

My sisters had her so convinced that she packed up her life and kids and moved home to Florida to spend more time with mom before she died. She stayed for ten months and seen that mom was fine and so she repacked her life and went back to Missouri. There's five of us daughters. After the story was told sister to sister it ended up being kinda like playing that kids game telephone. The story about moms health changed so much from sister to sister. This happened eleven years ago. Momma is still living and very healthy. Her Alzheimer's caused the family to put her in a nursing home six years after all of this happened.

Robbie, his crew man and I were going commercial fishing. It was Sunday night and we were going pompano fishing. I was so excited to be back on the boat again. I asked God to please forgive us for working on a Sunday but we really needed the money. As we were riding through the dark night my happiness turned to dread. I got this thought in my head what if the motor broke down. Then I told myself that was silly the motor was in great condition. But I had this strong feeling about the motor. I kept telling myself the motor was fine. It was a good running motor. We were about ten miles from the dock when the motor made a strange sound. Robbie stopped and shut the motor off. They checked the motor out and nothing seemed wrong. So Robbie tried to start it and it wouldn't start. They checked it out again and couldn't find what was wrong. So Robbie said we were going to have to paddle back to the dock. Robbie took the first turn paddling our twenty five foot boat.

Robbie and his crew man took turns paddling. I told Robbie that I would take a turn paddling but he said no. As they paddled I thought to myself why hadn't I said something to Robbie about my bad feeling about the motor. I questioned myself if we could have kept it from happening. But I know now the motor just gave out. They were hoping it just needed to be worked on. As I sat on the cooler I thought to myself the motor is blown. The tears welled up in my eyes and I prayed that I was wrong this time. After they paddled for a couple of hours with the wind blowing harder and harder against them. They were both getting so tired. So I started taking a turn with the paddle. It was so hard to paddle against the wind. It was hurting every muscle in my body.

The pain was so bad but I just had to keep on paddling. I knew the guys were tired and sore. I was in good shape but this was a hard workout. The wind finally got too bad to paddle against. So we paddled into a creek. We got to the end of the creek and tied the boat up. We got off the boat and we started walking through the woods. We didn't know exactly where on Pine Island we were. We were hoping we were close to home so we wouldn't have to walk far. Of course we didn't have a cell phone with us that night. We heard barking dogs ahead. This made us kinda nervous since we were in the woods at night. The crew man got his knife out just in case. I was smoking a cigarette and was thinking how I'd fight off a dog biting me with my cigarette. Robbie just kept walking. We walked on the opposite side of the dirt road as we passed the dogs. We were so happy the dogs didn't chase us.

We finally saw headlights coming down the dirt road. We stopped the guy in a van. We asked him where were we? We asked if we were close to the fish streets and he said yes. We explained our situation and hoped he'd offer us a ride when we told him where we lived. It was only about four miles but he wasn't a do gooder he just wished us good luck and he drove off. So we kept walking down the dirt road. We were so happy when we got to the highway and we started hitchhiking. No luck. Our happiness turned into pains in our feet, legs and backs as cars kept going by. We walked for quite some time. We walked about two miles down the hard road when finally a do gooder stopped and we crawled into the back of his truck. He gave us a ride to our front door. Thank God! We were all so tired. Bless that man's heart.

He told us his name but we were all so exhausted we didn't remember it. But I know the Lord gave him the blessings he deserves for helping us. We got home at 11:00pm. We were so happy to be home. We told each other we needed to replace the cell phone that Robbie had dropped into the water a few months earlier. The next morning we all got up and were very sore from our walk and our paddling. My legs, feet, back, arms, and stomach hurt so badly. I had to roll out of bed. I was in massive pain all day and night. It was about 10:00pm Monday night. I was sitting in Robbies chair watching TV. Robbie was standing behind me with the door open watching our dog Rascal that was outside. Some will think it was a cold chill from the door being open. But we lived in Southwest Florida at the time. It was very hot out that night.

I wasn't praying. I was just thinking to myself how in the world was I going to be able to handle this much pain the next day. I hurt so badly. Every time I moved the pain shot through my body. Then I got one of those cold chills I get quite often that makes my whole body jerk. But this one was so much more intense it felt like it went right through my chest. My whole body jerked really hard and I screamed AGH! Robbie seen and heard me and laughed like he always does when I get a cold chill. Then he said what he always says when this happens. He always says that someone just stepped on my grave. He said this one was a good one it made you scream. He shut the door and sat down. I told him that was a really good one, I don't have any pain in my body. I got up and I stretched. I did a little dance. I touched my toes. Just a few minutes earlier I couldn't hardly move because of the pain. He didn't know what to think. I got kinda scared at first I thought no pain maybe I was dying or dead. Then I realized I was ok. I went outside and sat in the dark and cried and thanked God for taking my pain away. I thought of my sister, I needed to call her and tell her. She would love this as much as I was loving it. She believes in healings like I do. It was too late at night to call her.

So I went back inside and talked to Robbie about my healing until I just about drove him crazy. He was happy for me but he was still in massive pain. I finally calmed down and went to sleep in the chair. I awoke in the chair at about 2:30am. Once again I was worried that I was dead since there was no pain. I petted my dog then went to bed.

I woke up in the morning and looked out the front door to say hi to the neighbor like I do every morning. He is the crew man that paddled with us. He wasn't out there on this morning. Boy did I get scared. So I went and woke my daughter Roseanne up. She talked to me so I finally was convinced that I was alive and well. I told Roseanne and John about my beautiful healing. They thought it was great. They love hearing about this kinda stuff when it happens.

Then I called my sister and shared with her this wonderful miracle. She was so happy and excited about my healing. Our faith had been tested the night our motor broke down. But Robbie and I kept each others faith going strong that night and many nights that followed. We kept telling each other that we would make it. We kept laughing together at the events in our lives. We didn't let the dark, negative vibes in our life take over our souls. We kept fighting back together. We kept our family strong and happy. The love and family bonding just got stronger each day. We will survive. This too shall pass. And yes we did survive those hard times after the motor blew.

We got a lot of help from a lot of do gooders. Too many to name and some don't like to be named. I know they all got the blessings that they deserved and I prayed for each one of them to get blessings from God for helping us during those hard times. The usual ones helped us out. Mom, sisters, brother, friends, then some surprise ones were the people from our church and the church. A agency that I had never heard of. The ones that touched my heart and all the way to my soul was my wonderful nieces and my ex brother in law. They gave so much. We're not really close now years later but I'll never forget their kindness in my time of need. That's exactly what family is all about. They're there for you no matter what. Some day I will pay them back even though they didn't want me to pay them back. That will make my heart feel as good as theirs felt when they helped me. I am trying to get close to them again.

I use to get heartburn once in a while until the past four years. I had heartburn all the time. I was to the point where I wasn't cooking Italian food too often. I'm half Italian and I love Italian food. I knew if I ate it I'd be sick with heartburn. I was always ready for the heartburn. I kept antacid medicine everywhere.

I had them in my purse, my car, on our boat, next to my bed, next to my chair, and in my pocket. Something everyday would give me heartburn. Then a few months ago I started reading Science and Health a key to Scriptures book. I've believed in praying and healings for years. But I didn't believe that my heartburn could be healed all these years. Until now. I've been heartburn free for three months. I can eat anything I want and no heartburn. It is totally amazing. About four years later the heartburn came back again. I would take several pills a day everyday. I went like that for about a year and finally I said thats enough and I prayed for my healing. I'm not sure what happened to bring it back on but for about four years I felt great. I'm not sure if its my stress level that has caused the heartburn to come back. Its not as bad as it use to be thank goodness. I do believe the heartburn is partly stress and partly being over weight. I now have lost twenty pounds and I have gotten rid of a lot of my stress and I've gotten rid of most of my heartburn. I can eat anything that I want to. I only get heartburn once in a while now.

It's April 21, 2005, the time is 12;15am. I just smoked my last cigarette. I'm going to brush my teeth then go to bed. Tomorrow morning instead of my morning cigarette I'm going to put a patch on and quit smoking. QUIT SMOKING! Finally after thirty five years. I'm ready to quit FOREVER wish me luck, I know I'll need it on this journey. It's 8:00am I've just put the patch on. I've got very high hopes for quitting. So I hope this patch helps. I want to live longer for me, my husband, and our kids. It's 9:30am I just got back from taking Bobby Ray to work. My first drive without smoking. It took two candies. Not bad. This is hard but I will beat this. It's 11:30am I ate the most wonderful, tasty breakfast of scrambled eggs and cheese, hash browns, bacon, toast and milk. I've been quit for eleven hours and already and I can taste food better.

I can't wait until I can smell stuff better. It's still hard not smoking. But I will make it. I've been quit smoking for six years. It was very hard but I survived it. I had a few set backs and smoked some cigarettes but I never inhaled so I reckon I never got the habit back. So now I'm trying to lose the fifty pounds I gained when I quit smoking. I'd rather have this weight then that horrible addiction to cigarettes. Here's how I finally quit smoking after all these years. My kids had been begging me to quit all their lives. I lost two fathers to lung cancer.

My fifteen year old daughter had a boyfriend who's mother was dying of cancer. I really thought she was going to be ok. But no matter what I thought when the boyfriend talked to me one day about his mom's cancer. His words went right through me. He reached a spot in my heart that day that no one else had ever reached. The emotion in that boys words were so intense, he loved his momma so much. I knew right then that I never wanted one of my kids to be going through this because I liked to smoke cigarettes. So I quit smoking. This boy and his mother helped me to quit smoking. They might have saved my life, who knows. His momma passed away about a year later. To this day every time I see this young man I give him a big hug. I'll always remember that talk we had that got me to quit smoking. He and his momma will always have a special place in my heart.

I was in a lot of pain from working too hard at work. My back, legs, feet, and arms all hurt very badly. Robbie and I went to bed early. I prayed for Robbie, my family, and like I always do a extra prayer for our healing. It was about 3:00am and Robbie woke me up. He said four or five woman spirits had just been there to heal me. He didn't know who they were but he explained them to me and one could have been my grandma Josephine who had passed before I was born. He said as they walked past him they said what a nice person he was. Then they were gone. So he made me get up to see how I felt. I was barely able to walk when I went to bed. I got up and I felt great. No pain. I did a little dance and then I thanked the spirits for the healing. Robbie and I talked about how cool it was that we were so open to the spirits coming when it was the good spirits. We wished that we would only have the good spirits come to visit us then it wouldn't be too bad.

It's the first of July 2005. Robbie and I have been reading Science and Health for a few months. This is my second time reading this amazing book. We're on page 325. He believes more each time we read. His healing has started to happen and I could tell the first day it started he was very surprised. So now he believes more then ever. He has always believed in God anyway but in his own way. He likes to see to believe. The only problem sometimes when I pray on him his sickness has been going into me and making me very sick.

The first time it was just a little bit. The second time it was a lot. I was so sick I went to sleep for a couple of hours. When I awoke I was ok. Robbie said I should go throw up like the Indians do in the movies. I've had this problem over the years when I'd pray on the kids when they were sick. Bobby Ray has seen it happen so many times he is afraid to let me pray on him. Sometimes I get it right and I don't get sick but sometimes I mess up and put the illness into me. But I still pray on him whenever he gets sick. Robbie did receive a beautiful healing but more important he has gotten closer to God. It's six years later and Robbie has had several wonderful healings but he hasn't had a complete healing. He is still sick from his thyroid and his back and legs are still in massive pain from his back operation that didn't fix his problems in his back. I get so upset that he still has to have so much pain. I pray all the time for him. I try to understand why he's still in pain. But I really don't know and don't understand it. He is such a good man and he is so connected to God he should have a complete healing. I'll never give up praying for him and believing that God will heal him someday.

How many miracles in one week? My best friend at work told me about one of our good friends that use to work with us had found out that she had cancer. I told her to start praying right now for our friend to get rid of her cancer. So we both started praying for her. We told other friends and family to pray for her too. I can't remember how long it was but every time we saw her daughters we would ask about her. Then on April 25,2009 she walked into the store and I asked her about her cancer. She said she went back to the doctor and they couldn't find any cancer. The doctors didn't have any explanations of what happened except it was a miracle. I was so happy for her. I told her that we had been praying for her. She said thanks. I know she had a lot of people praying for her cause she is one of those loveable ladies that everyone loves. She is so happy and she is glowing from this beautiful miracle from God.

The next day I was talking to my sister on the phone she lives in another state. I was telling her about my friends miracle cure from cancer. She told me a story about a friend of her's that had a miracle cure from cancer. I was just so blown away by this wonderful healing. It reminds you that God is busy at work helping and healing people all the time.

If they just have the sense to ask or if someone prays for them and asks for Gods help. Then the next day one of my customers that I had been praying for because his cancer had come back came into the store. I ask him just about everyday how he is doing since he told me the cancer was back. I'd been praying for him for a couple of months that his cancer would be healed. He is such a sweet man.

I enjoy talking to him so much. So I asked him on this beautiful April 29,2009 morning how are you feeling? I said you look great. He said he had gone back to the doctor about his cancer and the doctor said he doesn't have cancer now. It's some other ailment that can be cured. He was so happy. He is on top of the world. He is glowing from his miracle healing. How many miracles do you see or hear about in one week? Today is Wednesday and I've heard of three cancer miracles so far this week. It has been a wonderful week for miracle stories. So the next time someone tells you about being sick take a few minutes out of your busy day and say a prayer for that person. Who knows you might be involved in helping a miracle happen. It also makes you a better person for caring about someone else. God loves to hear our prayers so keep on praying.

CHAPTER 8
PSYCHIC, KNOWLEDGE, OR CONNECTION

December 26,2006 I'm on my way home from work. I'm listening to the radio while I'm driving home. I'm waiting for this song to get over then I'm gonna start talking into my new recorder that Robbie bought me for Christmas. I really like this song. The radio station went blank. So that was my sign to go ahead and record for this book. When I doubt my psychic abilities they show me they're still working just fine. I get so amazed that God lets us have these great gifts. I don't like to look at the kids relationships, friends, boy or girl friends with my psychic ability. I don't want to tell them completely how to live their lives. I tell them a few things. Sometimes they believe and sometimes they think I'm being a pain in the butt momma. I try to let them learn by their choices and mistakes in life without my butting in all the time. Robbie had been reading a Angel book. He had learned a lot about angels. We were laying in bed reading and Robbie turned to me and asked me, "Did ya know that everyone has the ability to do things and everyone has the psychic gift"? I said yeah I do know that honey. That's what my whole book is about. Our gifts from God and learning how to use them. I believe everyone has them they just don't know how to use them. They need to talk to God. God is there with you everyday.

It was New Years Eve 1999. Everyone was a little unsettled about it turning to the year 2000. We were going to our neighbors New Years Eve party that night. All the kids were going to another neighbors house for the evening. This way the parents would be close by to where the kids were going to be. We were all walking to the party so we could all drink. My husband and his buddy went out for drinks before the party. He was in a great mood when he got home. I was mad he had drank so much before the party. He had met up with my boss from the golf course so that was his excuse why he had stayed so long at the bar. He got on the trampoline with our three kids. They were all having a blast. I was freaking out yelling at him to get off the trampoline.

I knew he was going to get hurt. I finally gave up and I went into the house to finish getting ready to go out. A few minutes later they were all yelling for me from the trampoline. I went outside and Robbies knee had gotten hurt.

So I helped him into the house and told him that he should have listened to me. They all joked that I had put the fachanada on him. He was on crutches for two weeks and out of work. It wasn't the best way to start the new year but it did get a lot better as the year went by. It turned 2000 with no other problems so that was great. We had a wonderful time at the party. We went into our favorite Italian restaurant while he was on the crutches. The owner asked him what had happened to him. He told her that I put the fachanada on him. She was an older Italian woman and you could tell by the look on her poor face she believed in the fachanada. She asked me if I did and I said no he was just joking. But she never looked at me quite the same after that day.

My friend and I would always talk about her son that had died in a car accident. I loved talking to her about her son. But I'd get so upset during our talks. I'd try to not show how upset I was cause I didn't want to upset her. I'm not a medium but when we'd talk I'd feel her son was there with us. Sometimes I'd wonder if the words of comfort I said to her were coming from me. Or was someone putting them into my head. Were the words coming from her son? It was a very confusing time for me. At first I thought I'd get so upset because our son's were only a year apart. They had played on the same baseball team as kids. As time went by it felt like I was really feeling her pain during our talks. I may never know the truth or understand these strong emotions.

I'll always enjoy our talks and hopefully it helps her to talk about her precious son. I wish that I could say yes that I'm a medium and have a real session with her and her son. But I'm just not that far progressed into the spiritual world yet. I still second guess whats coming from me and whats coming from the deceased person that we're talking about. Hopefully someday I'll be able to open myself up completely to the spirit world.

When this does happen I'm going to look up my dear friend and have a real session with her and her wonderful son. He was such a special, sweet, young man. He was just having fun and living his life when it was taken from him way too young. He was here for such a short time but he lived a lifetime during those years. I was standing outside my house hanging fishing net in the yard. My neighbor drove by. She drives by several times a day.

She was going through a break up with her husband. She had already driven by a few times that day. But this time was different. Her dead daughter came to my mind. I don't know if these were my thoughts or her daughters thoughts. At the time I was planning on moving in two weeks. We had been neighbors for five years and I hadn't met her daughter. She died before I moved to this town. I had read her obituary before I moved here and I cried my eyes out for this young girl. Then a few years later I became her parents neighbor. Anyway I thought to myself I need to go talk to her before I move. We never got really close but we always said hi and waved.

I thought to myself while I was hanging my net. I need to tell her that her daughter said that she'd never be alone that her daughter would always be with her. Her daughter wants her to start living again and enjoying life for both of them. She's cried enough tears for the husband and daughter. It's her time to be happy. As these thoughts flooded my mind it was like the daughter was talking to me. I could see her daughter. I thought to myself when I talk to my neighbor, I have to re-word this or she'll think I'm crazy. I will give her the loving message from her daughter before I leave. Hopefully this message will help her to get on with her life. I don't claim to be a medium. So of course I wonder if the daughter really talked to me. Or if I just felt so much compassion for this woman.

I spoke to this woman before I moved. I told her everything the best I could and I didn't say any of it was from her dead daughter since I wasn't for sure if it was or not. I didn't want her to think I was nuts. Hopefully this was her daughters message. After I moved off that beautiful island I did hear that she was doing good and had started living again. I heard she was very happy with her new boyfriend. This was 2004 and mediums were new.

I'm much more at ease with myself and the spirit world. As I'm typing this book from all my years of writing it is all just really amazing to me. I have lived a very exciting, eventful, spiritual life. Sometimes when things happen I wonder if it is psychic or just knowledge. I know a lot of these things happen to a lot of people. I think its psychic and that some people are just more tuned in to their psychic powers. I believe everyone has these psychic powers. I think some people just forget how to use them.

I believe some people let their minds get clouded with alcohol, drugs, or their busy lives. I know when my mind is clear I'm more in tune to my psychic mind. Before there was caller ID, there was so many times I knew who was calling when the phone would ring. I have four sisters and I'm really close to all of them. My one sister is two years older then me. We are super close. Our minds have always been in tune to each other. There has been many, many times that we cook the same dinner. Our mother and her only sister have always been like that too. My aunt lives in New York and we live in Florida. My mother, sisters, and brother and I are all very connected. When ever one of us is having a hard time in life or sometimes just a bad day. You can always count on someone in the family will call you.

Sometimes when you get the call they'll say, "I've been thinking about you all day". Sometimes the first thing they say is, "are you ok"? Someone in the family always feels your pain no matter how many miles away they are. A lot of times I know what someone is going to say before they say it. I'm not sure if its psychic or just the situation I'm in at the time. Some of it could be psychic and some just knowing the person so well. On Christmas Eve one year my four year old son John got a boomerang from my husbands cousin. I freaked out and I didn't want him to keep it. When my little brother was that age he had one and got hit in the mouth and got stitches. I told my husband this story. He said don't worry John will be fine with it. I was very upset. So when the boys went outside to play with it I watched out the kitchen window. I watched John throw it and it came back perfect except it hit him in the eye. I ran out of the house screaming at my husband that John was hurt. I had to take John to the hospital for stitches, so was it psychic or just another freak accident.

A lot of the following things happen to people all the time. You think of someone then you see them or they call you. You think of a movie and it comes on TV. You think of a song then it plays on the radio. You wish or pray for a close parking spot at a busy store. You find one while the rest are packed with cars. You're at the grocery store and you think of a item you want but can only buy it if its on sale, you find it on sale. You're shopping and want to buy a certain brand of shoes or clothes. But they have to be on a really good sale for you to be able to afford them.

You find them and they're on a great sale. So are these psychic, prayers, or just consequences. This is the way I live my life. One of my favorite uncles got cancer. When I found out I cried like a baby. Two months after I found out I started writing him a letter. I started the letter before Thanksgiving. Then I wrote some after Thanksgiving. Then it was getting close to Christmas and I still hadn't finished his letter. I decided I'd finish the letter and send him a Christmas card. This year was a very hard year and I wasn't sending out Christmas cards. It was about a week before Christmas and I started looking for the right card in my old leftover cards from years pass. After days of looking I finally found the Foot Prints card. This was perfect. So the night before Christmas Eve I sat up until 1:00am finishing the letter and the card. The first thing I did the next morning was put the card in the mailbox.

I used my last stamp I had been saving to mail something special. The mail lady picked the card up in the early afternoon. About three hours later my sister came over and told me our uncle had passed away that morning. I was devastated. I didn't really know he was that bad. When I talked to my cousin who is his son we always talked about when he would get better. I never thought for a minute that it was going to cause him to pass away. His passing was so quick, too quick. His wife of about fifty years had passed a few years earlier.

I'll always think that they just really needed to be together. I hated that they passed away so young. But I know they're so happy being together. I saw them together in my mom's living room a few years after they had passed. They looked so in love. They were holding hands. They were younger then when they had died. They looked great. So was this card and letter just a consequence or a very special good bye connection.

I've always read the obituaries. I grew up in a small town so reading the town paper I'd know a lot of the people that passed away. It's a habit that's gone into adulthood. I read this obituary about a teenage girl. I cried my eyes out. I don't know why this girls death fifty miles away broke my heart. I didn't know her or the family yet. About three years later we moved fifty miles away from our hometown that I had no intention of ever leaving. We met the girls parents that I had read about. A year later we became neighbors with the girls parents.

Rozie and I walked into the restaurant for our fancy dinner on the graduation cruise. We were hoping we'd be sitting with someone we knew. We found our table and there was Frog and his mother and a few other people. I thought to myself cool we have someone we know and like. We all had a nice dinner. The next dinner we had together my brain started wandering. I'm a big believer in signs. So I started thinking maybe this means my daughter Rozie and Frog will finally get together. I'm getting to meet his mom. We're dining together in this beautiful setting.

Then one night a bunch of us were sitting at out Dixie County table near the pool. I looked at all the guys and asked why did I have to put up with Rozie being upset for two years with her ex-boyfriend? I told them "Ya'll are all so nice and just awesome". I said "Why wasn't she dating one of you guys"? They all said they were willing but she was in love with her ex. Then they all started joking about how Frog was willing and they could have little tadpoles. Frog is his nickname. I joked back and said oh no way not Frog. But I was thinking is this another sign that Frog is going to be my son-in-law someday.

So life went on and a month later I was supposed to be writing on my book. But instead I was looking at cruise pictures. I kept going back to Frogs pictures and studying them. I thought to myself maybe he is gonna turn out to be the one. We moved here in December. On Valentines Day he gave Rozie a box of candy. He said "Here's my heart and pulled a heart shaped box of candy from under his shirt and gave it to her". How romantic is that. Rozie just melted. He would ask her in welding class when are we going to date? She would tell him we're not going to date we're just gonna get married. I liked him so much for his personality. But also because he welcomed my daughter to Dixie County. He was a household name in our house. We were always talking about him. We were always asking Rozie when was she gonna start dating him. I was always asking her how he was doing? That all changed a few days after I was looking at the cruise pictures. July 4,2008 will go down in Dixie County history as the saddest 4th of July. I started crying that morning on the way to work for no reason. I kept crying all day over every little thing. I was so sad for no reason. I knew something bad was brewing.

That's the only time I get like that. I preached and preached at my three kids all day and evening to be extra careful it being a holiday. I didn't tell them of my horrible feelings. I was so happy when all my kids were safe the next day and still safe the next evening. Then Rozie called me crying her heart out and told me Frog had passed away on the 4th of July. He had accidentally been shot. I cried so hard for him. I cried even harder for Rozie. I cried the hardest for his mom, dad, and sister. I begged God for a miracle. Just bring him back I begged. I prayed so hard. No miracle came this time. I was heartbroken. No son-in-law Frog and no tadpoles. But we have the memories of a smile on this young man's face that always made you smile. We have our memories of our cruise to Mexico all of us in his namesake bar. We all had a blast hanging out with Frog. We had a great time getting back on the ship after our day in Mexico. We had walked back with Frog and we got some pictures getting back on the ship.

He didn't get to grow up but he did a lot of living in the short time he was here. He touched so many peoples lives with his friendly personality. His parents should be so proud of themselves for turning out such a awesome young man. His friends are better people for having known him. He brought out the best in people. He'd flash that smile and you were smiling and laughing with him before ya knew it. I decided to put a container up at my store to collect money to help Frogs family with the expenses. I was trying to decide what picture of Frog to put on the container to collect money. I had printed one of him on the cruise with a funny shirt on. I had taken this picture of him. I was having second thoughts on the picture and shirt being proper for this. I was fixing to print the picture of him in his suit from our fancy dinner on the cruise. But thats why I had a picture of him in this funny shirt cause he was so happy about buying it. His happiness was so contagious. He had me laughing so much about that shirt so I had to get a picture of him in it. I was sitting at my desk trying to decide what picture when my glass from the Mexico bar fell on my desk near me for no reason. I jumped when it fell and I said ok Frog. I reckon that was Frog saying to put the funny shirt picture on the container. So I did.

I was mowing the fairways on the golf course like any other day. It was a nice day out. I was in a good mood singing out loud all the songs I could remember the words to.

I had worked on the golf course for about five years. So I had a lot of airplanes fly over in five years. This plane on this day flew over just like any other day. But this time it was so different. I started crying. I looked at my watch and wrote down the time this crying started. I was getting use to strange things happening in my life. I kept mowing. The crying wouldn't stop it got worse. I was crying hysterically for no apparent reason. I thought I was afraid of the airplane. But why? It didn't make any sense. I knew something bad had happened, I didn't know what. I was crying so hard I had to stop my mower and cry my tears out. I was so confused. After about thirty minutes I finally got myself put back together. Later that day I found out the Oklahoma bombing had happened when my tears had started. I never told anyone. I figured they'd think I was crazy. But this book is all about me coming out and dealing with every strange thing in my life.

Robbie and I kinda inherited our fathers friends. Our fathers both passed away in their forties. This friend became our friend as we got older. He lived in a travel trailer on the property we rented from another friend. He became part of our family. The kids adored him. He gave our daughter who then was four years old a stuffed Mickey Mouse that was as big as she was. She loved it so much. He was known around town as quite a drinker. But our family got to know this sweet, loveable side of this man. He would take my laundry down if it was fixing to rain while I was at work. He'd pick oranges and make orange juice for the kids. He'd talk and play with the kids all the time. He had so many patience with the kids. He was a really good guy. We bought a house and we moved. It was so hard leaving him and the other two guys that lived there. We had become a family. Shortly after we moved he found out he had cancer. We took him to the doctor a few times. We had a benefit BBQ at our new house for him. We still kept in touch after we moved to our own house. We all knew his time was running out. We saw him this one day and he wanted to have a small cookout with a few of his close friends.

So we took him to the grocery store. He bought steaks and seafood. He got snacks for the kids. He'd never forget about the kids. We went and had the cookout and talked for a few hours. When we got ready to go he gave us the leftovers from the cookout. A few days later he passed away. When we lived on the property he would get me to go get him bingo scratch off tickets.

I started doing them with him. We had a blast doing our bingo tickets together. I still think of him every time I do a bingo ticket to this day. At the time of his death our town had a flood going on. They would plan his funeral then we'd get more rain and they wouldn't be able to bury him. I felt so bad for him and his family. This went on for over a week. I was worried about him not being able to rest in peace. One night during this he came to visit me in a dream. We walked through a big field talking. We stopped under a big beautiful tree. He explained to me that he was resting in peace. He said his soul was finally at peace. He thanked me for letting him become part of our family. When I think of him I remember him alive. But I always remember our last talk in the field under that tree. Some would say it was just a dream but I know the difference between a dream and a visit. This was my last visit with our friend.

I was working at a golf course. One of my coworkers got hit by a golf ball while working. It had happened to most of us that had worked there for a long time. My friend complained to me a few days later that it still hurt. I told him he needed to go to the doctor. I can't remember how long he let it go. But I kept griping at him to go get it checked out. He was hit on his back so there really was no reason to rush to the doctor. But I had one of my feelings and I kept bugging him. He finally went to the doctor to shut me up. He found out that he had lung cancer. They were able to remove the cancer. But there was complications and infections. He ended up losing his leg to these problems. So he was now in a wheelchair. I never saw him again after that. I heard stories from other friends. The last I heard was he might lose his other leg. Then I left the golf course and moved fifty miles away.

A few years later I had a dream about him. A few days after my dream I was on my way home and I saw the neighbors loading a pickup onto a trailer to tow it away. I had one of my weird feelings about my truck getting repossessed. I blew the feeling off. I had been talking to the lady from the finance company and as far as I knew we had a payment plan worked out. Then that night I layed in bed channel surfing and came across a repo show so I stopped to watch. I had just heard about the show the day before when I saw one of the actors on a talk show. I had one of my feelings while I was watching the talk show.

I watched for a few minutes and my strange feelings were getting very strong. I almost yelled out to my husband in the living room. But he had aggravated me that's why I was in my bedroom instead of the living room with the rest of my family. So I turned the channel and I couldn't shake the feeling. So I rolled over and went to sleep. Robbies cousin walked into our house at 4:30am and told us our truck had just gotten repossessed. He saw them going down the street with it. The guilt set in quickly. I should have followed my signs. I know I have this gift and I ignore it all the time. So Robbie and I got up and had coffee. We did what we always do in the morning. We played backgammon, drank coffee, and talked. I started blaming myself for not begging the credit company enough. I thought the lady said she was going to wait for the payment. Robbie said don't blame yourself I'm not blaming you. So I had to tell him about the signs I had saw. I had just vowed to myself to take this vision with me to the grave. After I told him everything he laughed and said you have another story to put into your book. I laughed. We would be ok. I sat down and re-read what I had wrote about my friends visit in my dream. He said everything will be ok. So I didn't cry about the loss of our truck. I just had a warm feeling in my body. Everything happens for a reason and we'd be ok. We will survive this set back.

I was sitting at the computer in the public library. A dad, mom, and daughter were having a conversation about what they were going to do after they left the library. They were talking about a friends birthday party in detail. I don't know why they caught my attention, but they did. I turned and looked at them and listened to their whole conversation. I didn't think much about it after they left. A few weeks later I was back at the library on the computer. I heard a family talking and the voices and conversation sounded familiar. I turned and saw the same family from a few weeks earlier. The whole conversation and argument was exactly the same as weeks earlier. I had such a hard time holding my tongue. I wanted to tell them how the conversation was going to turn out since I had heard it already. I didn't say anything cause I knew they'd think I was crazy. Sure enough it all turned out exactly the same as weeks earlier. I've heard of de'ja' vu before but this really flipped me out. About the same time this happened to me it also happened to Robbie. His experience happened at his old hangout bar.

Some will say well its a bar. Same ole people same ole stories. But it was more then that. He got there and people and stories were like he had lived through this night before. So he started paying close attention to all of it. He knew how the whole evening was going to go. He knew who was going to walk into and out of the bar next before it happened. He was really amazed. He came home and told me his story and I told him I know exactly what you're talking about. I told him about my library story. He tried to tell his friend his story but his friend just didn't get it. His friend was like oh yeah same ole people, same ole stories in that bar. But it was more then that. It was a night re-lived. Just like my day in the library was a day re-lived.

My husband Robbie and I know we are soul mates. We've had all the usual relationship problems like everyone else. We've wanted to be together since we were ten and eleven years old. I reckon that's why none of our relationships with others ever worked out. We got together when we were thirty and thirty one years old. We've worked through all of our problems and any new ones that come up. We just know we'll be together forever. Besides the love we have for each other our souls are connected. We're so in tune with each other. So many things have happened over the years, way too many to list. Here are just a few of them.

Our three kids and I went to church every Sunday. Robbie didn't attend church with us. After church we'd always go to the coffee social in the parish hall . This one Sunday all through church I felt like my husband was calling me in my head. I was kind of shook up by the time church was over. The kids started walking towards the parish hall after church and I said no. I told them we had to get home in case their dad needed something. They all argued and begged to go to the coffee social. They reasoned with me that dad was probably still sleeping. Usually the three of them can talk me into something when they all gang up on me with so much logic. On this day I said we have to go home and see what daddy needs from me. We got home and Robbie was sitting in his chair bleeding. Our dog Rascal was trying to wake him up so he could go outside. Rascals nails cut near Robbie's right eye. This happened shortly after we had left. Robbie told me he had been sitting in his chair trying to get it to stop bleeding. He said he was sitting there talking to me to come straight home from church that he needed me

He had told me to please don't go to the coffee social after church. I asked him if he had told me what was wrong. He said no he hadn't.

His message came to me loud and clear. I took him to the hospital and he got stitches. We were both so excited and amazed that this mind talking worked. A few years later I was sitting at the ballpark watching the kids play baseball. All of a sudden I felt like someone was talking in my head. I heard go to ice cream shop after the game. Well the only time we'd go get ice cream after a game was when one of the kids would get a home run. We got into the truck after the game and I announced that we were going to get ice cream. So of course everyone wanted to know why since there was no home runs. Then they wanted to know if it was for this good play or this good hit. I told them no we were just going. Then they wanted to stay there and eat their ice cream. I said no that I want to bring daddy home his shake. We walked in the door when we got home. Robbie said oh good you heard me ask you for a shake from the ice cream shop. He had been sitting there talking to me asking me to get him a shake and I had heard him. The kids all commented on how we were so weird. We just smiled at each other.

About a year later it happened again but I thought I was just wanting ice cream. So I didn't go. I got home and Robbie said couldn't you hear me ordering my shake? I said yes I had heard it in my brain but I was afraid that I put it there. So we went and got ice cream. We're always saying the same thing at the same time. So many times we decide we want the same thing for dinner. For some people it might not be a big deal. But we have a deep freezer that is always full of a lot of different kinds of meats. Our kids are always so amazed how connected Robbie and I are to each other.

Since Robbie and I are so connected it has made our family very connected. The five of us are very close. Most people can't tell that we're not a blood family. When the kids friends ask them if they come from a divorced family they say no. To them Robbie is their real dad even though he adopted all of them. We are so lucky that our family turned out so good. It was lots of love and the Grace of God. Our wedding day was not like the story book wedding, we had been living together for eight years. We had always been planning on getting married.

We had been engaged all those years. Time just kinda got away from us. About a year before we got married, I was driving with the kids and we were talking about some friends of ours that weren't married. When we said that Robbie and I weren't married our nine year old son John screamed AHHHHHHH YOU'RE NOT MARRIED, YOU HAVE TO GET MARRIED RIGHT NOW. Needless to say we started planning our wedding very soon after that. We just assumed the kids all knew we weren't married. Robbie adopted my three kids after we were married. Back to the wedding day. We both worked together at a fish house. So that morning we were getting ready for work. I knew whatever my husband put on that morning would end up being his wedding clothes. After work he was going out to get oysters for our small reception we had planned. Our big reception was already planned for a few months away. We had to move the wedding up so he could adopt the kids sooner. They were all ready to be the Weeks family. So I just knew the timing would end up that by the time he got back with the oysters that it would be time for the wedding.

So I tried to talk him into putting on his blue jeans for work. He said no he was going to wear his favorite tan work pants for work. I hated those pants. He said after getting the oysters he'd put on his blue jeans. We wore matching fishhouse shirts. This was a fisherman redneck wedding. I wasn't sure if I'd have time to change before the wedding, it all depended on how many fish we had to get packed. So I fussed at him about his pants. We got to work and of course we had more fish and crabs to pack then we had expected. We worked so hard and fast. During all of it I was in a bad mood about these stupid pants. He kept trying to get me into a good mood all morning. I kept griping. We finally got to our last vat of fish. We packed out all the fish.

I was cleaning the vat out with the water hose while he put the fish into the cooler. At the bottom of a vat I found a beautiful rock and shell. I've packed out a lot of fish over the years. This was the first time I had ever found a rock or shell in the bottom of a vat. I picked them up and held them. My anger about the pants disappeared. Robbie came out of the cooler and I gave him a big hug and kiss and told him I loved him.

I told him I didn't care what he wore when we got married. I told him how sorry I was for griping at him all morning about his pants on our wedding day. I showed him the rock and shell. We both knew it was a sign from heaven. I put the rock and shell in my pocket. He wore the tan work pants when we got married. It was a beautiful wedding. We had our white fishing boots on. Our rock and shell sit on our kitchen window sill. They're a constant reminder of our love for each other. They also remind me that some things just are not worth fighting over. You can just let some things go without commenting on it if you know its going to upset someone. We're happily married and he wore tan work pants to seal the deal.

It was a beautiful October morning and Robbie and I were sitting on our front porch drinking our coffee. Robbie and I know we're soul mates. We've known each other for thirty nine years. We've been together for seventeen and a half years at this time. We were always drawn to each other. Our lives were always going in opposite directions. I reckon we both needed to do some living before we could be together. The first five years were very tough but we made it. We didn't ever get to just be a couple. We were parents since day one. When we got together I had a eighteen month old son, a two and a half year old daughter, and a six year old son. We've had to work on our relationship while we were raising kids. We've gotten super close and we know we're both in our marriage till death do us part.

We've gotten to the point now that we read each other minds quite often. It started with just face expressions that we could tell what the other one was thinking. Then we'd finish each other sentences. Now we hear what each other thinks. Its a good and bad thing. We can tell when each other are mad without a word being spoken. So a lot of times we can solve the problem before any mean words are spoken. It's a lot of fun most of the time. So anyway as we're sitting on the porch talking and drinking coffee. I thought to myself I'm going to go------- then I stopped my thought and I thought about what I needed to do before I went. Robbie said where are you going? I said nowhere. He said you said you were going somewhere but you didn't finish.

I said but I didn't speak any words. He said I know but I heard you anyway. We just looked at each other and smiled.

We know how lucky we are to have this wonderful special love that we share. It still amazes us everyday. It's January 30, 2008 a beautiful Thursday afternoon and Robbie went into back surgery forty five minutes ago. I read and prayed with The Science and Health Book. I ate chips, candy, and cola for forty five minutes. Now its time to write. My love of my life is in surgery and there's nothing physical that I can do for him. Instead of feeling helpless I prayed and read for him. I may not be with him in the flesh. But our souls and minds are still completely connected. Our soul mate love keeps us connected. Hopefully I'll be able to go into the recovery room with him like the doctor said I would. I can't wait to see him again. This has been our biggest challenge so far together since Bobby Ray's surgery.

The love and prayers our family has for each other will bring us through this. Before Robbie went into surgery I was trying to think of something to say that would make him feel good. I tried thinking of words of wisdom. Not much came to me. I'm always so long winded and here I was speechless. All I could think was how much I love him. I was so very afraid of him being in surgery. Thank You God for my Robbie. Please take good care of him and bring him back to me soon Amen. I believe this surgery will bring us even closer if thats possible. It gave us both a reminder of how lucky we are to have each other and our special love.

I tried to wait for the doctor to come and get me like he had promised. I kept saying I'll be good and not pushy like I usually am. At 8:00pm I called the recovery room to see if he was still in the operating room. They said no he was out and awake, and that I could meet him at his room. So I got to see him at 8:15pm. He went in for his operation at 3:45pm. It was a very long day. This was the first time the kids stayed home alone for a few days. I begged all of them to please behave so I could stay at the hospital with Robbie. We stayed in the hospital for five days. After Robbies long recovery he still has pain in his back and legs so the operation was not a success. The kids five days alone resulted in everyone safe and one wrecked truck. I should have been pushy and called the recovery room sooner. The surgery was only supposed to take two hours. It took longer so when it was over the doctor didn't come tell me like he had promised. I sat there so worried while he was in the recovery room asking for me. I watched a lot of doctors come out I reckon we were forgotten.

I have three boy cousins close to my age. We were all best friends our whole childhood on up to our adulthood. When we were teenagers my two cousins would come down on spring break vacation every year with their parents. When they'd get here I'd start acting like a kid again. My sister would get so mad at me cause she was trying to help me grow up and not be a tomboy. I'd do ok until I'd see them. Then I'd be a kid having a great time again. We'd go fishing, play baseball, basketball, football, and all kinds of games. We'd camp out in the tent in the yard. We'd sit up most of the night talking and laughing. We had a blast together. When I was with them there were no worries, no pressures, just lots of fun. My other cousin came one year when we were teenagers then he didn't come back until we were in our twenties. But I'd go to New York on vacation with my family during the summer and all of us would be together again.

Moving away from them was so hard when my dad moved our family from Long Island, New York to Bonita Springs, Florida when I was eleven years old. I was sad for about five years then I fell in love with Florida.

So anyway we kept each other forever young. We'd sing songs and we laughed all the time. We'd tease each other. Life was wonderful and I'm sure we all thought we'd all always stay this close. But time changes things sometimes. I'm still very close to my cousin. We talk all the time on the phone. He knows everything about me and all my kids and my husband on a weekly basis. I know everything he's up to and what his family is all doing.

He is more like a brother then a cousin. I haven't been able to see him in about seventeen years. He quit coming down here and I couldn't afford to go up there while I was raising my kids. But we still talk on the phone for every holiday and usually once or twice everyday. We talk about new stuff and we talk about old stuff that happened when we were kids and young adults. He keeps me forever young. My other two cousins and I stayed very close for a lot of years. My one cousin and I were the same age. He had a younger brother. They both ended up moving down to Florida after their parents had retired and moved down. His brother went to college down here. My cousin that was my age had gotten married and divorced in New York before he moved down. I got married and I had lots of problems with my ex husband.

My other cousin graduated college and got a job close by to us. We were all so happy to be around each other again. We would meet for drinks at the local bars and have the best times together. It was like we were kids again but we were finally old enough to drink. Then his brother got serious with a girl. He couldn't commit at first. We teased him so badly about not committing. He finally got married. But then they moved back up north. My cousin and I would joke for years after that if we had known she was gonna take him away from us we wouldn't have pushed him to get married. But he was happy and that was all that really mattered to us. We missed him very much. But life went on without him. My cousin and I still had each other since I finally got a divorce. My cousin would come over several times a week to visit me.

My cousin took me to my first Rock and Roll concert. We'd go out dancing with some of my friends. We ate a lot of pizza. He'd play with my kids. We'd talk about when we'd get married again. We'd talk about when he'd have kids. He would have made a great daddy. He was so good with my kids. Life was great and we were best friends. Then it happened two years later. I fell in love. Life changed. They didn't dislike each other but there was a lot of tension there. So my cousin quit coming over. We didn't hardly talk when we'd see each other at his parents house. I was so sad. I had lost my best friend. Then just as quickly that our friendship had ended it was all ok again. He started calling and dropping by again. Not as often since I had a boyfriend. He recorded four tapes of some of our favorite 60's band songs for me and brought them to me. I was so happy I had my cousin back in my life.

Then a few years later his parents decided to move back up north to be closer to all their kids. He decided to go with them. I was heartbroken. I knew that I'd never see him again. I was so sad to lose all of them but I knew they needed to be closer to their family. I was just being selfish by wanting to keep them. I had them for quite a few years. They were like my kids grandparents and they were always like second parents to me. So I always kept in touch with them over the phone. Then my aunt got very sick but when you're miles away you just don't realize how bad it is. I was blown away when she passed away. I didn't think it was that bad. She had always been so healthy.

I always thought she was going to live to be really old like her mother had. So after that I'd call and talk to my uncle and cousin. Then a few years later my uncle got cancer and again I didn't think it was that bad. Maybe I was just in denial. Then he passed away so quickly. I was so freaked out. But I was happy that they were together because to me they were always the perfect couple. They always looked and acted so in love. I always wanted a husband that I could take walks with like they did together. I'm so lucky that I got one and I feel like the happy couple like my aunt and uncle. I felt so bad for all of their kids. They didn't deserve to lose both parents so quickly and so close. Some things that God does I just don't understand. My cousin and I talked more often after all of this. I felt so bad that he was all alone now. He had been living with his parents for about ten years before they died. We talked on every occasion.

We usually talked at least once a week, sometimes more often. Towards the end my life was so busy I was lucky if I squeezed him in once a week. Sometimes two weeks would go by and I felt so bad. My cousin in New York would ask me all the time how our other cousin was doing. I finally said call him and ask him. So I gave him the number and then they were talking all the time too. It was good for both of them. So then whenever two cousins talked they'd also talk about the one that wasn't on the phone. Then the two would call the other one and tell them will ya call your cousin Beverly or the guy cousins whatever the case may be. We went round and round like that for several years. We had a great time with it like we were kids again.

Always funny phone messages when you'd get home. Life was really good.

I laughed so much on Thanksgiving that year with my two cousins. We all cracked each other up so much. My cousin and I talked several times again before Christmas. My New York cousin and I talked and laughed on Christmas. Then I called my other cousin to wish him a Merry Christmas. I wanted to find out what he was doing for the holiday. I was always wanting to make sure he wasn't gonna be alone. He wasn't in the best of moods but I got him to laugh several times. We talked for a hour. It just didn't seem like enough. I felt very strange when I hung up the phone. So I called him back and we talked for fifteen more minutes.

He sounded a little better now. I told him if I didn't talk to him again that week I'd call him on New Years Eve or he could call me. That was the last time I spoke to my cousin. Our last phone call we both laughed at life. A good way to end it. We always made each other laugh so much at ourselves and at everyone and everything around us. I was gonna call him on New Years Eve but all the kids went out and my husband and I were having a romantic dinner. I didn't want to be hold on I need to call my cousin. But I should have. I should have called him like I always did when I was cooking on the BBQ. I remember sitting in the chair near the BBQ thinking about my cousin. I don't know why I didn't pick up the phone that night. It wouldn't have changed anything but I wouldn't have felt so guilty.

My cousin died on New Years Eve from his medications not mixing well and having a heart attack. The night before I had a dream that I was in my mom's living room and a man and a woman were in the living room. It didn't feel like a dream it felt like a visit. My mom said what are they doing here? I said I don't know. Mom said it like she knew them really well. I didn't know who they were. They told me don't worry its going to be ok. I didn't know what they were talking about. When I woke up I was worried that it was someone to come take mom. So then I was worried that mom was gonna die. My sister called me with the horrible news about my dear cousin passing away. When I got off the phone with her I went to my old pictures and found my cousins parents wedding picture. It was his parents in my dream. It was more then just a dream. I knew it was a visit. They were trying to get me ready for his death. I cried for weeks after losing my cousin.. My cousin and I talk about our cousin all the time. We joke about him and we laugh about all the good times we had all those years. My cousins kept me forever young all these years. I think I keep God in my life everyday so I'm Forever Young.

4/3/2009 My mom had been in the nursing home for about six months. I live three hundred miles away so this was the first chance I had to go see her. My step dad had died eight years earlier. My sons and I were walking up to the nursing home doors. We saw some people sitting outside, but one man caught my eye.

He was laying on a bed with the bed up so he was sitting up. He had dark hair and reminded me of my step dad. He was sitting and layed back on that bed exactly the way my dad was in my vision of my dad after he had died. So when we walked by I said hello to everyone I passed. I said hello to this man and the woman that was sitting with him. They both said hello back. So we went in and visited with mom.

4/4/2009 I came alone on this day to see mom. As I walked up I said hello to everyone as I passed them. The man that looked like dad was on his bed outside again with the lady. I said hello to them and they said hello back. I went into the nursing home and I stopped at the desk. The lady was on the phone so I was standing there waiting. The man that looked like dad was being pushed into the nursing home by the lady. She pushed the man right up to me. She said to me he wants to talk to you. I was very surprised but I said ok like it was no big deal. He put his hand out to shake hands. I'm not real big on touching strangers but I shook hands with him. We shook hands then he held my hand and kissed my hand. As this was going on I was looking into his eyes. I saw my step dad John in this man's eyes. He said to me Thank You, Thank You, Thank You. The man and I were in our own little zone. I knew it was dad telling me thank you for coming to see momma. I didn't want to let go. He didn't want to let go. It was a very awkward moment and then the woman spoke and brought us back. She said ok we've gotta go now. She told me I'm sorry and I said no problem. It was fine. I'm not real sure what she was sorry about. But it didn't really matter. I know what a wonderful, special, blessed experience I just got to have with my dad. I was a little shook up but I had to pull myself back together to go see momma. She has Alzheimer's and I wasn't sure if she really knew me the day before. I walked towards her on this day and I saw her face light up and I knew she knew who I was. She was so happy. We had a wonderful visit.

4/5/2009 As I walked up to the doors the man was there again and I said hello to him. I walked into the TV room filled with patients, with the nurses watching to see if momma would know me. As soon as she saw me she got really excited and happy and started saying my girl, my girl, over and over.

The nurses asked if she knew who I was and she said of course I do she's my girl, daughter. I was so happy. We had a wonderful visit. It was so hard to leave her there. I was leaving the next day so this was my last visit for a while. So I have to be happy with our phone calls. At least I get to hear her voice and make her laugh and she makes me laugh. Sometimes that just has to be good enough. I'm very lucky to still have my mother. When we talk most of the time she doesn't make any sense at all. But sometimes she talks like she's never had Alzheimer's. It's a very confusing disease for everyone that's involved. In the beginning I'd sometimes get my hopes up that maybe she was going to get better. That's the tricky part of the disease. I've watched the movie's about this several times and that helps me so much to deal and to try to understand what my momma is going through.

Sometimes we get so involved with what someone's disease has done to our lives and we kinda forget what it has done to the sick person. They're the ones that have lost everything to a horrible disease. Some people say the person with Alzheimer's can't remember them so they won't know if the person has called or visited them. As far as I know no one has come back from this disease and told anyone this so how can anyone say for sure if the calls and the visits are good and enjoyed by the sick person. It just might be the only bright spot in their very dark sad day. I could be wrong but I do know none of us will know for sure until we all pass away and talk about it in heaven. Some people just can't handle the phone calls or the visits to a nursing home. I never could handle sick people at all so I know how they feel. I just finally told myself if I could make anyone that is sick even a little happy then I've done a good thing. Hopefully I brighten my mommas days with our talks. She makes mine a lot better hearing her voice and laughing with her.

CHAPTER 9
SPIRITS

I've only seen one ghost for sure in my life. I've had a lot of dreams, visions, and feelings during my life. The only reason I know for sure that this was a ghost is because my husband Robbie saw it with me. We bought our first house from a elderly woman who had to move out to live with her family. She had lived in the house for about forty years. We don't know if the ghost was the woman who we bought the house from. It was about two years after we bought the house. Robbie and I let the kids sleep in our bedroom sometimes to watch TV late on the weekend. Robbie and I were sleeping on the sofa bed in the living room this one night. We were both sound asleep. It was just breaking daylight. I woke up and I felt a presence.

I looked to my right and there in the corner of the living room stood an elderly woman looking at us. I got very scared. I looked away. Then I looked back to make sure my eyes weren't playing tricks on me. She was still there. I put the cover over my head. Robbie whispered are you awake Bev? I said yes. He said do you see what I see? I said yes. He said the woman in the corner looking at us. I said yes. Then she just disappeared. Needless to say we couldn't fall back to sleep. She kinda glowed. She wore a beautiful long white nightgown. We were shook up over seeing a ghost in our house. But we knew it was ok because she didn't do anything but look at us. We didn't tell the kids about the ghost until we moved out of that house years later. They said we should have told them right away but they were way too young to tell them. We promised if we ever saw anymore that we'd tell them. We never thought we would have to keep that promise. Ten years later we bought a new house.

We bought the house November 2004. The spirits started coming June 2005. It was sometimes every few days sometimes every few weeks. No rhyme or reason to the visits. Our son Bobby Ray and his friend were driving their friends truck one night. It was the middle of June in Florida. No AC in the truck so the inside of the truck must have been about 80-90 degrees. All of a sudden it got very cold in the truck. The boys said it felt like about 40-50 degrees inside the truck. At this time they were friends but not best friends.

Bobby Ray came home and told us the story about the truck. At the time Bobby Ray wasn't doing anything real bad. He just wasn't doing anything real great. I told him it just sounded like his grandpa who is dead was trying to tell him something. Maybe to get him to straighten up or was warning him about something. Bobby told me he wasn't comfortable with ghosts and he wished grandpa wouldn't come see him. We tried to explain to him that he was lucky. He didn't think it was lucky to have a ghost riding with him. A few days later his friend got kicked out of his house. He came over and asked if he could stay the night at our house. We said yes. Bobby Ray wasn't home at the time.

Our friend from down south showed up and needed a place to stay for a few days so we said sure no problem. Bobby got home and him and his friend went out together. I told Robbie and our friend that Bobby and his friend would be best friends. They came home that night and they were the best of friends. They were together all the time for months. The next day Robbie saw a spirit in the living room. I later told him it was probably our friends dad coming to say thanks for letting his son stay. He had passed away about fifteen years earlier and he was a good friend of mine. The next day Robbie saw the same spirit again in the living room. Then the spirit left out the back door and a different spirit arrived looking for the first spirit. So Robbie told him which way he had went.

Later that day Bobby's friend needed a place to stay longer then just one night. So I told Robbie the second spirit was chasing the first to see how his son got to stay. Most people would be freaked out that their husband had seen a ghost, spirit, or whatever you want to call it. Not me I try to figure it out and rationalize what causes them to come to visit. The spirit world has always scared and amazed me. Three years later we joked about how the spirits came to our house. During the three years of ghosts and spirits, it was not a joking matter. I've decided that ghosts are the scary ones. Spirits are the friendly ones. Yes I've seen and dealt with both. We decided that when my sister and her husband came and stayed with us for a few days, that they brought the ghosts and spirits with them.

Before they came here they stayed in a well known haunted hotel. After they left we had our ghost problem so thats why we think they dropped them off at our house. We had lived in the house for six months and hadn't had any problems before their visit. So over the three years of ghosts the few people that we told our problem to all had different opinions on how to solve it. Of course some said sell the house and move. Some said look up the property on the internet. Some said bless the house. So we just kept doing what we always did. We'd read our spiritual books and our bible. We would buy spiritual pictures and statues that we liked. The following are just a few of the spirits that came during that three year period.

August 2005 We awoke at about 1:00am and we were so cold we shut the AC off. We layed back down. We got up about 3:00am Robbie said he was very cold. I was sweating. I walked over near him and it was so cold around him. I hugged him and almost three hours later I'm still cold with no AC on. September 4,2005 The ghost held us really tight. It held Robbie down first. Then it held me down with my arms crossed across my chest. It held me so tight that my chest still hurt for several days afterward. September 5,2005 I finally talked to someone about what had been going on in our house for the past three months. He was my customer at the store that was a retired preacher. He told me he would come and bless the house but I knew my husband probably wouldn't go for that. So he said he'd pray for us. So this night we didn't have any problems.

September 6, 2005 Our dog Rascal slept with us every night since we got him. Rascal woke us by sitting up in the bed in between us staring into the corner of our room. It was 4:30am. From that moment on Rascal was sick all day and night. I asked God to show us what our next step should be. September 7, 2005 We were woken by what we believe is a spirit. Sometimes we're held down, sometimes it just gets so cold in our room and our bodies that it wakes us up. It was 3:05am we turned the light on like we always do even if it doesn't make it go away it just makes us feel a little better. I had told my sister about the problem we were having and she told me to call her anytime of day or night. She was on the graveyard shift so we went into the kitchen and we called her. She is very spiritual and she keeps God in her life everyday.

So she prayed with us as we could feel this very cold spirit in our bodies. She prayed with us for a hour. She helped us so much. She was such a comfort at such a scary, crazy time in our lives. She told us different things to read. She sent us a box of books for us to read. She was our lifeline to God. We would have gone crazy without her help and her understanding. So after we got off the phone with her on this night we went back to bed with the light on. Rascal came into our bed for the first time since the day before he was really sick I was just finishing reading and the front door started shaking really hard. Robbie got up and let Rascal out. When Rascal came back in he looked healed. So then we started reading the marriage chapter it took us until 5:15am then we had to get Bobby Ray up for work. Robbie left at 5:50am to take the boys to work.

At 5:55am the water in the kitchen sink just started running without anyone turning it on. I tried to shut it off and it wouldn't shut off so I washed my hands in it then I tried to shut it off again. I was trying very hard to keep my sense of humor. It still wouldn't shut off. Then Rozie's bedroom door closed and I screamed. Rozie had gotten up and shut the door. So I asked Rozie to look at the running water in the sink. She finally got the water to shut off. September 8, 2005 We slept in bed until about midnight when the spirit came then we slept in the living room. September 9, 2005 We slept in the living room. Robbie heard something walking around the house. September 10, 2005 We slept in the living room. Robbie heard something walking around the house. September 11, 2005 Before I would sleep in the bedroom again I washed and bleached the sheets and blankets. I reckon I thought I could wash the spirits away. I was willing to try anything.

September 12, 2005 The spirit came at 4:30am we slept in the bed. September 13, 2005 The spirit came at 2:30am we slept in the bed. This was our lives now. Sometimes it was Every night for weeks at a time. Sometimes we'd get a day or two off then they'd come back. No kind of pattern no kind of reason. We were so exhausted. I was working during all of this at a Dollar Store. Some days I'd only have a hour or two of sleep then have to go to work. Life was so crazy. No one at work knew what was going on in my life.

They just knew I was very grouchy. Plus I decided to quit smoking April 2005 after smoking for thirty five years. This was two months before the spirits started. So to say I was being grouchy is putting it quite nicely. I was really cranky. Robbie was very sick so he wasn't working during these years. December 6, 2005 It was my day off. I had a great day with Robbie. When Rozie and John got home Rozie started putting Christmas lights up on the boys apartment. I made a big pot of sauce. As Bobby Ray got home from work some of their friends stopped by for a while. They had to take them home so we ate dinner then they ate when they got back. We had this family night planned for a week. We decorated the Christmas tree. Then we made Smores and ate them. We all joked about where we would watch the movie since our bedroom was haunted.

So we all got into our king size bed and watched the movie together. It was Robbie, Rozie, John, Beverly, and Bobby at the foot of the bed. Our family dog Rascal was near Bobby Ray. Rozies dog Rebel was between me and John. It was so cozy and loving. We laughed and joked and enjoyed. After the movie the kids went to bed. We went to sleep about midnight. At 2:22am Robbie started yelling get off me. In the name of Jesus get off me. I jumped up and turned the light on. I asked what happened even though I knew. I thought here we go again. I read to him until 3:18am. The spirit was laying between us. It got Robbie in a arm choke hold and had his head against Robbies head and ear and was whispering in a different language five or six words about three times. Robbie couldn't move. Robbie finally shook it loose and it left. He thought maybe he was dreaming so he checked the clock and himself.

Then he layed back down and a black shadow came across his head and grabbed him again. It didn't get a good grip so he shook him off. He was awake and saw this one coming so he shook it off easier. So then I layed down to go to sleep. I knew I wasn't sleeping yet and I felt something rolling me back and forth gently. It didn't hurt me but it scared me very badly. I said Robbies name about ten times but could only get very quiet whispers out of my mouth. When it finally quit rolling me I said are you ok to Robbie and he said yes. Then I got up and read. I was sitting outside waiting for Robbie to pick me up after work. I was trying to figure out my life. I want to make my living with my words and knowledge.

I try so hard but the almighty dollar doesn't come to me. I'm so tired of being stuck in that Dollar Store everyday. I've gotten a chance to meet a lot of nice people. The past few months with all the spirits and ghosts in the house. I just expected Something Great to happen. I'm kinda disappointed. I've learned a lot and nothing will ever surprise or shock me again after all that we have been through. Maybe I'm supposed to make Something Great happen. I'm not sure how but I'm gonna really start trying and we'll see what happens. My healing ability has puzzled me lately. Why can't I heal Robbie? Why can't I heal myself anymore? I've got to find my peace again within myself. Then hopefully my healing ability will return. Thank you God for letting me stay off of cigarettes. I did get my healing ability back as well as my peace of mind.

May 24, 2006 It usually got onto Robbie but this night when the spirit came it held me down. I fought and tried to yell. I finally broke loose and I kicked Robbie several times. One night when it got on me I was fighting it as hard as I could. I was trying to yell for help but no words would come out of my mouth. When I finally shook it off I yelled really loud for my oldest sister to help me. Our life continued like this for three very long years. As the years went by I started telling some people about it. I told partly so they could maybe understand why I was so tired and not acting like myself. And partly cause I hoped someone could help us get rid of them.

The first person besides my sister was of course my Aunt in New York who is my moms sister. She talked with her niece who gave us some prayers to say and told us about some books to read. We needed all the help we could get. These people didn't really know or realize what a big help they were being in our lives at this time of need. Every prayer, every suggestion, every time someone cared it helped us get through another night, week, month, and year of ghosts and spirits. I told a few of my close friends at work. They both had experienced spirits in their lives so they were really understanding. As the years went by we made it a house rule that we would tell anyone that was going to stay the night. Some believed. I reckon some thought we were crazy.

Robbie was really sick and we didn't know what was wrong at the time. He had been to so many doctors and we had spent so much money. He was so sick of doctors and medicines. So he thought maybe if he took it easy for a while and rested up he'd get better. He was going in and out of what the doctor later told us were mini comas. His thyroid was so out of line. It took the doctors four years of playing with his medicine and they still don't have it right yet. Every few months they check his blood and change his medicine. So Robbies cousin was very sick with cancer at this time. He had been fighting cancer for a few years but he still looked really good, We had just seen him a few months earlier. We thought he was going to beat the cancer.

So when Robbie called me into the living room one night to see his dead Grandma I got really scared. I wasn't afraid that I was seeing a spirit I was afraid that she was there to help Robbie pass away. We sat there looking at her for a few minutes. A few days later we got the phone call that Robbie's cousin had passed away. We decided she stopped to see how Robbie was doing on her way to help Robbies cousin pass away. The night before this we were in bed sleeping and Robbie awoke to some spirits. They were in the closet. He saw a tall older man, a short older man and a older woman. She floated over the bed to Robbie. She asked very nicely How are you feeling? He said not so good. She said ok and floated back to the closet and the three of them left into the closet. Another night of spirits.

December 2007 The spirits only come once in a while now. This is what we've chosen to call them. It sounds so much more friendly then GHOSTS. The mean ones are GHOSTS. We hadn't had a spirit for a while. So when Robbie started yelling I woke up not knowing what was going on. I finally got my senses together and I lunged for the light switch. We always feel better once the light is on even if the light doesn't scare them away. The last one's were a few weeks ago. We always hope they're gone for good when we don't have one for a few days or weeks. Then they start right back up again. We talked and prayed then we went back to sleep. I woke up to use the restroom and the light was already on from the spirit earlier in the night. I looked at my husband Robbie sleeping and he looked like he was fighting for his life. He was thrashing all over the bed. I was scared.

I knew I had to wake him up. I was so afraid for him with all that fighting that he'd have a heart attack. I was afraid for me that he'd think I was whoever or whatever he was fighting. I shook his leg and foot and said his name Robbie wake up. No luck. So I got more forceful and yelled his name. This time he woke up. He was fighting a spirit that was grabbing our daughter Roseanne. He got up and went and checked on Roseanne sleeping in her bed to make sure she was ok. She was fine.

Our lives had overwhelmed us. We just weren't sure how much more we could handle. We had read so many books, we had bought so many beautiful crosses, statues, and pictures of angels, Jesus, and Mary. The house was filled up. My youngest son John would tell friends that would come over my mom isn't really a religious freak she just likes all of this stuff. So three years after this all started Robbie found a Christian Store and bought me some presents for my birthday. The next month his brother and sister in law were coming up to visit us for the first time. He wanted to go back to the Christian Store and buy them something. So he brought me to the store. I saw the holy oil and I asked him if I could buy it to bless the house. He said yes of course you can. That night I prayed and blessed our house and our sons apartment next to our house.

This was April 2008. As I was blessing the houses I remembered my mom saying that you had to get your house blessed by a priest when you moved into a new house. I thought to myself I hope my prayers work as good as a priests prayers. I put the sign of the cross all over the house with the holy oil as I prayed. I put crosses on all the windows with the holy oil. I put crosses on all the peoples foreheads that were home even if they were sleeping. I put the sign of the cross on all the dogs foreheads. It had been one year since we had a spirit. We still read and buy spiritual stuff. It was a very scary three years and a great learning experience. Robbie and I can face anything now after all that. Our family became stronger and more caring about each other from having to deal with the spirits all those years. There was a lot more events of spirits then what I was able to list in this book. I just wanted to give ya all a idea of what we went through.

The next time a young child says they saw the boogeyman try to be more understanding they just might be telling the truth. We saw it and felt it for three years. Its Scary. No spirits for one year and four months. The night before Robbie was going away for a few days we talked about the spirits. So that night when I woke up to Robbie chanting some words. I jumped up and turned on the light. I tried to wake Robbie up. When I touched him he was ice cold. I thought Oh no not again and not when he's fixing to go out of town. I kept trying to wake him up. Finally after about five minutes I woke him up. He said he wan't sure if it was a dream or a spirit. He kept saying hopefully it was a dream. He had been planning this pool trip for months. So I told him sure it was probably just a dream. I wanted him to be able to leave without feeling guilty. Besides the last time he left town the spirit came to me the first night. Then it found him in South Carolina in the motel room. So we knew there was no running from them. It wasn't just the house it was something to do with us too.

So Robbie left the next day. Later that day I blessed the house. I wasn't taking any chances this time. I like living without ghosts and spirits. No offense. I don't mind talking to spirits but I just don't want to do it when I'm trying to sleep. I don't like when they hold me down it hurts and scares me. I don't like when they get into my body, it's too cold. I believe there's a place and time for everything. Having ghosts and spirits hanging out in your house everyday was just too much. They even had come during the day when we would try to take naps cause we weren't sleeping at night. So hopefully the blessing of the house with the holy oil worked again this time. It's been three years with no spirit visits.

CHAPTER 10
FORGIVENESS

December 2008

My husband Robbie and our oldest son Bobby Ray went back to our hometown to go commercial fishing. They were in the best spot in Southwest Florida for great chicken wings in Bonita Springs, Florida. They saw my brother and his buddy. My brother and I hadn't spoken in two years at this time. That was the last time he had allowed me to speak to our mother on the phone. Thanksgiving 2006. I have had nothing good to say about my brother since he took my mother away from me. She has Alzheimer's. When I talked to her all the time she knew me. We had great talks on the phone. We'd laugh, we'd cry, we'd just be mother and daughter. Two years later she doesn't know who I am some of the time.

They put mom into a nursing home in October 2008 so now I talk to her all the time on the phone. I live three hundred miles away for the past four years. Some of the time it might just be my wishful thinking that she knows me. I was very close to my mother all my life. We'd talk almost everyday. Sometimes several times a day. He knew how to hurt me. It almost destroyed me. He had one sister on his side. Then another sister joined in. It was ok cause I still had two sisters that loved me and knew I didn't deserve this horrible treatment. My cousins, aunt, and uncle just couldn't believe that no one would step in and let momma call me during those two long years. They all offered to call him and try to talk some sense into him.

But I said no this is between me and my brother. We use to be so super close no one could believe or understand what could have caused him to turn on me like this. They say its because I moved and left them mom, but I begged momma to move with us but she said she wanted to see what they were made of. I hated him so much and I told everyone who would listen to me. I got plenty of sympathy from everyone but I still hurt so badly. I went down on vacation about eight months after he started doing this to me. I didn't tell anyone exactly when I was coming except one of my sisters since I was gonna be staying with her. So I was able to sneak into town and go see mom at her daycare. The first day she had no clue who I was or she was being her old self. She might have been making me pay for staying away and not calling for so long.

Whatever the reason it killed me. The hurt was so deep and unbelievable. A few days later I went back to see her. She yelled out my name when she saw me from across the room. I'll remember that moment until the day that I die. It was such a wonderful, warm, amazing feeling. My kids Rozie and John were with me both times. They were so happy during the second visit. Not only did he take my mother away from me but he had taken my kids grandma away from them. They were all very close to their grandma. So then vacation was over and I had to go back home three hundred miles away from my mother. Then it was one and a half long years of not being able to talk to her. I kept calling and hoping he'd pick the phone up one day and let me talk to her. No luck. I was so angry. It got worse the more my Aunt who is mom's only sister and my sister from out of state would tell me how bad mom was getting.

I told everyone if he died I wouldn't go to the funeral. The hate was so deep it was eatting me up. I was not me anymore. I was a hater. It was April 2008 and my husband Robbie and our son Bobby Ray went down south to our hometown to pick up our boat. They saw my brother and he told them that he was so sorry about not letting me talk to my mother. He said that I could call mom anytime and he'd let me talk to mom again. I told them he was lying and was just afraid that they would kick his butt for everything he had put me through. So for six months here I was all excited again and trying to call my mom. He never let me talk to her. Sometimes he'd pick up the phone and I'd get all happy and then he'd just hang it back up. No words, no nothing. No one will ever know or understand the torture to my heart and soul he was causing me.

I always treated him like he was my own child. The love I had for him had turned to complete hate. I could not figure out what would cause anyone to turn against someone that badly. Most likely I'll never know. So then it was October 2008. All of a sudden I was falling apart for no reason. I was dreaming about mom, thinking about mom, crying about mom. I was worrying that she was dying. I was crying over nothing. I was crying over everything. I was totally freaking out for two weeks. My husband Robbie and our kids didn't know what to do with me. I didn't call any of my family during the two weeks of my break down. I was too crazy to talk to anyone. Then my brothers sister that use to be close with me called me on October 23.2008.

She told me mom had been in the hospital for a week very sick. Then the hospital wouldn't let her go back home, they sent her to a nursing home. She had been in a nursing home for a week. So my two weeks of hell was caused by my mom's two weeks of hell. We were always so very close so this all made so much sense to me. I was so mad that no one had called me sooner. What if she would have died in that hospital. If they would have called us from the very beginning then my family and I wouldn't have gone through those horrible two weeks of me falling apart. I only live five hours away. I could have come down to see her in the hospital. So I let my sister know how pissed off I was at all of them. But me being pissed off didn't make any of it any better it just made me very sad that none of them cared enough about me to have called me.

Today is December 12,2008. So back to my husband being in our hometown. I got a phone call from Robbie on my way home from work. He said he saw my brother and his buddy. After a while the buddy left my brother there with Robbie and Bobby Ray. I don't know if it had anything to do with the last time they had seen Robbie together and my brother had promised to let me talk to my mom six months earlier and never did. So my brother pleaded his case to my men. He of course blamed a lot of it on everyone but himself. He said how he wanted me to meet his daughter. He said how he was so sorry. So then it was time to leave and he had to ride with my husband and son. So he climbed into the middle of my two men in the cab of Robbies pickup.

He asked them is this the time where you drive me out to East Bonita woods? Robbie said why do you deserve that. He said yes. So Robbie took him home. So when Robbie was done telling me all this I got mad at Robbie for being so nice to my brother. I felt so betrayed by the person who is so close to me, my soul mate, my husband. Robbie heard the anger in my voice. He said stop yelling at me. I hadn't even raised my voice. But he knew how mad I was. I said you're always telling me how I'll be the first one to forgive him and then its you. So we decided we'd better talk later and let me drive home from work. I had a thirty four mile drive. I cried and then I called Rozie our daughter for a pick up speech. I put myself in her shoes if this was her and one of my sons fighting like this. Should I forgive my brother is all I could think about. That was the big question that I couldn't find the answer.

A few hours later Rozie returned my call with bad news about a friends family that she knew. The boys Aunt had passed away and the boys dad the Aunts brother had found her. Oh Lord is this a sign? I felt so bad for this wonderful family who didn't deserve to be hurting like this. So I prayed for them. Then I had to get back to my problem. Should I forgive. I asked Daddy, my big brother Ray Ray, my step dad, and my grandparents all who are deceased to please help me to decide. I asked God for a big sign not a small one that I wouldn't understand. Then I went to take a bath. This is where I do my best praying. It's such a peaceful spot for me. I got a very simple sign. My prayers were answered. It was time to forgive. All I heard was Joseph forgave his brothers who had sold him into Slavery. What a beautiful sign. I thanked everyone. I thanked God.

I got out of the tub and the phone rang. It was my cousin who is like a brother to me. I named my first born child after my cousin. That's how close we are. So I ranted and raved to him about my brother. He listened like he always does. He told me to let it out. He made me laugh at me and at my brother. That was part of my forgiveness. So then I sat down to watch some TV. I started channel surfing. I stopped on some Gospel music not because I needed to hear some which I really did. But because I saw a guy on the TV that looked exactly like a cross between my dead brother Ray Ray and my brother that I was trying to forgive.

Cold chills went through my body as I backed it up and paused it and sat there and I cried as I looked at this man. I knew this was Gods big sign for me. It was a sign that went straight to my heart and soul. It was really time to forgive. I sat there and I really enjoyed the gospel music. I really enjoyed watching this long haired man with all of his emotion he put into the songs and his amazing voice and the way he looked just like my two brothers. He was the final sign to help me become a good person again and be able to forgive my brother for taking my mother away from me. I'm really as surprised about this forgiveness as everyone else is. I feel great since I heard the sign and then saw the sign on the TV. I knew seeing this man sing for the first time when I needed to forgive my brother was a huge sign.

I really shouldn't ask for signs from God but I just get overwhelmed sometimes and just don't know what to do without help. I can forgive my brother and his two sisters. They can be my sisters again if they want to be. I will have a brother again. Now its all up to them. We'll see what happens. No matter what happens I get to feel better about myself. I also get to talk to my mom anytime I want to which is great. We laugh together again. We tell each other how much we love each other and how much we miss each other. I tell her stories. She tells me stories. It doesn't matter if either one of us understands the stories. We have each other again. I sent her a package of new clothes and shoes and I know she got them. The nurses tell me how nice my mom is. This one day mom and I were having a great time on the phone. The nurse got on the phone and asked if I was still on the phone. I said yes. She said mom was having such a good time she just wanted to make sure mom was still talking to me.

I laughed and said yes mom and I always have a lot of fun together. I now have my momma back. I hope and pray that God will let me keep her for a long time. I feel so much better with her in my life. I'm forty eight years old but I still need my mommy. The sound of her voice just soothes me. I'm going to go see her for the first time in one and a half years. We had some illnesses, a knee operation, and my husband had major back surgery. So there hasn't been any vacations during the past one and a half years. I can't wait to hug my momma. The best hug in the world is my momma's hugs. The love just pours out of her and into me. It makes me so happy. I can feel the happiness all the way to my soul.

I've met so many people along the road of my life. They come and go. There's reasons to the seasons of life. I always figure anything new is a new adventure in my life. A time to meet new people. Some people stay in my life for a long time. Some stay in my life for a short time. Some come and go in my life a few times. When the new adventure is over I look back at all the people that had traveled through my life during that adventure. I think about how they effected me and how I effected their life. the good and the bad effects. My husband Robbie has been in my life for thirty nine years. He came and went during our childhoods, our teens, and our twenties. He's been a constant through our thirties and our forties.

I've always wanted everyone I meet to like me. I'm always looking for approval. I believe most people do like me. But there's been some people that just dislike me for whatever the reasons. That use to drive me nuts. I was always on a mission to get them to like me. Now I am just as nice and pleasant as I can be to everyone I meet. Hopefully they'll all like me but the ones that don't are missing out on having a really good friend. Me. A few years ago Robbie and I started out on a new adventure. We moved three hundred miles from home. This was the hardest move of my life. I was leaving my mother, my three sisters, and my brother behind. Plus all my friends. It had been home for thirty two years. I was so afraid plus not wanting to leave everyone. The move made complete sense for my husband and three kids lives.

So it was something I had to do to stay in their lives. You don't always have complete control over your life. I could have had a fight with my husband over this or at the worst left him to stay close to my family. But no matter what, I knew I wanted to keep our family unit together. I knew this move would be great for our two youngest kids that were just getting into high school. It was hard leaving lifetime friends behind. But the worst was leaving my one sister and my brother since we were in the middle of a fight. This would either mend our relationship or destroy it. Three years later the relationships were pretty much destroyed. But the up side was my life with my husband Robbie and our three kids was PERFECT. So I had been having this war of hurtful words and thoughts going on between me and my sister and brother for three years. It hurts me everyday that this is going on between us.

They didn't want me to leave and not help with mom anymore. They felt like I was dumping her on them. After three and a half years of fussing with them I was dreaming about them a lot. So Robbie said its time you mend things with them. So I sent my sister a forward email. She wrote back that she had been thinking about me too. It was getting close to Christmas so my next step was to send them both Christmas cards. So we'll see what happens. They may hate me forever. But for the sake of my mind and soul I need to make peace with them. So after the ice breaker with my sister we talked on the phone one night for over a hour.

It was great just like no time had gone by at all. I heard through the grapevine of the family that my brother wanted to talk to me again. The same thing he had told my husband So then we got a wedding invitation to my nieces wedding in April 2009. At first I said no way would I do that to my niece. What if our first meetings turned out bad I didn't want that to happen at her wedding. Then we talked about it and we decided it would be perfect time to become a family again. My nerves about drove all the family crazy leading up to our trip back home for the wedding and for the forgiveness between me and my sisters and my brother. The wedding was the perfect spot. The forgiveness was perfect. It was like there was never a problem to start with. We talked about it just a little bit. For the most part we all just enjoyed each others company. We were family again. I got to meet my beautiful four year old niece for the first time, my brothers daughter. She is the sweetest little girl. I'm looking forward to many more visits with her and my brother. It was a wonderful homecoming. I had three great visits with my momma at the nursing home. I had been able to forgive and they were able to forgive me. We are a family once again.

Momma has always been very psychic. She always said way before she was even old or sick that no one better ever put her into a nursing home. It kinda became a joke. She would say how she would fatuchanada them. I reckon she always knew she'd end up in a nursing home. How sad that must have been all those years always worried about that even when you're in good health. She sure didn't have much faith in all of us kids. I only hope and pray my kids don't have to put me or my husband into a nursing home. Forgiveness is moving forward in life. If you move the bad out of your life you make room for some good to come into your life My brother took care of mom the best he could for as long as he could..

I was getting ready to type this piece on my computer. So I went to the TV to put music on like I always do when I'm going on my computer. I was channel surfing for music. I stopped at the first music it was gospel music. So I sat down and watched it. It was the gospel band that the man who looks so much like my brothers was singing. I didn't type that day I just sat and I enjoyed the music.

CHAPTER 11
BEV'S THOUGHTS

My cousin is like a brother to me. He has been my rock in my life forever. He's always there with love, time, caring, and smart words for me. I thank God all the time for him being in my life. Thank God we've always been there for each other. I wish my real brother loved me as much as my cousin loves me. God really blessed me when he gave me him as my cousin. Our mothers are sisters. My Aunt is my second mother. She has always been like a mother to me. We have always been super close all my life. She has helped me so much during these hard years with my mom. God really knew what he was doing when he gave me my cousin, my aunt and my uncle, I named my first son after my uncle and my cousin. My son's middle name is after my daddy and my brother Ray. My aunts daughter has also felt like having another sister. Just a nicer sister. She always had more patience with me then my real sisters. Her husband felt like my brother in law. This family has always been my second family. Thank you God for my second family.

My third family was my daddy's brothers family. My aunt and uncle were so totally amazing. They were like my kids grandparents. We all lived close for quite a few years so we'd go to their house to visit. We'd see them at church, the beach, and at stores. We'd be at all the family parties together and the small get-togethers at mom's house. My uncle fixed our TV's. Our first house we put a new living room addition on and he gave us all the electric stuff we needed. They were there for all the baptisms, communions with their camera snapping. It was like having and hanging onto a part of my real dad my uncles brother. At least my kids got a piece of my daddy from my uncle. When they moved away I was heartbroken but I knew they needed to be closer to their kids and grandkids.

Then for some reason that I'll never really understand God took them both back home to heaven within a few years of each other. I was so totally blown away by their passing. I just can't ever imagine what their kids and grandkids are feeling. I'm just so glad they had a chance to live closer for a few years.

Families never really know how much time they have together that's why forgiveness is such a wonderful thing. My daddy's sisters family was a big part of my life when I was younger. All of her kids were older then me so I didn't spend as much time with them as I did the others growing up. The other families had my playmates. I was always close to my aunts kids when I'd see them. I remember when I was a teenager up in New York for a visit. My aunts son and I were sitting in the back of a pickup truck watching a baseball game just talking our heads off. He was a lot older then me but I was so happy that we were still close enough to have stuff to talk about. My aunt always made me feel so special when we'd go to her house when we were kids. The love she had for us was such a great feeling. The last time I saw her was at my aunt and uncle's house a few years before they moved back up north. She still made me and my kids feel so loved. What a special, wonderful. loving aunt she is.

We'd go years without seeing each other and then see each other and it was like no time had gone by at all. I use to be really good about doing Christmas cards to everyone to keep up with all my cousins and their lives. Then my life, my kids, and not enough time came along. I always kept up with everyone's lives through my cousin. I should have kept in touch myself. When my cousin died I called my daddy's sisters daughter. We talked like no time had passed. It was about twenty years since the last time I had saw her. A few weeks later I talked to my cousin's sister and we talked like no time had gone by and it had been about seventeen years since we had talked. Families have that special bond that knows no time. Thank Goodness.

The first time I saw my best friend at the retail store I knew we'd be best friends. She looked and acted like a combination of my mom, and my three Italian Aunts. I just loved her personality the first two minutes. We were laughing together that quickly. We've been working and laughing and griping together for four years now. She has become part of my family and me a part of her family. The only problem is we live thirty five miles from each other. No matter where our lives take us I'm pretty sure she and I will stay best friends for life. Our customers just have a blast with us. We get everyone to having a good time. We've even met with our husbands and her mom at our favorite BBQ restaurant a few times. We're family.

The rest of this is going to be some of my thoughts. That doesn't make them right but I think they make some kind of sense. They're about all different kinds of things. So here they are.

2/2004 I've been writing this book for almost two months now. Life has been hectic because I've been getting ready to move since I started writing this book. But my mind has been clear and I've been able to write. I've gotten moved and only lost one day of writing. Last night I had a vision of my son and I was so happy. I was worried that since I had moved back to the city I might lose my inner peace that I had found on that beautiful island we had lived on for six and a half years. I'm so happy that I've kept my inner peace. We moved back to the town Robbie and I had grown up in. This town has grown a lot while we were gone. Being back around all the people and traffic will be a challenge. But my husband had a feeling that we needed to come home. I fussed with him for a few months. Then I finally realized his feelings are like my visions.

We've got to believe and trust them. There's a reason that we needed to come home and someday we'll find out why. For now we are putting our lives in Gods hands and letting him lead the way. God has never steered us wrong before so we just have to keep the faith. We believe that everything happens for a reason. I'm sitting on a dock right now with birds chirping and flying around. I'm watching fish swim by. That's Gods way of saying yes everything will be ok.

I believe you should have God in your life everyday. Not just on Sunday and Wednesday nights. If you see someone walking down the road or riding a bike and you can tell that its not for exercise. Say a prayer for them. They need it. If you see someone broke down or a flat tire. Feel bad for them. Say a prayer for them. I would say stop and help but we all know the world we live in now we can't always stop and help strangers in need. That's not our fault that's because of the few that ruined it for all of us. If you see someone driving a old clunker car, feel sorry for them. Say a prayer for them. Maybe they're just in a bad spot in their life and a nice prayer might just help them out. You should Thank God for all the little things in life as well as for all the big things in life. For example: a parking spot, a good sale, a ball hit, a ball caught, a fish caught, your car or truck, flowers, kids, parents, your life. Some say you'd be thanking God all the time and yes what's wrong with that. Since without God you wouldn't have a life to begin with.

Every night when I tuck my three kids into bed we'd say our prayers together. Some nights it was a very serious thing. Some nights there would be one of the kids that would just get the giggles and then we'd all be wrecked. This was our time to pray, laugh, and reflect on the day we had just lived. Some nights when my son's wouldn't feel like praying they'd speed pray to get it done quicker. It didn't really matter at least they were praying. We'd always say a special prayer for their daddy Robbie when he was out Commercial Fishing. We'd pray for his safety, and for a good catch of fish. Then we'd always say a special prayer for my parents, the kids loved their grandparents so much. Then they'd take turns reading the Ten Commandments. Sometimes they'd argue over who's turn it was so I'd let all of them read the Ten Commandments. The oldest boy would get the younger ones mad because he knew them by heart and would just say them while the younger ones were trying to read them. In the end at least they got to learn them and hopefully obey them. We had a lot of fun during prayer time. Rascal our dog loved prayer time.

Sometimes mothers just know things or maybe it's just me, I really don't know. We were at a Halloween party at my sister's house. My daughter Rozie was four years old. She was a very active child. She was playing on the monkey bars with a bunch of kids. She fell off the monkey bars and came in crying and said her arm hurt. So I was ready to take her to the hospital but I thought maybe I'm over reacting. She was always climbing trees and playing rough on the swing sets. So everyone said she probably just bruised it and was crying cause she was tired. So I put her down to sleep. So the next day I asked her all day long did her arm hurt and she said just a little bit. So the next day was Monday so we asked her again how she felt and she said fine so we sent her to Pre-K. A few hours later I got a call from her teacher at work that I needed to take her to get a x-ray cause her arm hurt. Oh I felt like the worst mother in the world. Then it got worse. We got it x-rayed and she had a broken arm.

I knew I was the worst mother in the world. The doctor must have seen that look on my face because he said it happens all the time and that it wasn't my fault. That it was such a small break and it didn't really swell much. But of course I still knew just knowing me and who I am I should have gone with my first thought and I should have taken her that night.

There should be spiritual support groups like meetings. If there already is spiritual groups there needs to be more since I've never heard of any or seen any in any of the newspapers that I've read. I know all the churches have a lot of support and prayer groups. But your spiritual needs don't always fit into a specific religion. I could have used a support group all those years. I had more needs and questions then the Catholic Church could help me with. I remember my best friend at church on Pine Island was trying to help me find some of my answers. She was telling me to get some books from our church's library to read. Which I did and they were really wonderful. But I needed more so I went to the public library and found a lot of books there that helped me to understand what was happening in my body and my life.

Everyone needs to know that they belong. Life is much easier when you belong to a group or something and you can feel normal. I feel so much better about myself after all my reading and studying for the past eight years. I've learned that I'm not weird. I'm just one of God's children that kept my gifts that were given to me when I left heaven to come down here for this life. There are so many kids and adults out there in this world that have these gifts and they don't understand them. Some people are afraid of their gifts like I used to be. I want to reach everyone and tell them don't be afraid anymore. Embrace your gifts. Enjoy your gifts.

I was talking to a woman one day about colds and flu season. She told me that she gets pneumonia every year. I told her to start praying right now that she doesn't get pneumonia this year and she probably wouldn't get it this year. She looked at me like I was nuts. I told her how I use to get tonsillitis every year all my life. The last time I had it was shortly before I had turned back to God. It was about 1994. I was sick in bed for about a week on all the doctors medicines. My sister had been helping me find my way back to God and I finally got there. Thanks Sister I will always be grateful. Some people don't like people talking to them about God but I'm so glad my sister kept talking to me about God all those years. I just couldn't imagine how my life would have turned out without God in it. My kids are better people for having God in their lives. People say three's a crowd. For my marriage its the perfect number to make it work. My husband Robbie, Me, and God.

Sometime in life at a certain age you have to get over all the crap that happened to you during your childhood. A lot of people have had very bad childhoods. Some were completely horrible. Some were abusive. Some were physical abuse others were mental abuse. To me its all abuse and it all leaves very bad scars on innocent children. All the babies in the world that are born and grow into children and then on to be adults should only be loved. There should never be any kind of abuse on any of God's children. You have to take responsibility as an adult on what kind of person you want to be and move forward in life. You have to start enjoying your life. A lot of people have very bad childhoods but that doesn't mean they have to have a bad adulthood. You need and can take control of your life and say I want a GREAT LIFE! Then you need to start doing everything you can so you can enjoy your life. Everyone deserves a wonderful life. GOD WANTS US ALL TO HAVE A GREAT LIFE!

You shouldn't try to change the person you fall in love with. You fell in love with that person for who they were. So many times the deeper the love grows the more you try to change them. It seems like the more you learn about them, you think you can fix them. The only person that can change them is themselves. Everyone changes some as the years go by. You should just try to change together. No one is perfect. Not even you or me. You can't change them into the perfect person. You're not perfect so why do you think they should be perfect. Change is very hard for people. It's even harder when someone is forcing it on them. Don't try to change the one you love. You should change the way you love them. If you change them too much they won't be the person you fell in love with in the first place.

It only takes once, you can play chance with your life. The first time you do drugs you can overdose and die. No one knows when it will happen to them. It could be the first high you get or it could be years down the road when you think you know how much your body can handle. I've known so many people in my lifetime that have died from drug overdoses and accidental medications not mixing right with their other medications. Some have been personal friends some have been singers and actors. What they all have in common is they're such sad and senseless deaths no matter who you are.

Some people say when its your time to go its just your time. I think God gives us the chance to not be in the wrong place or to be doing the wrong things. I think if you're not there doing something then you might get to live. The poor people that die from their medications not mixing right have put their trust in doctors that just didn't know that it was going to cause death by mixing the medications. God wants people to make the right choices. God doesn't make all your choices for you. Before you do anything you have to think to yourself how is this action going to affect my life. You have to think to yourself how is this action going to affect my kids lives. How is it going to affect everyone's lives that I love and care about. If people slowed down and thought about that before they made rash decisions there would be a lot more happiness in this world.

The reality of life is the first time you have sex you can get pregnant. No one ever knows when it will happen to them. Most people just think about the sex part and the passion. A lot of them don't think about the baby part of it. This is how we make babies. Before you have sex with someone you should be thinking do I want to have a baby with this person. If the answer is no you shouldn't have sex with them. Before teens have sex they should be asking themselves if they want to be teen parents. If the answer is no why take the chance when you're too young to raise a baby. Some people say every baby is a gift from God. I do believe that too. I also believe everyone is in control of their own life and what will happen. I've just heard so many teens say after they had the baby that they should have waited until they were older and more ready for all the work and responsibility that comes with raising kids.

Who are we to judge? Why should we be able to say who marries who? We don't have to agree with it but we shouldn't be able to tell each other what to do with our individual lives. We all come into this world alone and we all die alone. Our souls make this journey alone. In between being born and dying we should all be able to do what we want with our lives. As long as we don't hurt anyone or do anything against the law on our journey through our lives.

Robbie and I went to buy a boat and motor. We grew up with the guy we were buying it from. He told us about this great deal he could make us on this motor. So we said yes to the deal. Then we were walking back to the office after looking at the motor.

The salesman found a dollar bill on the ground. I thought to myself he got a gift from God for being so nice to us. When you're cleaning the house or doing laundry and you find change or dollars. Your first thought might be it is such little payment for such big jobs. You should think thank you God for the money. What you received is better then nothing. Some people throw their pennies away like they're not worth anything. Enough pennies saved up will one day be dollars. I've seen some cashiers say stuff and look down on people paying for their purchases with change. Those people worked just as hard for that change as they did for the dollars that the cashiers take without saying a word.

Rozie was fourteen years old and our finances were tough because our motor had blown on our commercial fishing boat. Times were really tough. Rozie and I were talking and I was real sad. I said we're going backwards because of the money problems we were having. Rozie said we just stopped, we're paused. She said its like somebody put us on pause then they'll come back and push play and everything will be ok again. That is a wonderful look into a fourteen year olds take on life problems. She and I both laughed so hard at this and at life.

Some people don't believe in the hereafter until someone close to them dies. They find out that they need to believe so they won't go crazy. They need to believe so they can look forward to seeing that person in heaven someday.

I have two best friends. They've been my best friends for thirty nine years. We never hung out as a threesome. I'd spend as much time as I could with each one. They are the two people that have always known me the best besides my husband, my three kids, my sisters, and my brothers. I'm sure they're gonna be in for a few surprises as they read this book. I'm sure my family and everyone I know will learn a lot about me when they read this book. I shared some things with some people. But not everything with no one. My two best friends and I stray away from each other with our busy lives but we always come back to each other. When we live away from each other we write and call each other. When we talk on the phone its like we've never been away from each other. When we get to finally see each other again its like we've spent no time away from each other.

The past six years while I've been writing this book I haven't kept in touch as much as I use to. Between my book and raising my kids most of my time has been taken up. I was very lucky to get to live next door to my best friend for three months before I moved to Dixie County. We got to visit with each other quite a bit. It was so hard being that close cause I wanted to go over to her house everyday, but I didn't want to intrude either. It made my move away from our hometown harder but I'm so glad we got to have that time together.

I'm just passing through this life. I'm over there then I'm over here. I'm in people's lives then I'm out of their lives. Nothings forever. If you're lucky enough to find someone you can call your best friend. Someone you can trust and totally count on. Someone you connect with physically, mentally, and spiritually. They're most likely your soul mate. You should marry that person. Jobs come and they go. Everyone you meet is for a reason. They needed you or you needed them in your life. Everyone makes a difference in your life. Some make a good difference some a bad difference. You have to have the bad to enjoy the good.

All I want to do is live my life. I don't want any upsets in my world. I don't want to have to fight or argue with anyone to make it through my day. I want someone to love and I want them to love me with all their heart and soul. I want to live happy. I just don't think thats asking for too much out of life.

Everyone is looking for their paradise. They go on vacations to beautiful beaches. They think that they've found their paradise. Some people move to these vacation spots to live in their paradise. They start working and living day to day. Sometimes they lose their paradise. You don't have to have a sandy beach to make you happy. Your paradise is where ever you are. You have to make your life a paradise where ever you are living. Your paradise is in your heart and soul.

Some call him a redneck, country boy, or a Florida cracker. I call him my friend. People can't always handle or deal with a guy/gal friendships. They sometimes say that there's more to it. Not always. I've had a lot of boy/girl, man/woman friendships over the years. We've been buddies for thirty years. Never a kiss just buddy hugs.

A shoulder to cry on sometimes. A smile to make you laugh at life. We both have a lot of like, love, and respect for each other. We go years without seeing each other but that doesn't change the friendship that we started all those years ago. There is always a big bear hug when we see each other again. We have been through weddings, kids, divorces, deaths, and our friendship keeps going on and on. He asked me about thirty years ago to be a pall bearer in his funeral and I said yes of course I would be. I told him I hope its not anytime soon. The way he's going I'm hoping to be the first hundred year old woman pall bearer. Thanks for our friendship friend.

I believe you never really die if you've touched someone during your life. You'll always be remembered for the things you said and the things you did. You'll live on forever through the people's lives that you touched. When those people touch someone else with something you had touched them with. A act of kindness, a saying, some advice you gave, a recipe, just caring about someone. You never really die if you've touched someone in your life.

My sister and I had been fussing with each other. So I got to church and I prayed to God to give me a sign if I should call my sister. When I got done praying a bird flew past the church window. I thought to myself well that wasn't much of a sign. So I went about the rest of my day. At 8:30pm that same night I sat down to read my church bulletin. The first thing that caught my eye was Forgiveness. So I read that first. It said if a bad person wrongs you. Forgive them lest there be two bad people. So I picked up the phone and called my sister and we talked for two hours.

They have all kinds of classes at school that are supposed to get you ready to become a adult and live out in the world. I think there should be a class on how to choose a husband or wife. That's a spot that a lot of people seem to have a lot of problems doing. Girls try very hard to be all pretty and girly for the guys all through school. When a guy gets ready to get married he wants someone he has a lot in common with. He likes the pretty girls but he sure likes his wife to like to watch sports and do guy stuff with him. Some woman don't like to help with the yard work but they want to give their opinion. Some girls like a tough, manly guy. Then they marry him and they buy him all kinds of clothes that they think he should wear.

Saying good bye is hard. Saying I'll miss you is true. We all say we'll keep in touch, that's the hardest thing to do when life takes hold of you. It's much easier nowadays to keep in touch with the internet. New friends come, old friends go. Some we keep, some we never know again. We spend years with some friends, then you see them a few years later and they treat you like a stranger. Graduation happens to everyone. Some don't receive the piece of paper but everyone moves on from school. It's a exciting, scary, fun time of the unknown to come. Some go through those graduation doors with boyfriends, girlfriends, best friends, new babies on the way. What ever the case may be it's the way God meant it to be.

You helped me so much while we were growing up. I was ten years older then you. But you were my best buddy. I got to stay a kid much longer then most. I always had to have you with me so I made the best of it. I loved playing with your race tracks and cars. We loved to wrestle like on TV. We played baseball but you always wanted to be up to bat. My friends sometimes griped about you tagging along. But I didn't care. I enjoyed having my best buddy with me. We'd sit for hours playing in your sand box. We went fishing almost everyday. We loved to go to the beach. We'd swim forever if we could. My best buddy, my little brother. We had the time of our life together. You were always with me. We didn't think it would ever change. Then we grew up and apart. Oh my best buddy, my little brother please come back into my life.

My daughter Roseanne your sweet smile brightens up my whole life. Those words I love you make my day. That sleepy little face in the morning turns into a smile that lasts all day. I can tell when you're sad or when your feelings are hurt. The beautiful smile turns to the saddest little face. A few kind words from me and that smile comes back even bigger. Your happiness spreads to everyone you come close to. When someone is sad your kind words or actions put a smile back on their faces. You are so special just like a Rose. I will miss my Rose when you go. You've been my daughter, my best friend, my sister since I never gave you one. You've turned out to be such a loving and caring young lady. I'm so proud of the woman you are becoming. When you have a daughter she will be so lucky to have you as a mother. You have mothered your brothers all these years. You love and care so deeply.

My son John keeps me young. He always wants me to play with him. We play a lot of games together. When we're at the beach we are always the last ones out of the water. He is quiet and shy to the world. But around me he is very outgoing and always has something to say. Whenever we're really happy we do our happy dance together that we made up years ago. He's always been my musical child. He loved to play all instruments. I hope he sticks with it. Now that everyone is grown and he's the last child home. Robbie, me, and John still play games together. When he moves out he will take my heart with him. We've spent the most time alone. We help each other get use to the older ones not being home as much and moving out. He still enjoys going to church with me. He still likes me to come watch him perform. That makes me so happy. I love the sweet young man you've turned into. You are a loving, caring, nice person. I'm so lucky to have you as my son.

Bobby Ray turned eighteen years old. Where did the time go. You were my little boy. Now you're a man going out into the world alone. I'm still as afraid for you as when you were a little boy. I'm not ready to let go. You feel the need to be on your own. I can think of a million things I need to tell you before you leave. I remember the day you were born. My first child. I never knew complete happiness before that day. I'll always remember the first time I held you in my arms. When they wanted you back I didn't want to let go. Everyday since that day you have made me smile at least once a day. Usually about one hundred times a day. I'm going to miss your happy face everyday. I enjoyed everything about raising you, even the crazy things. When you were by my side I felt like I could face anything. You made me a stronger, braver person. Thank you for that gift.

I've talked about my wonderful husband Robbie all through this book. I'm sure you can tell I'm happy with my marriage and husband by now. He plays on a pool league on Tuesday nights. I go with him sometimes. I haven't been able to go in three months since I got my head injury at work. Earlier in the day I was telling him how I wished I had something chocolate to snack on. I told him I would probably find something to bake homemade tonight while he was gone. He left for his pool night but before he went there he stopped at the grocery store.

He got me chocolate ice cream, two cake mixes and icing. He didn't have time to bring it back to me so he called our daughter to bring it to me. When she got here with my surprise I was so blown away after almost twenty years he can still surprise me and be so romantic. I am the luckiest and the happiest woman in the world.

Pine Island, this is where I've dreamed about being all my life. It's my paradise. I always knew I was looking for a place I would just feel at home. I was seven years old the first time I heard of Pine Island. I wanted to be there. It sounded great. Lots of water, woods, and sunshine. All I needed to survive. It took me four years to get there. Then all my parents would do was drive around the island and say it looked like a swamp. It looked like paradise to me. I wanted to stay forever. It just wasn't meant to be right then. I knew in my heart I'd find my way back to my paradise someday. So I made the best of life everywhere else I had to go. Then twenty five years later my husband took me for a ride on Pine Island. It had changed some in twenty five years. But not as much as the rest of the world had. It was still my paradise. We decided to move to paradise. We found a place to live. We fit right into this town just like we were meant to be there. I thought to myself I'm finally in my paradise and I'm never going to leave.

I thought this is where I'm meant to be. Our kids loved it there just as much as we did. They're lucky they got to enjoy paradise during their childhood. They love to swim so what better a place to live then on a island. Pine Island was my home for six and a half years. Then Robbie found his paradise in the newspaper called Dixie County. I didn't want to leave the island but I figured he gave me my paradise that I'd give him his. Five years later we're done raising our kids in our families paradise. We all love Dixie County. The lifestyle is so layed back and relaxed. The people are so caring and loving. I believe we have found our home and paradise.

There's another life waiting for me to live. It's far beyond where I can see. I know it's up there waiting patiently for me. I'm in no rush to get up there. I still have so much to do here. When the bills, kids, love and job get to me. I sometimes think I'm ready to go see what lays beyond where I can see. Then I look real hard at this life the Lord gave to me. I realize none of it is really all that bad. I call to the Lord to help me. His response is quickly to the point.

Only I have the power to be sad or change my life to be happy. I choose HAPPINESS. My daughter Roseanne Josephine wrote this for me about four years ago, she was almost sixteen years old. Moms are angels Moms are angels sent from above to teach us kindness and how to love they kiss away the pain when we fall down make us smile when we have on a frown work so hard and come home late and still finds time to make dad a plate If you ask me your like no other thats why I'm happy your my mother I know your an angel I know its true your not just my mommy but my best friend too.

By Rozie

Oct 7,2005

Love ya Mommy!

I volunteered to work on July 4, 2009 the evening shift so my coworker could enjoy her 4th of July. She had worked the evening shift the year before. I make the schedules so I didn't have to give up my 4th of July but I just wanted to do something nice for her since she always has a lot of the night shifts. So I was putting stock away. When I got done I took my rolltainer into the stock room to close it. I tried to close it and it was stuck which wasn't anything new. So I tried again and when I did it came loose and part of it came off the hinges and went up into the air. I was trying to move out of the way but I wasn't fast enough.

A metal gate that weighs about sixty pounds came down on the right side of my head, neck and back. It knocked me to my knees. It hurt so badly. I got up and went up to the cashier and asked her and the customer if I was bleeding. I was really dazed out. They said no so I went and got some ice and wrote a accident report. I was so upset and hurt. The only person I could call to come in was the lady that had worked the morning shift that I was trying to give a break to. I called Robbie and told him about my head. I had a very hard time with my paperwork that night that I've been doing for four years. I was very scared. When I started my thirty five mile drive home after my shift was over I called my husband and talked to him for a while. Then I called and talked to my aunt in New York so I wouldn't fall asleep while I was driving. I didn't tell her about my head I just wanted to talk about happy stuff. Just in case this was gonna be the last time I spoke to her.

I wanted it to be a fun talk. I don't believe in doctors unless I have to go. The next day was my day off so I figured I'd rest all day and hopefully be fine the next day. I always like to try to pray before I go to the doctors. So I prayed all day on Sunday. It still hurt a lot. On Monday I knew I needed to go to the doctor but there was no one to come in and open the store. So the good person that I am I drove the thirty five miles and opened the store and stayed there until ten o clock am when my boss got there. I had Robbie meet me in the next town over to take me to the doctor. I got to the doctor and I had to sit there for a few hours. I had a head injury I didn't think to call and make a appointment. I finally see my doctor and he sends me to the hospital fifty miles away. During all this driving Robbie was doing, it was pouring down rain. So now I'm really scared. So Robbie is driving in the rain and I start telling him what I want done if I die.

We get to the emergency room and they do a cat scan and we sit at the hospital for a few hours. They said I had a concussion. So I go back to my doctor a week later still in so much pain. He says to take this prescription of ibuprofen and come back in a week. So I do with no improvement. So he refers me to a neurologist. So I go to him and he checks me all out and says ibuprofen after a while causes headaches. So he prescribes me some stuff and says I need a MRI. So I'm waiting on the MRI appointment. Today is August 15,2009, I have asked myself, my family, my friends, and God why did this happen to me.

I was just trying to do something nice for someone else. I was very angry at first. I layed in bed or on the couch for the first ten days. I didn't do anything while I waited to get better. It didn't work. I started getting up and doing a few things hoping that would help me to feel better. The doctor told me I need to do more so I have been but it hasn't made me feel any better. When my head allows me I write in my book. My book was very close to being done before I got hurt. So this book is being finished with me with a head injury. My aunt and I were talking about why this happened to me. She said maybe this is a good thing. She said I needed a little rest and it gives me time to finish my book. I thought about it and I wondered if God would do that to me. I thought yes that makes sense because anything else I could think of didn't make any sense at all. There was no reason for God to hurt me like this since I hadn't done anything wrong. So the pain is very bad. My memory is very bad. I'm driving my poor husband and son crazy. It's very sad and scary. This memory problem has given me a peak into my mothers world.

I now know how my poor mother felt when her Alzheimer's started. I've begged my family if this gets worse to please don't put me into a nursing home. My family had to put mom in one last year. I never want to feel that kind of loneliness that the people in nursing homes feel. I know a lot of families have no choice in the matter. I don't know how this head injury is going to turn out. I just thought everyone should know that the end of this book was done with me having a head injury. I got my MRI done on September 8, 2009. The MRI didn't show any injury. So that was good. It is May 4, 2010 ten months after my head injury and I am still in pain. It hurts all the time everyday. It feels like I was just hit in the head. I have headaches everyday. I still have some memory problems. I pray all the time for my healing. I just don't understand why I can pray some pains and illnesses away. But I can not pray this head pain away. I will never lose faith. I will always believe in the power of prayer. I believe when it is my time God will give me my healing. It has been two years since my head injury. I am still in pain. The doctors can't find anything wrong with me. I am still praying for my healing. Thank you for letting me share my life and my gifts from God with you. Hopefully I've touched some of your lives. I hope and pray everyone that picks up my book has a very blessed life.

Here in Dixie County a lot of us don't say have a nice day we say have a blessed day. It's all about keeping God in your life, heart, and soul everyday. Have a blessed day and a blessed life.

I need to add a few things that I left out of the book by accident. My kids think they were important events in our lives. My sister, her son, me, and my kids were going to houses on the island that we lived on and my sister was wanting to move to. We were at this pool house. I kept telling Bobby Ray to be careful, slow down, you're going to get hurt. Sure enough as I was saying that he tripped on a wire in the yard and he got hurt. He asked me if I did that to him I said no I just knew you were going to get hurt. I was so connected to my kids I'd ask them quite often if they were ok before they got hurt. When they were young and around all my family a lot they thought it was the fachanada curse. As they got older they began to understand me and realize that I just knew what was gonna happen a lot of the time before it happened. Years later after proving to the kids over and over my psychic abilities they started to trust them and believe them. My husband even became a believer.

One day Robbie and I were in our yard on our three acres. I was just walking across the yard and all of a sudden I thought I was having a heart attack or stroke. I got so sick feeling. I felt like I was gonna faint, I had a sharp pain in the left side of my chest. My face went numb so then I thought great I'm having a heart attack and a stroke at the same time. I yelled over to Robbie. After about ten minutes I was ok but I was very scared. Then I got worried about the kids but I didn't say anything to Robbie. I took it easy the rest of the day. A couple of hours later I got a text from our twenty year old daughter. She told me what she had been going through at school. All the symptoms she told me sounded like a stroke. I told her go to the hospital right away. It turned out to be Bell Pailsey. When I had my attack in the yard she had one at school. Her face drooped just like a stroke. The doctor said it was from stress. It made sense. She had just started massage school, got a new boss at work, my truck was broke down so I was driving her car. I had told her the day before to calm down. Also a local hero police officer was killed in the line of duty.

He was trying to keep Dixie County residents safe from a gunman on a shooting spree from a town a couple hours away. The gunman stopped in our quiet little town and He lost his life keeping us safe. I will forever be grateful to him for that day since my three kids were all in that town that horrible day. He stopped that man from killing anyone else. Rozie knew all the police officers since she worked at the sub shop in that town. We got her calmed back down and a lot of facial massages at school and her face went back to normal in a few weeks.

My teenage son John was having a few new friends spend the night for the first time. My desk wall is covered with religious pictures. My shelves are covered with religious statues. I love all of them. My husband and kids know I love them so they buy me them and I buy some for myself. So when he brought his friends into the house for the first time. He told them my mom isn't a religious freak. She just really likes religious pictures. I was sitting in the kitchen watching the boys. They all said cool. I was so happy for my son. So then he showed them all my statues. Then he was able to be proud of who we are. The next year he went on a school trip to Washington D.C. He bought some clothes while he was there. His and my proudest purchase is a Jesus belt buckle.

My friends son was in a horrible car wreck. The doctors gave the family no hope. I knew better, there is always hope if you are alive. I kept telling her he was gonna be ok to just keep on praying. The hospital was seventy five miles from her home. She stayed at the hospital and they got her a spot at the local house for patients families to sleep. We started collecting money to help her stay with her son. Her life stopped when her son's life stopped. My best friend and I got a prayer chain started. Every quarter and dollar that was given we asked for a prayer for him. Our prayer chain was all over the U.S. Me and another good friend went to the hospital to see her and him. Only family visitors were allowed, we became family that day. On our walk through those hospital halls she told me the doctors told them to be ready for the worse.

I told her don't you ever believe that unless you are burying your son then you can believe it. I told her he depends on you to be strong and will him back to you. You can't have any negative vibes in his room. I could never had been prepared for what I saw when we walked into this teenagers hospital room. I was so overwhelmed. I tried to hold the tears back but I couldn't. I thought to myself Oh My God am

I giving her false hope. He looked dead. They had him in a medicine induced coma because of the bad head trauma. I pulled myself back together and I started praying. I prayed everyday. I got my three kids to pray a lot. I got everyone I knew to pray for this boy and his mother. I can't remember how long he was in the hospital. I know it was at least a month. Then a very long recovery with his mother by his side. He lived. He lives again. He thanks me all the time for my prayers. He is so thankful for his life. I got to know my friend a lot better. I admire her and I'm in total awe of her. She became this strong mother/ woman. She was not leaving her son's side. I will always believe she brought him back. Her love brought him back.

Every ending isn't a happy one and I don't know why we were so lucky to have a happy ending. We all feel very lucky that God answered our prayers. I don't understand why sometimes God doesn't give us a chance to pray a loved one back. A few months ago we got a call from Robbie's cousin that still lives on the island. He keeps us up on the island news. Robbie told me about a friends son had died in a car accident. I cried my heart out and asked God why hadn't we had a chance to pray for his recovery. I knew between me and my friend we could have prayed him back. Why didn't we get that chance? It was so unfair. We had worked together on a small boat for six months. We had talked about all the mothers that had lost sons and daughters. We had prayed for those women. We had gone to kids funerals. We always said a prayer that our kids would be ok. I learned a lot about God from this woman. She didn't have to sit in a church to be close to God. Sitting on that boat we were just as close to God as the people in the church. The next day I bought a card to send to her. Four months later and I cannot find any words to put on that card as it sits on my desk. Our sons were friends. They were fishermen sons.

There was a bond since they were being raised the same. She and I had respect for each other as workers, wives, but mostly as mothers. We both were good mothers and we loved our kids with our hearts and souls. No words could tell her how badly I felt for her and her family. So I prayed for her son, her daughter, for her, and her husband

My best friend from work had her mammogram done like she always does. Her mother is a breast cancer survivor. So this time they saw something. So there were more tests. I started praying right away. I kept telling her it was gonna be ok. She kept saying she wasn't worried. But when I'd go out to the car to talk to her mom when she would come to the store we'd talk about her. We both said she's worried but won't admit it. We were worried too. So we got our prayer chain going in full action. We weren't taking any chances. So they set it up to remove it. When she and her husband came out of the doctor she called me. She said that they didn't remove it. I got mad. Then she told me that it was gone. There was nothing there to remove. I reckon we prayed it away. We were all so happy.

After my head injury my daughter saw how we were having problems paying the bills while I was out of work. She did everything she could to help us. Then she turned to God. She started to pray more. She started reading her bible again. She found her spiritual life again. She got back to her old self praying for everything. She had God in her life everyday again. I was so proud and happy for her. Then she had her best friend believing and praying all the time too. Her best friend is like having a second daughter. I had prayed a few years ago for a special best friend for my daughter and God sent this wonderful, special, sweet, loving, awesome, best friend into Roseannes life. So now they are both very connected to God and to each other. They are on a beautiful spiritual path. They truly are spiritual sisters.

I don't lie. My mother always said not telling was just like lying. So I've always told too much probably. I tell it like it is and not all people like to hear the truth all the time. I bring out good and bad reactions from people. Most people like me. But some people don't like me and I get very offended when someone dislikes me. I think that I'm a very nice, honest person. I'm very much to the point and I think I freak some people out by it.

My life has been a wonderful adventure so far. Robbie always says I don't like any kind of change in my life but we have had so many changes over the years and I have embraced them. He usually has to talk me into each change so I reckon he is right about me. I've worked at a Store for five years. Its the hardest job I've ever had. You'd be very surprised how hard those men and woman work so ya'll can come in and get good deals. We all need to treat everyone with respect. We really need to be nicer to the people that are working trying to make a living that are taking care of you in a store and anywhere else. We're all just trying to make it through life the best we can with what we have to work with.

I worked on a private golf course in Bonita Springs for seven and a half years. I loved that job and a lot of the guys I worked with became more like family then just co workers and friends. The other night I had a dream about my first boss from the golf course. I found out I was pregnant a few months after he hired me. He knew the work was too hard to do for a pregnant woman. He begged me to go get a different job. But I couldn't since my ex husband had just left me. His wife had just had a baby so he was fresh from all the pregnancy drama. He dealt with me really good during my pregnancy. He always made sure I wasn't around any chemicals. When I told him at six months along that I couldn't fly mow anymore he took me off of it. I had the easiest delivery with my son John. I believe it was from staying so active during my pregnancy. The family jokes about how John is my tallest child that the fertilizer worked. My best friend at the golf course had the same name. Everyone teased me so bad that I didn't name my baby John. I always knew that should be his name after his grandfathers and after the guy that helped me through my hardest pregnancy. He legally changed his name to John when he was ten years old. I have a lot of great memories from my years on the golf course. From me and my best friend Red fighting in the bunkers to us laughing ourselves silly working on that golf course. She got me the job. I made a lot of friends over the years but they were mostly men so you just can't keep in touch after you leave. Three of my best friends stand out in my memory all these years later. We were super close. This woman taught me so much about the golf course and about life. She was there for me and I was there for her everyday. The guys and I became like family.

We had a great time together during coffee time in the morning, mid morning smoke break, lunch breaks, afternoon talks, cleaning our equipment together, rain out breaks, meetings, and even after work refreshments at the local bars. Once my husband came into my life there was no more after work hanging out. The one guy I think about every time I see his cigarette brand or when someone asks for a sip of my drink. We always sipped out of each others sodas and water. I have always been worried about germs except with him. My other best friend I think about when I see or hear about his baseball team. Some friends stay in your head and heart forever.

I had been planning this trip to New York for over ten years. I wanted to go see my uncle, aunt, and cousins. I wanted to spend most of my time with my favorite cousin. My brother/ cousin. I almost took the trip with my mom about eight years earlier but my sister went with mom instead. I cried and felt bad but I knew it must not be my time to go. So I decided that I'd go after I got my last child graduated from high school. That way I wouldn't feel guilty about leaving the kids and using the money for myself. My cousin and I talked about it year after year. So my trip was getting closer and my uncle got sick. I prayed so hard for him to hang in there until I was able to get up there. He fought cancer for quite a while. Shortly before my trip he was put into the hospital and then the nursing home. When I arrived my cousin took me to the nursing home to pick my aunt up and I got to see my uncle. I felt so bad for not coming sooner. I should have come for a visit while he was doing good. It had been thirty one years since my last visit. They had been down to visit us in Florida over the years. I had a wonderful visit with my cousins and aunt. My cousin and I had a blast for a week. My uncle got sent back to the hospital a few days after I got there. My cousin and I had to go pick up my uncles things from the nursing home. It was a very sad day for us since we both knew he probably wouldn't be going back there. We made the best of it like we always do everything in our lives with our humor. We joked about almost forgetting his teeth at the nursing home.

When my aunt and I went to the emergency room to see my uncle I was so sad for my aunt. The doctors started telling us what was going on. I was so happy I was able to be there with my aunt during all of this.

At that moment I felt like God sent me to New York at that time in our lives. I figured since my mother who is my aunts sister couldn't be there he sent me there. My uncle passed away a few days after I went back to Florida. I was so happy that I was able to go to New York and say goodbye and that I loved him. My cousin and I were always close and we always talked on the phone a few times a week. After spending that week together we try to talk everyday on the phone. Some days we talk several times a day. My husband is very happy that I have my cousin in my life. He supports our friendship completely. My husband and cousin talk through me about sports and they also bust each others chops. They have a friendship through me.

I had a dream about my son's great grandma. She had passed away about eighteen years earlier. There was no reason for me to dream about her except she must be trying to warn me about Bobby Ray. He was very close to her and he was my only child old enough to remember her. He had just bought a car a few days before the dream. So of course I thought the worse. I thought she was trying to warn me that he would get into a car accident or worse maybe die. I was so scared. I started praying for his safety. I prayed for days. I told Bobby Ray and the rest of the family about this dream about Grandma. I told Bobby Ray "Please don't do anything dumb for the next few days." He laughed it off and said he'd try not to do anything dumb. I told him no I am very serious about this Bobby Ray. Please be careful. He promised that he would be careful. The next few days I reminded him several times about my dream of his grandma.

His girlfriend at the time was giving him a real hard time. He had broken up with her about a month before and then she begged him back. I told my husband that she wanted to be the one to break up with him. I knew nothing good was going to come out of this. So for this month she would not allow my son to come over to her house. So of course we all thought the worst. We all knew now that he got his car he would go over there. This one evening he was going to drop me off in the same town she lived and she kept telling him no he couldn't come over. She even drove twenty miles to our house to visit him so he wouldn't come over to her house. As Bobby Ray and I rode we talked and had fun like we always do together.

I was still nervous and I reminded him to wear his seatbelt. I told him he could be anything he wanted to be even a Country singer. I told him his soulmate was out there in the world looking for him. I might have ended up pushing him to go find out the truth about his girlfriend. I almost rode home with him so he wouldn't go to her house. I decided he was almost twenty five years old and I had to let him go. I was so afraid with the dream weighing heavy on my mind. Will I regret this for the rest of my life or will he finally be able to move on with his life. The truth shall set you free. I told him one more time don't do anything stupid. He smiled that huge Bobby Ray smile I knew he was going to find out the truth.

When we got home that night and his car wasn't in the driveway I said to my husband this is not good. My husband got in the door and heard the answering machine going with our son calling from jail. He yelled out the door to me Bobby Ray is in jail. I asked is he ok. He said I didn't talk to him. So I got into the house and he called back and we were able to talk to him. It was that call every parent prays that they won't get. I was sad for him being in jail but I was so happy that he wasn't hurt or dead. I thanked God for taking care of my son. I thanked Grandma for coming to me in my dream and warning me that Bobby Ray would be having a problem. It made it a lot easier to be able to deal with him going to jail. So he got put into jail for being in love with the wrong woman and going to find out the truth about what she was telling him. When he got there he found another man there. So as it was told to me the three of them did a lot of yelling. The now ex girlfriend and the new guy told the police their stories and my son was arrested. My son says he doesn't know why they would lie about him and what he did. My son's bond is so high we cannot get him out. Now our family is very upset over Bobby Ray being in jail. He will turn twenty five tomorrow in jail. We will go visit him. We are all praying that Bobby Ray will be over this woman. This is a very big and hard life lesson for Bobby Ray. I heard this on one of her last shows and it stuck with me and I will always think about it and share it with others as I shared it with Bobby Ray in jail. If someone tells you by their actions that they are mean, uncaring, addicted, hateful, unfaithful or whatever, they are usually telling the truth. I told him that woman had been telling him all these things for two years.

Listen to people's voices and actions. Voices can lie, actions can lie but actions don't lie for long. No matter what happens if my son is innocent or guilty he still is in jail. His perfect record of never being in any trouble is gone forever. He still lost his job that he had just put in for a promotion just a week earlier. This whole family from us that are in his life everyday to all his aunts, uncles, cousins, and his friends are all going through this with him and praying for his release. His best friend who was with him when he met this girl gets a lot of kidding from me over these years. Our kids best friends become part of our family while they are in our kids lives. His best friend is in Ohio during all this so he calls me to keep up with what's going on with Bobby Ray. Its so sad that they are not together planning a birthday bash for Bobby Ray for tomorrow. My other son John came home today and told me he had spent the night at his best friends house over the week end. I was happy for both of them. They have been best friends for six years since they were fourteen years old. They have grown apart the past few months. It's hard on me when the best friends grow apart. My husband and I are very involved in our kids lives so we get involved in their best friends lives too. Hopefully these three best friends that my kids have will stay in their lives forever.

I have been writing this book for a very long time. Now that I'm almost done with it I want to try to make sure I don't leave anything or anybody important out of it. But I know in my heart that you can't get fifty years put into one book. So I reckon if I left anything out it will be in my next spiritual book. Rozie has wanted to be a singer since she learned to talk. She would sing to you when she would talk to you. When she was four years old we were watching some country music awards show. She said when she got older she wanted to be on a big stage and sing like that show. When she was young she wanted to get started. We wanted her to have a normal childhood. Then when

I was ready for her to start she was busy having fun and finishing high school. So finally we are both ready for her at the same time. She just finished writing her last song for her first album. She is already planning how the music videos will be for all the songs. I am sure you will be hearing a lot from Roseanne Josephine Weeks better known as Rozie. I received the following letter from Bobby Ray after he was in jail for a few days.

John asked me if I'd add it to the end of my book. I said yes maybe this story will help some one to not have to go through this or help someone that is going through this in their own lives.

Visitation Tue-Sun

LOVE Y' ALL

Dear Mom and Dad I heard that u came to see me I didn't have my form in I got it in now. I love u all so much. I should have just took yals advice and just went home that night. U know every thing happens for a reason. And yes I'm done with her, she lied on me and said I hit her, I pray everyday I get out. My cell mate gave me this paper and envelope to write yall. He is very spiritual, he is helping me so I'm not such a wreck. Mom I promise u when I'm done with this path in my life I'm coming home and doing right by the grace of God. Live right find my soulmate and settle down and be a man that dad and u raised me to be. Not being with a married woman and doing wrong committing a sin that has not been the right way to live. And everyone has been trying to tell me but I have ignored everyone and said they were wrong. But all along I was the wrong one and the blind one I really in my heart thought she loved me. I'm doin fine to be locked up I really miss freedom though. Tell Rozie and John I miss them so much. I think of the argument me and John got in and just want to tell him that I haven't been a very good big brother hear lately. But if he will let me show him I really want us to have the best relationship. I love him so much. His forgiveness means the world to me. I really miss my little big brother. No matter what happens he is my favorite brother. I Love u John. And Rozie I miss her smile she told me about her too but like a dummy I turned my head. I hope ya'll aren't ashamed of me I really don't.

I Love Rozie so much. I just want to get a great big hug from her. An mom u r my best friend and hero. U mean the world to me I'm so sorry I didn't listen to u and did this to this family. I really am I love ya'll with all of my heart. I'm hardheaded we all know that but I've seen the light and know what I have to do now. I really know what to do. I go to bond reduction on Thur. So pray that the Judge R.O.R. me so I can come home. I pray everyday and night God will help me. I know he will no matter what happens. I will be ok. I love ya'll so much. I miss all of ya'll and yes I will finally help u clean the yard dad. I love ya dad. I miss ya'll so much really miss ya'll

Love Bobby Ray

I cried my heart out when I read this letter from my son in jail. He didn't get released at bond reduction because the man claimed he was in fear of his life of my son. As I sat there and heard that I thought to myself you can keep the girlfriend just give my son back his life. No one was hurt but this is he said, she said. We always told our son something bad like this would happen if he stayed with this woman. So its been three weeks now and life goes on. This has changed all of our lives. We all pray everyday for Bobby Ray to get to come home soon. How sad is this if he really didn't do anything he is being excused of. He should have just walked away when he saw the man at the girlfriends house and he wouldn't be in jail right now. Two months later and he is still in jail. We are hoping and praying he will get out next month.

I was living with my parents after I left my ex husband. I wanted to get moved out and start my new life with my two kids. I finally found a efficiency apartment that I could afford to rent. I had enough money to get moved in. I wouldn't get another paycheck for two weeks. I didn't have enough money for groceries. My best friends mom asked her church for help for me and my kids. She and my best friend got me the help and went and did the grocery shopping for me. They also put some of their own money in too so they could get me more. Her mom also would leave me a big pack of diapers on my porch once in a while. That wonderful love and caring helped me get through a very hard time in my life. A month after I moved in I found out I was four months pregnant with my son John. Life wasn't easy but we survived it because I always believed better days and a new husband were coming into our lives.

I always loved to write but I never thought I was smart enough or talented enough to be a writer. I always wrote stuff down for years and just saved all these books and pieces of paper. I was thirty five years old and something about housing for low income people was in the newspaper. I didn't agree with what they were saying so I wrote my one and only letter to the editor. When my mother read my letter in the newspaper she called me up. She told me that I was a very talented writer. She told me how proud she was of me. Momma couldn't believe that I was this old and she never knew that I could write. She told me she was sorry that she didn't know sooner. She asked me if I ever wrote anything else.

I told her about all my stuff I had wrote down. She told me I should start writing songs and books. Momma made me feel so great about myself that day. A few days later I started writing songs. I have thirty six songs wrote now. I now have this book wrote. She was so proud of my songs and that I was writing this book.

I have not been able to decide if I should put this into my book. That is why its at the end of the book. I've finally decided that it was the reason why my life went the way it did, that it had to be included. I want people to understand no matter what you have gone through, or are going through in your life. You never know where or when help will come to you and change you and your life. I was twenty seven years old in a very bad marriage with a two year old son. This was twenty three years ago. I would put my son down for his nap everyday at the same time. I would watch my soap opera and then my favorite talk show that was still kinda new back then. I just loved this new talk show host. Her shows made me feel good about myself and I needed that. This one day she had some sisters on that had been molested by their father. This kind of talk was new on TV. It was just what I needed to hear about since my father had molested me when I was a child until I was thirteen years old.

I always thought and felt like I was the only person in the world this happened to. After that day I read and watched everything I could find on being molested. I had beat myself up for so many years now I knew it wasn't my fault. This show inspired me to take charge of my life. I took my life back that day watching that show with my two year old napping next to me. I had my struggles but I became a stronger and happier person as the years went by. Two years later I was able to divorce my ex husband. During the past twenty three years I've been able to put myself back together. I am now a whole person again. I did not let the abuse win. I was just telling my cousin the other night on the phone, that I had just touched on this subject in a small way because it was a small part of my life. It ran my life for twenty seven years. Thanks to the talk show host for knowing what a important subject this was way back then. She got me started on my journey to finding Beverly. I've found me and I've been able to write this book and hopefully I'll be able to help some people with their lives with my words.

When my husband and I moved to Dixie County almost seven years ago I knew I'd have a hard time finding a job. I finally got a job that I didn't want but my husband was sick and we needed a paycheck. I got a job as a cashier in a retail store. The money was very bad for how hard they expected you to work. I worked very hard like I do at every job I've ever had. I have done a lot of hard jobs in my life. The retail store job was the hardest. I kept getting promoted. My district manager kept moving me to different stores. I had gotten a job down the street from my kids school. But to keep my job I was driving thirty five miles to work. So I drove 350 miles a week with the promise from him as soon as a spot came open he would bring me back home. There was a store six miles from my house. He finally left me alone for four and a half years at the far store. I would ask for all the openings close to home and he always had one dumb excuse after the next. If I wasn't psychic maybe I would have believed him.

I had eight different managers that told my district manager that I'd make a good manager. I was a assistant manager for five years. He kept telling me that he would let me be a manager of the store I was at when my manager left. I loved the store I worked at even though I had to drive so far. The customers were like extended family. My co workers were like family. My one co worker became like a sister to me. She and I still keep in touch and I've been gone for one and a half years. My manager requested a transfer which I was kinda sad since I really enjoyed working with him. I was happy because I thought that I'd get this store. I had proven myself for years. But there was one thing standing in my way. My district manager did not like me. He said I was too forceful. What ever that means. I am very truthful and I say it like it is. Some people don't like that. He gave my store to someone with a few years less experience then me. I was heartbroken. He tried to sugar coat it but it was so wrong.

A few weeks later he said he was sending me to the store six miles from my house. I had already heard what a bad mess they were in at that store. I told him he was sending me there so he could set me up to get fired. I knew I was fighting a losing battle. I went to the store and was not welcomed by a lot of the employees. They thought I was a spy since I did just about everything different then they did. It was the worst few months of my life.

I was not use to being treated so badly for no reason. My district manager set me up to take the manager test which I passed no problem. I know he thought I would fail the test. I was also getting ready for vacation during all of this. I was going back to New York for the first time in thirty one years to see my aunt, uncle, and cousins. My uncle had been fighting cancer. My new manager was also a friend of a lot of mine and my husbands friends in our pool league. She needed her job and had to do what it took to keep it. I was not happy with it but I did know what was going on. It was ten minutes before my vacation started and I was called into the office for a meeting with my manager and district manager. They both started tearing me apart. I was blown away. My district manager told me that he and her had decided that I would not make a good manager. I was told I wouldn't be getting the store that had been promised to me. I took it and then I told them everything that had happened since I got to that store. I went on vacation and had to act like life was wonderful while being heartbroken. My beloved uncle passed away a few days after I came back home. I was so happy that I was able to go and say goodbye to him. I felt blessed to be there with my aunt and cousins while they went through this sad time.

I came back to work for a few days when I got back from vacation. It was just getting worse. I talked to my husband and we decided that I would quit my job. I had a few job offers so I thought I'd be able to get a job. I went in and told my manager that I quit. I told her that we both know what went on here but we would leave it in that office because we will have to see each other a few times a week at pool. Then I hugged her and told her goodbye. A year later and I am still job hunting. I was shopping in that same store about eight months later. My husband called me on my cell phone and said he had just gotten a phone call from the publisher. They wanted to publish my book. What a perfect place to find out my dream had come true.

GOD CHOOSES WHAT WE GO THROUGH,
WE CHOOSE HOW WE GO THROUGH IT!

CPSIA information can be obtained at www.ICGtesting.com
Printed in the USA
LVOW120140170112
264140LV00001B/16/P

9 781462 631643